Sociology of Culture
and Cultural Practices

NEW DIRECTIONS IN CULTURE AND GOVERNANCE
Series Editor: Terry Nichols Clark
The University of Chicago

This series has a combined focus on innovation in local governance and new developments in the field of cultural policy. Culture functions, much like society itself, as a complex system of elements that often acts to strengthen attachments to place. New Directions publishes scholarship that is thematically diverse—examining culture, for example, as a trigger for economic renewal or as a tool for intercultural understanding—and while books in the series may use differing methodologies, we are especially interested in creative applications of social science research.

Titles in the Series

Tampering with Tradition: The Unrealized Authority of Democratic Agency Edited by Peter Bogason, Sandra Kensen, and Hugh T. Miller
Local Politics: A Resource for Democracy in Western Europe? By Angelika Vetter
God and Karate on the South Side By Joseph Yi
The City as an Entertainment Machine Edited by Terry Nichols Clark
Sociology of Culture and Cultural Practices By Laurent Fleury, translated by Michael Lavin

Sociology of Culture and Cultural Practices

The Tranformative Power of Institutions

By Laurent Fleury
Translated by Michael Lavin
Preface by Terry Nichols Clark

LEXINGTON BOOKS
Lanham • Boulder • New York • Toronto • Plymouth, UK

Published by Lexington Books
A wholly owned subsidiary of Rowman & Littlefield
4501 Forbes Boulevard, Suite 200, Lanham, Maryland 20706
www.rowman.com

10 Thornbury Road, Plymouth PL6 7PP, United Kingdom

Copyright © 2011 by Armand Collin
Translation copyright © 2014 by Lexington Books
Originally published under the title *Sociologie de la Culture et des practiques culturelles* by Armand Collin

All rights reserved. No part of this book may be reproduced in any form or by any electronic or mechanical means, including information storage and retrieval systems, without written permission from the publisher, except by a reviewer who may quote passages in a review.

British Library Cataloguing in Publication Information Available

Library of Congress Cataloging-in-Publication Data

Fleury, Laurent.
[Sociologie de la Culture et des pratiques culturelles. English]
Sociology of culture and cultural practices : the transformative power of institutions / by Laurent Fleury ; translated by Michael Lavin ; foreword by Terry Nichols Clark.
p. cm.
Includes bibliographical references and index.
ISBN 978-0-7391-7481-4 (cloth) — ISBN 978-0-7391-7482-1 (electronic)
1. Culture. I. Title.
HM621.F565 2014
306—dc23
2013046981

∞™ The paper used in this publication meets the minimum requirements of American National Standard for Information Sciences Permanence of Paper for Printed Library Materials, ANSI/NISO Z39.48-1992.

Printed in the United States of America

Contents

Acknowledgments — vii
Preface: A New Perspective — ix
   Terry Nichols Clark, University of Chicago
Introduction: An Institutional Approach — xv

I: Sociology of Culture and Cultural Practices — 1

1. Sociologists and Culture — 3
2. Culture's Publics — 17
3. Explaining Social and Cultural Hierarchies — 35
4. The Question of the Democratization of Culture — 49
5. Contemporary Reorientations — 65

II: The Transformative Power of Institutions — 83

6. The Work of the Institution: The Democratization of Culture in the Light of the Legacy of the TNP — 85
7. The Influence of Mediation Apparatuses on the Structuring of Cultural Practices: The Pompidou Center's "Correspondents" — 99
8. The Discourse of the "Failure" of the Democratization of Culture: Sociological Observation or Ideological Assertion? — 115

Bibliography — 127
Index — 141
The author — 145

Acknowledgments

This book would not have been possible without the help of a number of people who gave me their trust. I would like to take this opportunity to express my gratitude to them.

First of all, I would like to thank Terry Clark for having recommended the project to Lexington Books and for writing the preface to this volume.

I would also like to thank Michael Lavin, who translated this book. I would like to thank him for his continuous commitment, his perception of semantic nuances, and his critical vigilance. The quality of his translation owes a good deal to his intellectual involvement and his keen awareness of the theoretical issues involved in the translation of social science texts.

I would also like to thank my publisher, Armand Colin, who invited me to write about the sociology of culture for a broad public and who supported the English language translation project. My thanks also to the journal, *Lien social et politique* and to the publishing house L'Harmattan who allowed me to have articles initially published in French translated for the second part of the book (chapters 6-8).

My thanks also goes to the institutions who contributed financially to the publication: the Association de Valorisation des Etudes sur la Culture (AVEC) and the Ville de Rennes, and my research center, the Centre de Sociologie des Pratiques et Représentations Politiques / Laboratoire du Changement Social et Politique (CSPRP / LCSP) at the Université Paris Diderot / Sorbonne Paris Cité.

And finally, I would like to express my gratitude to the students in my "Cultural Policy" Master's program at the Université Paris Diderot, and also to all those who, thanks to their questions and fascinating conversations to which they gave rise, helped me, over the course of time, to develop my approach to culture, institutions, and politics.

Laurent Fleury

Preface

A New Perspective

Terry Nichols Clark, University of Chicago

We often look to Paris for leadership in cultural theorizing. This volume gives us reason to do so once more. It offers a new perspective on cultural theory and cultural policy.

Laurent Fleury explicates a framework where institutions (can) play a key role in (re)shaping the cultural activities and experiences of the young as well as adults. Many past theories posit that cultural activities are driven largely by primordial, unchanging factors like race, class, gender, and national origin. Yet if they dominated all, cultural consumption would be static, with minimal change from the past.

Laurent Fleury provides a framework for a dynamic, evolving view of culture. His general theory grows from a broad reinterpretation of past work combined with detailed original analysis of two major Paris institutions, the Théâtre National Populaire and the Centre Pompidou/Beaubourg. His account shows how the workings of these two institutions challenge more static past theories. His new approach is conceptually original yet empirically grounded.

Both Paris institutions combined brilliant theatrical staging and innovative programming, but these were joined with active efforts to mobilize visitors, to engage them as participants—via active mentors, newsletters, frequent small group discussions, even a short summer school.

TNP actor/director Jean Vilar carried a message of ironic alienation in theory and performances, from Molière and Shakespeare to Brecht. Emerging from a left-leaning Paris suburb, the TNP moved to the white marble traditional Palais Chaillot, one of the most prized Paris locations, directly facing the Eiffel Tower across the Seine River. Vilar's populist/anti-establishment approach in turn inspired Fleury's second institution: Beaubourg. Its architecture shouted Beaubourg's message: radically red/orange walls in industrial style, framed by steel girders and an exterior escalator—drastically shocking the rest of Paris. This anti-establishment statement continued in its programs of art, lectures, and discussion groups.

The dramatic results: the TNP became the lead theater in Paris and the Centre Beaubourg a lead arts/museum combination. They became charismatic scenes for *le tout Paris*, hugely successful with the general public. Beaubourg could attract as many visitors as the Louvre and the Eiffel Tower combined. The TNP and Beaubourg publics included many non-elites, persons of moderate educational and cultural background. Both institutions were self-consciously anti-elite in the playwrights and artists selected, in the mentors' interpretations, in newsletters, and discussions. This active, socially engaged style grew out of the progressive political commitments of the leaders of the TNP and Beaubourg, supported or tolerated at the beginning by political leaders and government staff. Both were state-sponsored institutions. Yet later, the political climate changed, and top political leaders decreed that the stronger left/progressive activities should be trimmed or ended. Both institutions then precipitously dropped in popularity.

There are other past and present examples if we look. One of the most famous was Bertolt Brecht's East Berlin state-sponsored Theater am Shiffbauerdamm, which launched a theatrical style of irony and alienation similar to the Paris TNP. Joining the Hollywood film noir tradition, it helped shape the post-1968 counterculture, touching many, many other institutions globally. The internet provides huge further potential, and many achievements, for individuals and small groups to post music and theatrical performances and critique established institutions.

The power of this book comes from combining three analyses, each elaborated in three full monographs in French. The core ideas are synthesized here for the first time. The result is an integrated, comprehensive statement important for readers globally. The original theory of culture is outlined, stressing how dynamic institutions can transform citizens through powerful aesthetics. A new cultural experience may be accidental, initially, but some citizens report that "their lives were changed" by exposure to an event like a play or concert. Aesthetic experiences can be deeply emotional and drive toward further cultural exploration. These can be active, not just receptive or following parents' examples. Adults and young shift consumption patterns as new options emerge, from new theater to electronic music downloads. Past theories are reviewed, critiqued, and extended, thus providing an original introduction to a restructured sociology of culture. The general analysis is embedded in case studies of the TNP and Beaubourg, which are discussed not as descriptive ethnographies, but integrated with the theory. The two are consciously chosen and presented as "deviant cases" to much of cultural theory as it is widely understood and practiced globally. How so?

Many core ideas in cultural analysis around the world are rooted in a broadly neo-Marxist background. These were sharpened in Germany by the Frankfurt theorists T.W. Adorno and Max Horkheimer, then Marcuse and Habermas, in Italy by Gramsci, and in France by Althusser, Foucault, and Pierre Bourdieu. Extensions of these to the third world stress cultural dependency, communication imperialism, and related concepts. These include ideas such as class-inspired interpretations of culture, e.g. where elites reshape cultural content, or in cultural participation where the disadvantaged are seen as participating less, where culture is used as "distinction" to mark higher social status, and there are conflicts between the dominant and dominated in cultural activities, consumption, and more. There is much critical discussion of how much official, especially government-sponsored institutions like the national Ministries of Culture perpetuate cultural inequalities through the specific policies and institutions they subsidize. These past ideas mix (1) theories of how the arts and cultural institutions operate and (2) descriptions and data about their operation, with (3) normative evaluations, often using the benchmark of cultural egalitarianism.

This book is all the more powerful as it does not challenge this last point, the normative goal of more equal cultural access. It simply details better means to the same end. Thus it faults the many institutions and their specific rules that discourage broader access. But Fleury differs from the past in that he does not just offer cultural criticism, but features specific alternatives that work. He does not declare that all institutions should seek the same patterns, but that by offering multiple options, a rich and diverse set of cultural activities can engage different subgroups on distinct themes and subtypes. And all can participate more. He stresses precise mechanisms involving personal involvement by mentors of various sorts with "members" of specific groups that meet and pursue active discussions. These can lead adults to new discoveries and aesthetic interpretations. We are not culturally frozen after childhood, but learn and adapt through social interaction. This insight links with the analogous theoretical breakthrough of Habermas and Joas in joining the American pragmatist tradition stressing social interaction with the broader institutional and macro focus of European social theory, leading to a conceptual stress on institutions like the coffeehouse. An earlier European/American synthesis was the Katz and Lazarsfeld *Personal Influence* approach where opinion leaders worked like Fleury's mentors. The strong party/union model of the European left was a clear inspiration here; these theorists sought more supple versions and discovered multiple specific manifestations from the salon to the voluntary association. Others write of bowling leagues (Robert Putnam), tiny publics (Gary Allen Fine), liminal spaces (Victor Turner and Mikhail Bakhtin), and scenes.

The French legacy is globally critical to help clarify the critical role of institutions, especially those connected to a strong national state. This is distinctly absent from most British and American cultural experiences and theorizing. Yet in many European and Asian contexts, the national state incarnates a powerful bureaucratic logic. It traditionally resisted initiatives from others as it often sought monopolistic control of fundamental policies. Why? Earlier largely from military preparedness for war, but in the globally important French case, after the 1789 Revolution, the monopolistic state bureaucracy was legitimated through a combination of the principles of liberty, equality, and fraternity. This republican logic drove the state to impose limits against its classic enemies, the Church and royal/aristocratic legacy. This left no space for independent cultural institutions like theaters, or voluntary associations of all sorts, which were legally prohibited in much of nineteenth-century France, and were similarly weak in twentieth-century Asia. But as education and sometimes income rose, unskilled labor declined, and media and travel increased, the hierarchy of bureaucracy came under attack. After the political uprisings of 1968, demands for more democracy by average citizens rose, leading to more of the new institutional forms which Fleury details and theorizes.

These challenges to a dominant, hierarchical perspective coincide with and incorporate major cultural developments from France and near-globally. Similar debates about possible change have informed cultural policy from Singapore to Brazil to France to the United States. Broad ideas are debated about how distinctive are high and low culture and how broad and differentiated are cultural participation in each. There are big debates often driven by small academic studies and large-scale government surveys, often seeking to assess how hierarchy or inequality of access operate.

Consider the U.S. example. One of the most visible debates surrounds the surveys of the National Endowment for the Arts (NEA). For many years the NEA "benchmark" activities (art galleries, museums, classical music concerts, opera, etc.) were cross-tabulated with education, race, and income. Results generally conveyed a hierarchical pattern of cultural consumption: those of higher status consumed more culture (in studies by Paul DiMaggio, NEA staff, and others). Critical discussion of these results and the overall approach grew in the years after 2000. This in turn led the NEA to commission several reports reanalyzing these same data by others. One of the most dramatic was by Jennifer Novak-Leonard and Alan Brown, who in 2008 reported very different results by looking beyond the "benchmark" activities of classical concerts, opera, museums, and the like. They also included creative participation such as playing in a band, painting pictures, or singing in a choir. Their results challenged past studies: many cultural activities were more popular among less educated and minority ethnic groups, such as gospel singing, listening to radio, playing in a band, and other cultural activities, even though they could not include many of the newest most popular cultural activities as they were omitted by the NEA surveys.

Similar concerns have driven decades of surveys in France, but often more comprehensive than the U.S. NEA study in the types of cultural activities included. The French surveys added electronic music downloads and internet-related entertainment, for instance. So while the NEA analyst can only speculate about U.S. trends, new items in French Ministry of Culture surveys add detail to the magnitude of some of the more populist/egalitarian patterns: electronic music downloads and performing in cultural groups are highly popular among younger French citizens, such that overall, there is a rise in cultural consumption rather than a decline, especially among the young, if these new modes of cultural participation are included. Most NEA studies by contrast generally suggest that young persons are declining in cultural participation.

David Throsby in recent work in Australia and elsewhere for instance moves in a similar direction. And Terry Nichols Clark and Filipe da Silva showed a rise in cultural consumption by citizens in many countries of the world using the World Values Survey of national samples of citizens: a tripling in the Netherlands over some twenty years, doubling in the United States, and near doubling in Canada, Sweden, Korea, and other countries. These results drastically contradict the traditional NEA results. How to reconcile them? Basically by noting that the World Values Survey results come from asking about all cultural activities, especially new activities that have emerged like electronic-related entertainment, or creating small arts groups that are too volatile and informal for official counts.

These new forms of institutional access and participation are dramatic illustrations of Fleury's general point: create institutions that attract people, and they will come. Including rap concerts in the favelas of Rio, cafes that feature storytelling, comedians, small dance groups, small bands that post on the internet, and personalized music selections individuals choose on their electronic players. This broader perspective provides new insights by transcending the high/low culture conceptual distinction which has misled theorizing and empirical studies of culture for decades.

Fleury's originality here is not unique: there are parallel developments in other fields that document a diversity of institutional mechanisms and influences on participants. For instance studies of school effects and changing values in college from T.M. Newcomb on Bennington College, through P. Jacobs, J.S. Coleman, and S. Raudenbush show that some schools have huge effects; others are barely noticeable. Or organizational studies show that many institutions seem leaderless, while others have leaders with dramatic impacts (like Bill Gates at Microsoft or Steve Jobs at Apple). By noting this diversity of impact, the questions become why and how. This opens a different window, through which Laurent Fleury here shows us how, if we look, we can see further and identify new dynamics of culture.[1]

NOTE

1. On a personal note, I can testify to the emotional experience stressed by Laurent Fleury when I attended Vilar's TNP performances in Paris, and the TNP Avignon summer school when I was twenty years old. These in turn led me to multiple pilgrimages to Brecht's Theater am Schiffbauerdamm in Berlin. Alas I have seldom felt such drama in the theater ever since. I debated related issues with Pierre Bourdieu and Jean-Claude Passeron in the 1960s and 1970s, when I was the first and main American social scientist they knew. I lived in Paris for about five years doing fieldwork for my PhD (*Prophets and Patrons*, Harvard University Press, 1973) and later teaching twice at the Sorbonne. I met Bourdieu and Passeron soon after their *Les héritiers* was published, attended their famous Colloque de Caen, and had multiple dinners and conversations with them. I published the first U.S. reviews of their books, especially in the *American Journal of Sociology*, stressing their fresh empirical work but critiquing their simplified model of stratification. Laurent Fleury here goes much further in using Vilar to make sense of Bourdieu, and far more.

Introduction

An Institutional Approach

"All authentic research consists in transgressing limits."
—Hermann Broch

After providing an overview of the major theories of the past, this book goes on to introduce an original perspective on the sociology of culture. What is new about it? Most of the thinkers of the past addressed in these pages hailed from France, the United States, and Germany, arguably the most significant centers in terms of both empirical and theoretical research on culture. But in recent years there has been a series of changes that have contributed to the new perspective that I elaborate here. The book is underpinned by the idea that, in the field of culture, there are no simple, univocal links between attitudes developed in childhood and choices, preferences, and practices deployed in adulthood. Forged over many years of research, this idea contradicts a number of studies that insist on determinants such as social class, gender, and ethnicity. The original approach outlined in this book runs counter to a current of the sociology of culture based on concepts—including "cultural socialization," "cultivated *habitus*," and "distinction"—developed by the influential French sociologist Pierre Bourdieu.

The new conceptual perspective outlined here is elaborated by means of a detailed analysis of two atypical cases presented in the second part of the book, namely Vilar's Théâtre National Populaire (National Popular Theater) and the Beaubourg, otherwise known as the Pompidou Center, in honor of the late French president. This analysis enables us to address both the very French problematic of the democratization of culture, and to reappraise our categories of sociological thought. This double perspective, at once theoretical and empirical, highlights the novelty of a dialogue between the French and American traditions and the recent changes that have taken place in both of them.

1. Current challenges and an original thesis

This book offers a discussion of the *historical model* of the theory of cultural legitimacy proposed by Pierre Bourdieu, an important figure in France in terms of the sociology of culture. It also refers to earlier authors who influenced Bourdieu's work, including Max Weber (who helped him develop his notion of legitimacy); Norbert Elias, Thorstein Veblen, Edmond Goblot and Marcel Mauss, whose thought contributed to his development of the concept of distinction; and Emile Durkheim, whose ideas helped him elaborate an epistemology that, as Jean-Claude Passeron has ably demonstrated, is far from explicit about its relationship with values. Similarly, the book implicitly questions Bourdieu's status as a *scientific reference point* by taking issue with the assertion, based on his somewhat deterministic theory, that the project to democratize culture has failed, and examines the status of his work as a *theoretical paradigm*. Bourdieu's ideas have been hotly disputed by members of the scientific community, both in France (not by only Bernard Lahire, but also by Bruno Péquignot, Emmanuel Ethis, Jean-Louis Fabiani and, others), and in the United States (by Paul Di Maggio, Richard Peterson, and Terry Clark).

1.1 Presenting three original theses

From a *theoretical* point of view, the book takes an original position, reappraising the concept of cultural socialization by positing, as one of its central theses, the idea outlined above that, insofar as culture is concerned, there are no simple and unequivocal links between childhood attitudes and the choices, preferences, and practices of adulthood.

My research on the spectators of Jean Vilar's Théâtre National Populaire (TNP), on the correspondents of the Beaubourg/Pompidou Center, on visitors to the Louvre, and elsewhere, on subscribers to the National Theater of Brittany (TNB) highlights the value of a sociological approach to the analysis of cultural socialization, an open process that, in spite of what is implied by Bourdieu, is not definitively determined by the educational establishment and the family. Instead, cultural socialization is a continuous, lifelong activity. In this regard, the analyses presented in the book enable readers to approach the notion of the cultural *habitus* in a non-deterministic manner, to imagine ways in which its effects can be subverted by amicable sociability (Georg Simmel), the work of cultural institutions (Laurent Fleury), and the ambiance of urban neighborhoods (Terry Clark).

Another genuinely novel aspect of the book is the introduction of the *political* variable in the sociology of culture. Its socio-historical explorations of the actions of Vilar's TNP and the Beaubourg Center, which, in France, have become points of reference, provide a description of the sometimes harmonious, sometimes fraught relations developed between institutions and their publics over substantial periods of time. The examples of the TNP, an organization founded in 1920 with the goal of providing "elite theater for all" and directed by Jean Vilar from 1951 to 1963, and the Beaubourg (later the Pompidou Center), the huge, multidisciplinary arts center opened in Paris in 1977, show just how much can be achieved by political voluntarism in terms of attaining the ideal of the democratization of culture. Better, the book bears witness to the historical advent of a form of cultural democratization that can be viewed not only as a process of reaching out to a greater number of publics characterized by inter- and intra-class variations, but also to the kind of transformation in attitudes to the way in which works of art should or could be viewed and "received" made possible by encouraging a degree of familiarity with culture capable of modifying aesthetic hierarchies and calling into question the *autoritas* of the canon. All these actions are part of a process establishing a relationship with culture; they point to the concept of the *political* institution of cultural practices. Furthermore, if, as Terry Clark, Stephen Sawyer, Filipe da Silva, and others suggest, cultural activities can influence political participation (Sawyer and Clark, 2012), the embeddedness of culture and politics is also manifested in *reciprocal action* (in the sense of Simmel's *Wechselwirkung*).

Last, from a *methodological* point of view, the book suggests the value of an intellectual approach articulating sociological understanding, historical depth, and critical thought. Critical thought makes it possible simultaneously to jettison categories of thought that have become redundant, and to distinguish between various orders of "fact." In this regard, it is worth quoting Max Weber who, in 1917, pointed out that, "all we can ask for is an act of intellectual probity: to recognize that, on the one hand, the observation of facts, the definition of mathematical and logical realities, or the description of the internal structure of cultural goods, and, on the other, the formulation of a reply to the question of the value of culture and its contents, constitute two orders of problems which are absolutely heterogeneous" (Weber, 2005: 14). The dichotomy between facts and values is clear.

The notion of historical depth obliges us to focus on an empirical point of reference and carry out a detailed analysis. From Weber to Passeron, scholars interested in fostering an understanding of the internal dynamics of institutions and the influence of policy initiatives on the way in which institutions function have highlighted the heuristic value of proceeding on a case-by-case basis. This is the type of approach applied to the analyses of Jean Vilar's forgotten revolution and the misunderstood revolutions of the Pompidou Center.

The two institutions are atypical. With their emphasis on popular participation, they are "deviant cases" that run counter to the dominant paradigms of the sociology of culture theorized by Passeron, paradigms that emphasize primordial/family socialization over and above the influence of later life experiences, such as theater and the arts.

Last, the sociological perspective characteristic of the intellectual tradition founded by Weber provides an insight into the meanings that individuals accord to their practices and to the processes of symbolization that constitute aesthetic reception. The sociological perspective also makes it possible to glean an understanding of various kinds of internalized attitudes (or *Gesinnung*, to use Weber's term) that mold lifestyles and ways of living. This perspective, understood in the broad sense of an intellectual approach, is vital in terms of gaining an insight into the effects of social contiguity that explain the singular trajectories of individuals, trajectories that are themselves crucial in understanding cultural practices and aesthetic experience. Similarly, if we accept that people can use their aesthetic experiences to free themselves from the shackles of predetermined social categorizations, even if only in a temporary way, then the influence of *sociability* and social interaction on the development of aesthetic judgments goes some way in explaining the identifications and dis-identifications based on such judgments.

Adults undergo strong emotional experiences, from religious and ideological conversions to divorce and grief from the death of loved ones. Similarly, adults change aesthetic outlooks, and try new cultural experiences—from going to a theater to visiting an art exhibit. These are not determined by their childhood upbringing. This may be from chance or they may in part choose, but once they have felt the shock or surprise of a new cultural experience, they may look for more in new places. Many adults report such experiences in exactly these terms ("it was a life-changing experience"). Such remarks were common in studies of these two institutions, the TNP and the Beaubourg, as is attested by documents unearthed in the archives, as well as in numerous reviews by art critics and evaluations by other social scientists. The frequency of such comments by persons who were low in education or cultural experience was particularly dramatic, as they contradicted so deeply the "dominant" cultural theories. This is not, of course, to say that childhood socialization has no impact, just that it is only moderately important, and that over the full life course it may shift trajectory many times. Or not, depending on the individual. Statistical studies show this by reporting that approximately 80 percent of the variance in cultural participation (going to films, theater, bookstores, art galleries, museums, and more) is not explained by race, class, gender, or national/ethnic background. This is clearest in studies that seek to measure such issues, for example, the journal *Poetics*, but can be seen in many other empirical studies of culture, for example Terry Clark's *The City as an Entertainment Machine* (Clark, 2011: 33).

Last, applying a sociological perspective reveals doubtless temporary spaces of *disaffiliation* or "desocialization" sometimes characterizing potentially life-changing aesthetic experiences. Since emotion suggests dispossession, the fundamental experience of aesthetic emotion can be defined in terms of a paradoxically "de-socializing" process of socialization, or of a "socializing" form of desocialization. Understanding emotion as a mode of knowledge and as a heuristic key to assessing what affects us and what we affect reveals the social connotations of the word's etymological roots: a "putting into motion", a transformation of identity, a process of re-socialization, the establishment of a new relationship with the self, the world, and one's own life.

1.2 The specificities of a paradoxical context

While the theoretical and epistemological approaches referenced in this book largely derive from German and American sociology, the historical context in which those approaches emerged was, initially at least, French. This observation requires some explanation if we are to understand a paradox inherent in the sociology of culture in France, which tends to elude the political context of its emergence (in the sense of both politics and policy) even though that context influences the way in which relationships with culture are imagined. This book focuses on policy, leaving politics (the impact of which has been substantial), the variables of partisanship, and the New Political Culture (NPC) so ably described by Terry Clark, to one side. What it does do, however, is to highlight the considerable influence of public policy on the development of approaches and attitudes to the formation and structuring of cultural practices. And it also demonstrates that cultural institutions not only make an important contribution to the implementation of public policy but that they also play a role in defining it.

France has a history of political intervention in the field of culture. Since the *Ancien Régime*, a centralized state has either aided the cultural cause by setting up the Academies and following a policy of royal sponsorship, or constrained cultural practices by political means, the imposition of censorship, the deployment of a stifling morality, outlawing voluntary associations, and more. This interventionist approach to art and culture was mirrored in more recent times by the voluntarist approach characteristic of the Fifth Republic in presidents and government ministers—one thinks particularly of charismatic figures such as André Malraux, Georges Pompidou, Jack Lang, and François Mitterrand—who played a leading role in implementing cultural policies. A prime example of political intervention in the field of culture was the setting up of the Ministry of Cultural Affairs in 1959. The first head of the establishment that was to become the Ministry of Culture and Communication was Malraux. The political problematization of questions touching on culture can doubtless be traced back to this very French tradition, which culminated in cultural policy being equipped with a body of doctrine in 1959. That doctrine expressed the ideal of the democratization of culture.

This tradition is also reflected in the constant tensions between heritage and innovation, dual principles of the Ministry of Culture, which have been non-deteriministically debated and modified under the leadership of, among others, André Malraux and Jack Lang. If individuals can have such impact, then "structures" are not as well established as deterministic theories would suggest. This openness at the top parallels and complements the openness displayed by ordinary people who have "life changing" cultural experiences after walking into a theater or an art museum.

Paradoxically, the specificity of the French state's interventionist attitude to culture is characterized by a polemic over whether the project to democratize culture was doomed to failure from the outset. The ideological connotations of this idea are examined in chapter 7. But first we should have a look at the background. Because, at least since 1959, democratization has provided the political foundation of public intervention in the field of culture, with the cultural policies introduced after that date regularly being judged by the standards of that doctrine. Against the background of the institutionalization of the cultural administration, of the professionalization of the artistic field, and of the elaboration of successive points of reference for public action (cultural action in the 1960s, cultural development in the 1970s, cultural mediation in the 1990s), an originally symbolic approach to policy was replaced by a more technocratic one.

The aim of this book is to describe the central categories of sociological analysis and apply them to an examination of public cultural policies, while developing the tools required to foster an understanding of the political issue of the democratization of culture, assessing the degree to which that project has succeeded, and appraising the influence of cultural institutions in the process. The book is based on the critical observation that the ideological discourse on the vanity of the project to democratize culture was replaced by a more strictly sociological observation that members of some socio-professional categories visit cultural institutions more frequently than members of others. The idea that the project to democratize culture had failed was replaced by a more ideological discourse invalidating the project itself, a discourse accompanied by the disappearance of many institutional innovations associated with cultural democratization. An example of this phenomenon is provided by the decision taken in 1968 by Vilar's successor at the helm of the TNP, Georges Wilson, to put an end to cheap subscriptions and other approaches introduced by Vilar to encourage working class people to go to the theater. It led to a spectacular fall in attendance figures and, eventually, to the closing of the institution in 1972.

These observations oblige us to highlight the effectiveness of policies designed to encourage the loyalty of the public, policies that explain the quantitative successes of Vilar's TNP, as well its qualitative successes (identification with the institution, trust and a sense of belonging, the establishment of a relationship of meaning with the plays produced by the company, the pleasure associated with the aesthetic experience it provided). On the other hand, when Wilson's TNP abandoned such approaches, spectators left in droves. It should be pointed out here that these conclusions concerning the usefulness of policies designed to encourage loyalty on the part of spectators have a methodological value.

By definition, researchers active in the social sciences rarely have the advantage of laboratory conditions in which they are able to isolate specific variables in order to test causal hypotheses. However, this case, in which a relationship with the public proved positive and the end of that relationship led to the disaffection of that same public, suggests that institutions are capable of structuring cultural practices. Similarly, when analogous public policies involving citizen engagement were abandoned at the Beaubourg, membership fell dramatically (from 50,000 in 1996 to 2,000 correspondents in 1997). These examples provide powerful, if negative, demonstrations of the social and political effectiveness of specific public policies.

In this instance, the embeddedness of knowledge and power calls into question the supposedly self-evident nature of the discourse on the "failure" of democratization which, in certain cultural arenas, has the force of law. Some observers even regard the absence of political reflection about how to, if not efface then at least attenuate the effects of the kind of symbolic obstacles highlighted in the late 1960s—symbolic obstacles that limit most people's access to culture—as a sociological inevitability. Today, it is considered proper to regard the "failure of democratization" as axiomatic. Indeed, some commentators like to present the social *determinants* of practices highlighted by researchers in the sociology of culture as *determinisms*. However, far from taking this fatalistic attitude, institutions like the TNP and the Beaubourg/Pompidou Center strike a voluntarist stance that prompts us to recast the question in the following terms: how do cultural institutions represent a possible vector of the democratization of culture?

The question is all the more worthy of attention in that sociologists of culture seem to have forgotten about cultural institutions. Previously unmentioned in the literature, the cases of the TNP and the Beaubourg/Pompidou Center throw light on cultural policies and practices. The first functioned and the second continues to function in ways that contrast to approaches taken in traditional high art institutions like the Louvre. Vilar's TNP has no equivalent in France. The fact that the organization acquired the status of a cultural reference point can be explained by Vilar's modus operandi ("theater as a public service"), by the success encountered by the TNP amongst wide and varied audiences, and by the positive and, indeed, negative reactions that it aroused. The same applies to the Beaubourg/Pompidou Center, which emerged as a kind of revolutionary force that shook the institutional landscape of cultural life in France to its foundations.

While there is a lacuna in the literature concerning the place and role of institutions in the implementation of public policy, there is another gap, of more interest to us here, concerning the role of institutions in realizing the ideal of the democratization of culture. In spite of many years of government intervention in the field of culture—if we accept that cultural policy originated in France with the creation of the Ministry—some suggest that inequalities in terms of access to cultural objects are as pronounced as ever. Here again, the argument is presented as being self-evidently true. But the TNP and the Pompidou Center provide two counter-examples (two deviant cases) in terms of the discourse on the democratization of culture. Without wishing to falsify the statistics, we can take an alternative view of the situation by supposing that, in changing contextual scale, we can glimpse elements of reality that were previously invisible. Indeed, it is impossible to exhaust the question of the democratization of culture by focusing exclusively on practices. The conditions of possibility of those practices must also be taken into account. Addressing the issue of democratization implies studying the conditions of its realization, including the policies of cultural institutions in regard to the public. According to Nathalie Heinich, "voluntarist policy mirrored the regime of cultural action of the 1970s" and, she seems to concede, was "a regime that had, on the margins, a number of undeniable successes" (Heinich, 1994). It is on these marginal successes, these counter-examples that we must focus in order to call into question a traditional, somewhat ideological discourse on failure.

Far from being neutral, the way in which the relationship between people and works of art is organized produces effects symptomatic of the power of cultural institutions. That is, at least, what we see in examining impacts of public policies implemented by the two main cultural institutions considered here. Focusing on the recipients of those policies, this book takes a "bottom-up" approach to the analysis of public policy, rather than a "top-down" approach emphasizing its development by the elite. This analysis implies questions of political sociology such as citizenship, democracy, and the public sphere. In view of the effects of public policy, we can conclude that cultural institutions are, in terms of public policy on culture, actors in their own right. Once again, in terms of culture, there is no simple, univocal link between childhood attitudes and the choices, preferences, and practices of adulthood. The cultural institution forms and informs practices, in terms of both behaviors and representations. In this sense, it too can be viewed as an arena in which norms and values are learned, or, in other words, as a sphere of socialization capable of consolidating, or, on the contrary, reversing the effects of primary socialization, of instituting social bonds and sociability, and of facilitating processes of identification and subjectivation.

2. *Two atypical cases and a socio-political issue*

The fashionable discourse of "the failure of cultural democratization" is based on the idea that cultural institutions are incapable of countering factors determining the social distribution of social practices. However, the argument presented in this book is that cultural institutions are spaces in which collective identities are expressed and crystallized, and that such institutions make an important contribution to structuring cultural experiences, social practices, and ways of experiencing relationships with art. Because Vilar's TNP represented a break from bourgeois codes governing a night out at the theater, and because, twenty years later, the Beaubourg/Pompidou Center affected a similar revolution for the museum visit, the two institutions have become points of reference. Recalling their originality helps us to understand the profound and still influential ideas on which these sometimes silent, sometimes invisible revolutions were based.

2.1. The forgotten revolutions of Jean Vilar's National Popular Theater

Jean Vilar is a paradoxical figure. Although he could be thought of as belonging to the past, he incarnates an idea that retains its validity in the present. Vilar claimed, without false modesty, that he had "made the theater of his time." It is undeniable that he bequeathed a heritage. His unwavering commitment to the cause of the theater, at both Avignon and with the TNP, which he directed from 1951 to 1963, fashioned the French theater of today. An heir of the Enlightenment, Vilar was a Republican in the French sense of the word, stressing the 1789 ideals of liberty, equality, and fraternity in an activist manner. The stage was his guillotine. He promoted the *freedom and liberty* of the artist and the spectator—the freedom to create and to think—just as he promoted *equality* by means of the public space that he established in Avignon (*Le Verger*, the *Rencontres d'Avignon*, a sort of summer school/theater festival), where spectators were encouraged to dialogue freely and use their reason publicly (this is how Aristotle, Arendt, and Habermas define the public space), sharing the aesthetic and emotional experiences of the night before.

Vilar not only sought to introduce equality in the form of open discussions at the Avignon Festival or mentored sessions at the TNP's Paris base, the Palais de Chaillot, but also fraternity through the establishment of a shared world forged in the togetherness of the theatrical experience, in the collective memory of subscribers, and via the togetherness of a working class audience gathered to see a play. Indeed, Vilar combined "the cult of virtue, a rejection of demagogy, a hatred of social constraint, a disdain of committees, a secret predilection for eloquence, a penchant for partying, and an absolute disgust for money" (Lacouture, 1995: 65).

As the head of a troupe of actors and, as such, a boss, Vilar was responsible for three revolutions. Through his actions, he asserted the principle of "theater as a public service," which he defined as a theater that excluded no one. He focused on the concrete aspects of the audience to such an extent that he turned it into a category of action. And, last, he elaborated a whole series of institutional innovations, described in chapter 6 of this book, which radically transformed the codes governing a night out at the theater by getting rid of the practice of tipping, and introducing earlier performance times and access to dress rehearsals. By breaking with the bourgeois codes that, until then, had defined the theater-goer's experience, Vilar's TNP opened a breach and founded what is now referred to in France as the public theater. Thus, *cultural practices* were transformed by Vilar's revolutions. The assertion of the idea of a non-exclusionary "theater as a public service" introduced new practices that were seen by spectators as a kind of emancipation from the bourgeois theater's rituals of intimidation and distinction and that, consequently, opened up a space in which they were free to express their own judgments, as well as to have fun and enjoy a sociable experience. The codes governing the theater-goer's experience as we now know it derive from Vilar's innovations. We are all, at least as spectators, Vilar's heirs thanks to the revolutions that he introduced and of which we are the beneficiaries.

The TNP created a role for cultural institutions: it introduced a revolution in terms of practices and representations, asserting itself as an institution that *instituted* both cultural practices and public policies. The organization served as an inspiration for the public theater and, more broadly, for other cultural institutions, as is attested by the number of theatrical men and women who, at the heart of their institution or company, develop a public service ethos combining a responsibility to artists, the public, politics, and the city. By realizing the ideal of the democratization of culture, Vilar rendered the unthinkable thinkable. Better, through his actions, he undermined the ideological discourse of the "failure of democratization," a discourse doubtless elaborated as a smokescreen to obscure certain failures on the part of the public authorities in the field of the arts. By attaining the ideal of democratization, he rendered the impossible possible.

Remarkably, all this happened before the foundation of the Ministry of Culture and continued for a number of years after public cultural policies were developed and introduced. Crucially, the organization continued to experience substantial success in its own, and, indeed, in absolute terms, even as Pierre Bourdieu and others theorized the impossibility of achieving precisely what Vilar had achieved and this, in a period when Vilar and the TNP were rising to the summit of French theater, summoned from a poor Communist suburb to move their headquarters to the Palais de Chaillot, one of the most prized locations in Paris, directly facing the Eiffel Tower across the Seine, and adjacent to the Museum of Modern Art, in the heart of the socially chic sixteenth *arrondissement*. But this generous official sponsorship did not "tame" Vilar's message, which he continued to deliver as if he were still addressing left-leaning workers in his old suburb of Suresnes to the west of Paris. He could play *Le*

Bourgeois Gentilhomme (The Bourgeois Gentleman) himself and show how disgusting the politics incarnated in the person of Molière's protagonist really were. His ironic alienation in theory and performances, from Molière and Shakespeare to works by Brecht, was shared with Brecht, the theater director and social critic, who theorized it in more detail. Both were broadly committed to the ideas of Revolution in a period when many leading intellectuals in France and Germany were broadly Marxist, even if they differed substantially in how to define Marxism. He and his staff were leaders of the 1968 revolt against De Gaulle and the hierarchical French state, and the TNP was in turn abolished.

The *cultural policies* introduced in 1959 were heir to Vilar's idea that art of the highest quality and the ideal of the democratization of culture, two notions that were too often hermetically separated, could be combined effectively. When the adversaries of the *Charter for Public Service Missions for the Performing Arts*, which emerged in 1998, brandished against its advocates the charge of "Vilarism" as an anathema, it became apparent just how much the idea of public service orients debates and struggles to define theater policy. Venerated or contested, he is still a model.

The TNP thus provided a template for the democratization of culture. It prefigured the development of public policies in the arts. The popularity of Vilar's TNP meant that what had previously been considered *illegitimate* was now *legitimate*. The legitimacy of government intervention in the field of culture is based on his success, which combined excellence in terms of artistic creation *and* a breakthrough in cultural democratization, and which enabled the Ministry of Culture, founded in 1959 and headed by André Malraux, to pursue both objectives simultaneously. Vilar's TNP also introduced the possibility of attaining the goal of cultural democratization by means of the idea of "theater as a public service" and the development of audience policies. Once thought to be mere wishful thinking, an inaccessible dream, and an unattainable utopia, the democratization of culture became a reality. Thanks to the approaches applied by the TNP, seemingly insurmountable problems were resolved. And, in spite of being prone to feelings of anxiety, Vilar's perseverance was enough to render *possible* what had previously been considered *impossible*. Vilar's TNP made what had once seemed *unthinkable* distinctly *thinkable* for tens of thousands of people. For a manual laborer or a clerical worker in the France of 1945, the idea of spending an evening at the theater was unimaginable; by 1951 it was clearly a viable option. Vilar's TNP exerted a positive influence on social and cultural practices, bringing light into the existence of a considerable number of people, many of whom claimed that it had "changed their lives."

Because the TNP effected a transformation in the order of practices and representations, it became a *model* for cultural action. It was later used as a template, as is demonstrated by numerous institutions which took inspiration from the approaches developed by the organization. The term *model* applied to these institutional innovations deserves an explanation. Jean Vilar did not attempt to elaborate a model as such. The term emerged from the judgements of politicians, artists, and art professionals, as well as social scientists, about the approaches implemented by Vilar's TNP.

In terms of the democratization of culture, the successes of Vilar's TNP are still relevant today. It is hard to imagine them being otherwise. First, because they are alive in the hearts and, indeed, the work of theatrical men and women who, against all opposition, apply a public service approach, thus demonstrating the value of a form of theater that respects artists and members of the public, who had been poorly served over the course of the preceding years. But Vilar's theater is also alive and well in terms of its symbolic value, for against the finalism and fatalism of a liberal approach obsessed with the present, Vilar's experience reminds us, as Françoise Proust has pointed out, that "events shine in the starry sky of history. Pure sparks of light, they are always already in the past, always already gone, and only live again when history awakens from 'its dogmatic sleep'. Then they flicker and glint, sending out a few notes to say that *new beginnings* and dawns are always *possible* and that history is watching over them" (Proust, 1991: 347). In this sense, Vilar's TNP is still a source of inspiration, a model for potential new beginnings.

2.2 The misunderstood revolutions of the Pompidou Center: The case of the Beaubourg

The Beaubourg is one of these new beginnings. The ideal of the democratization of culture, seemingly demolished in 1968, acquired a second wind with the founding of the center in 1977. The Beaubourg was revolutionary in three ways, first in that it applied a public service model, second because it displayed a concern with the public in general and publics in particular at a time when the sociology of culture was becoming institutionalized, and last because it introduced a series of innovations in the field of museums and public libraries.

In founding the Beaubourg Center, Georges Pompidou was attempting to bridge the gap between modern art and society. "I am struck by the conservatism of French taste—particularly the taste of what is termed the elite—and scandalized by government policy in the arts over the last hundred years; that's why I'm trying to react", he told *Le Monde* in 1972. "I was passionate about Paris having a cultural center . . . that would be both a museum and a center of artistic creation. . . . The library would attract thousands of readers who, at the same time, would come into contact with the arts." We should not forget Pompidou's attachment to the French Republican model and to the project to encourage reading among members of the public; nor should we forget the utopian sentiment shared by the founders and their unwavering desire to create from scratch a new site built specifically to support the most diverse and contemporary forms of artistic expression. And, underpinning theses ambitions was a desire to promote the idea of openness and freedom of circulation.

Approaches to introducing the general public to the arts were based on the central principle of freedom of circulation between spaces and disciplines. One of a series of institutional innovations established by the Beaubourg, the active promotion of the idea of *openness* deserves special mention. *Temporal* openness through the introduction of longer opening hours, unusual in the France of the time: from 10:00 am to 10:00 pm every day of the year, except Tuesdays. And *spatial* openness, not only thanks to direct entrances to the cardinal points of the building from the street, but also in the sense that access to many parts of the Center were free (the Forum, the upper floors via the escalator, debating rooms, contemporary exhibition galleries and the galleries of the Center for Industrial Creation, regular events put on by the museum and the Public Information Library, or BPI, a bastion of liberty and equality of access); and, last, *social* openness, facilitated by the invention of the *Laisser-passer permanent* pass and of the membership system, equivalent to Vilar's subscription system, with its two aspects—individual freedom, since it provided free access for everybody to all the Center's spaces, and an enlargement of the public, since it was based on correspondents whose role was to provide a link with the institution. This critical success added to the positive curiosity aroused by the steel and glass architecture of the Beaubourg Center, with its lively reds, blues, and greens (considered, by its detractors, as an eyesore in the heart of the French capital's historic Marais district). The architectural shock of the new acted as a catalyst, luring people in and encouraging them to pay a cultural visit. Egged on by their curiosity, members of the public would visit the Beaubourg's facilities, take up membership, and perhaps even become correspondents.

The Beaubourg's institutional innovations had an immediate impact. The "Beaubourg case," presented in chapter 7, provides a second, emblematic example of a viable approach to democratizing culture. Like the TNP, the Center was immensely successful with the public. From the outset, there was a "Beaubourg phenomenon." Although, prior to its opening, the most generous estimates peaked at 10,000 visitors per day, or three million visitors a year, the Center attracted 25,000 people per day on average—with high points of 40,000 per day—or, in other words, between 7 and 8 million visitors a year. The Beaubourg immediately became one of the most visited institutions in the world, with its temporary exhibitions proving especially attractive: *Paris-Berlin* (407,524 visitors); *Paris-Moscow* (435,013 visitors); *Paris-Paris* (473,103 visitors); *Vienna: The Birth of a Century* (450,000); *Dali* (840,662); *Matisse* (735,896). In terms of numbers of regular users, the Center is one of the most successful cultural institutions in the world, with the Public Information Library proving particularly alluring. The Center's immense success is also linked to the number of new members attracted and retained every year. Initially, 50,000 people a year took up membership and the Beaubourg achieved 8 million visitors per annum. Internationally, only the Metropolitan and the MoMA in New York boast comparable membership figures, and it took them decades to reach that level. In France, the Beaubourg was positioned as a pioneer and as a point of reference, wielding considerable influence on new cultural establishments that were either set up or refurbished over the course of the following twenty years. Orsay, La Villette, the Grand Palais, and the Louvre all adopted the policy of expanding their respective publics, involving them actively and encouraging them to remain loyal.

2.3 The issue:realizing the ideal of the democratization of culture

In attempting to understand how the TNP and the Beaubourg/Pompidou Center affected a revolution in cultural practices and representations, I have sought to shed light on how institutions can succeed in asserting themselves not only as *organizations*, but also as *instituting* structures generating new beginnings. The democratization of culture is the product of a kind of reciprocal relationship between the visitor and the institution. Highly original in the French context, this public policy approach can be thought of in a relational way. An object of study in and of itself, the cultural institution becomes key to understanding the ways in which cultural policy and cultural practice are articulated. In the light of Vilar's TNP, cultural institutions appear to be not only the result, but also the condition of possibility of public policy in the arts. *Instituted* by policy, the TNP was also an *instituting* agent of new cultural practices and new public policies. Vilar's TNP was a real actor in terms of the definition of public policy in the field of culture, both as an event and a model, a possible vector of the realization of the ideal of the democratization of culture. That is why I have developed the idea of a *political* institution of cultural practices.

In order to posit successfully the ideas expressed above, it was necessary to start with cultural institutions while bearing in mind that, in the social sciences, it is in the variation of the scale of contexts, generating a quasi-experimental variation of scientific constructions that the most interesting knowledge effects emerge. This perspective characterizes the intellectual approach of this book, an approach that accords a double status to institutions: on the one hand, as objects of research, and, on the other, as a mode of analysis or access. They are objects of research in their own right, giving us a clearer vision of the lessons to be learned from Jean Vilar's TNP (1951–1963) and from that of his successor, Georges Wilson's (1963-1972), as well as from the Beaubourg, which, in homage to the late president, became the "Georges Pompidou Center of Art and Culture" in

1975. But they also provide a mode of access, to the degree that the TNP and the Pompidou Center are key both to an analysis of cultural policy and to a sociological examination of cultural practices. Indeed, both could be defined as synecdoches of cultural policy in that that they condense the tensions and issues that have characterized that same policy in France since 1945.

I have accorded a simultaneously empirical and methodological status to cultural institutions with a view to analyzing the democratization of culture in light of their actions. This approach is informed by a desire to combine general reflections with empirical fieldwork based on the study of specific scenarios. The choice of two institutions (the TNP and the Pompidou Center) derives, negatively, from my desire to avoid the bias inherent in the monographic approach, and, positively, from my intention to extend the lessons learned from one institution and apply them to another, neighboring one in order to produce a "configuration of events," or, in other words, the most consistent ensemble possible capable of generating a number of general propositions. In this regard, it should be observed that the Pompidou Center functions within the paradigm defined by the TNP in that, beyond the heuristically useful comparability of the two institutions, there is a genuine historical filiation between them due to the fact that the public policies underpinning the Beaubourg were developed by Georges Guette, the former Secretary of Vilar's TNP.

As well as the TNP and the Beaubourg, it would be worthwhile examining another case that, in terms of orientations and conclusions, is of a similar nature. In 1996, free entry to the Louvre was introduced on one Sunday per month. The controversy opposing the advocates of free entry and the supporters of payment for access to cultural goods is an often stormy affair and the arguments presented are often based more on rhetorical conviction than on empirical reality. The emotive nature of the question of whether or not culture should be free is at once its strength and its weakness. Indeed, that emotiveness should be viewed as symptomatic of its power and of the breadth of values that it encompasses. The question of entry prices to museums and historical monuments was, until recently, left to the care of public administrators. Indeed, the introduction of a free Sunday every month had the positive effect of refocusing public attention on the debate. Since the turn of the last century, an increasing number of sites have been offering free entry; the variety of free offers is now so broad in the field of cultural practices that it has become legitimate to ask whether the connotations and ramifications of the issue have changed radically. It thus seemed important to reflect on what is specific to free entry as applied to heritage and, following on from my previous work on the function historically attributed to the practice, to examine its evolutions and its effects at the Louvre and at other cultural institutions with a view to suggesting a theoretical model describing the way in which it is experienced today by museum visitors. Although the Louvre enjoys an exceptional status due to its size, reputation, and history, it nevertheless seems that its unmatched prestige encourages the public to express their opinions, and makes of this museum a paradigm for heritage sites and centers all over France. Indeed, the impact of the reintroduction of free entry has been substantially similar in the Louvre and in other museums and historical monuments and confirms both the plurality of modes of cultural socialization and the plasticity of the *habitus* that, as has been demonstrated, is open to modification (Fourteau: 2007).

Before concluding this introduction, I would like to recall the infinite diversity of cultural configurations, the difficulty involved in fully understanding them, and the fact that modesty is a prerequisite of sociological research. The fact that a number of empirical works have helped to render explanations based on sweeping generalizations obsolete suggests that Max Weber's views on the social sciences are still valid. He insisted on a *rejection of causal monism* (overestimating the influence of social class or academic background, for example), which consists in questioning simplistic descriptions of cultural practices. And he promoted a *sociological perspective*, indispensable for accessing the sense and signification accorded by individuals to their evening at the theater, their visit to the museum, or the literature that they read. Indeed, this type of understanding reveals that people establish, at the very heart of their cultural practices, a relationship with values—sometimes ultimate values—expressed in the classic statement, "it changed my life." Aesthetic experiences can, in other words, provoke an "upheaval" or a "transformation."

Furthermore, Franco-American dialogue presupposes at once a degree of modesty and the need to accept and embrace the labyrinthine task of comparison. In order to make a small contribution to that dialogue, this book suggests a few hypotheses common to my research and to that of Terry Clark. The first involves the *conception of cultural socialization*. An initial observation—fairly disconcerting in view of this thematic, chronological presentation—is the idea that, in terms of culture, there are no simple, univocal links between childhood experiences and adult behaviors. Such a conclusion obliges us to think of cultural socialization in complex terms, taking into account both transformations in primary spheres of socialization (family, school, peer groups), and secondary spheres of socialization (processes of individuation, phenomena of contiguity, cultural institutions). Taking an interest in secondary socialization highlights its *incomplete* nature, constitutive of the very process by which it defines itself. However, sociology must rise to the challenge of understanding and explaining the experience of a cultural act.

This introduction will have achieved its goal if it demonstrates both the fecundity of the approach and the originality of the perspectives outlined, as well as the way in which the conjunction of various intellectual traditions enables us to glimpse what emerges from the intertwining of art and emotion, the association of culture and politics.

These examples suggest the range and diversity of institutional mechanisms and influences on participants. Rather than thinking of cultural policy solely from the viewpoint of the production of the discourses and bodies of doctrine of a central administration, we should attempt to understand the influence of links forged between the cultural institution and the individuals making up its public on the definition of policy. Reciprocally, rather than considering cultural practices exclusively from the point of view of the relationship between a given individual and a cultural offer, an attempt should be made to analyze the possible influence of policy decisions and institutions on those practices. Applying a sociological perspective to understanding the governance of behaviors ultimately initiated by cultural institutions introduces a political dimension to the sociology of culture.

In lieu of a conclusion, it should be pointed out that it is impossible to summarize the sociology of culture in an introduction as brief as this one. Indeed, this introduction does not lay down the law for the book that follows it. It is therefore up to the reader to develop her own conception of approaches to understanding the cultural sphere. Because processes of interpretation escape analysts who address themselves to a public, because the production of an interpretation can be defined in terms of a collection of structuring traits, the process of production in itself generates meaning. A work of art drifts and, during its wandering, is transformed: it lends itself to the metaphor of the "journey" through both time and space. An "invitation to a voyage," to paraphrase Baudelaire, whom Terry Clark echoes by providing us with "an idea" of things. This book owes much to him. In effect, Terry Clark *invited* me to write this book after we met and enjoyed a series of fascinating conversations. I would like to take this opportunity to express my gratitude for his invaluable advice and constant encouragement. Finally, I would like to thank him for his invitation to seek a deeper sociological understanding of culture and politics and share them with a wider public.

Laurent Fleury
Professor at the Université Paris Diderot

NOTE

Hermann Broch. 2005. *Logique d'un monde en ruine. Six essais philosophiques*. Translated from the German by Christian Bouchindhomme and Pierre Rusch (Paris: Éditions de l'Éclat, « Philosophie imaginaire »), 53.

I

Sociology of Culture and Cultural Practices

ONE

Sociologists and Culture

Among the problematics inherited by the sociology of culture from cultural anthropology, *ethnocentrism* is of fundamental importance in any attempt to understand the tension between *culture*, in the singular, and *cultures*, in the plural. Ethnocentrism is a refusal and a rejection. A *refusal* of the diversity of cultures and of the relativity of one's own culture, but also a *rejection* into the realm of nature, or, in other words, outside culture, of the person who does not share the same norms and values as the society of reference. Ethnocentrism is not reserved to historical figures ("barbarians," "savages," "primitives"); it is also present in a state of prejudice in class or gender ethnocentrism.

A second problematic derives from cultural anthropology, which insists on the diversity of culture in general and the specificity of cultures in particular, an approach typical of culturalism. This approach defines culture according to specific traits common to members of a particular group, traits which form a unified, coherent system and which are handed down from generation to generation without undergoing any substantial modifications. Ralph Linton's concept of "cultural heritage" (*The Cultural Background of Personality*, 1947), Abraham Kardiner's notion of "basic personality" (*The Individual and His Society*, 1939), and Ruth Benedict's idea of the "cultural model" (*Patterns of Culture*, 1934) are all examples of this tradition. In her comparative studies of the social personalities of the ethnic groups of New Guinea (*Sex and Temperament in Three Primitive Societies*, 1935), Margaret Mead (1901–1978) distinguishes a number of ways in which culture is transmitted. However, when culturalism is used as an exclusive explanatory approach describing a conception of culture as a closed, immutable, and homogeneous universe, it generates confusion in terms of identity, substantializing *cultural* traits to such a degree that they appear *natural*.

Last, the definition of the term *culture* represents a third problematic. For both cultural anthropology and the sociology of culture, all culture is "arbitrary." The idea of the arbitrary should not be confused here with any notion of correctness or a lack thereof. The arbitrary in this instance refers to the *arbitrary nature of the linguistic sign* that Ferdinand de Saussure defined in his *Course in General Linguistics* (1908) by making the *arbitrary* character of the relationship between signifieds and signifiers the basis of all language. It also refers to the prohibition on incest which, according to Claude Lévi-Strauss, is an *institution* as opposed to an *instinct*, and which founds not only the family but also society (*The Elementary Structures of Kinship*, 1949). Culture, as its anthropological definition would suggest, is informed by an ensemble of institutions, each of which is situated in a historical narrative and characterized by certain particularities. Nature, defined, on the other hand, by means of the rule of law as a universal principle, is thus opposed to culture, a field of rules characterized by their variability. The anthropological opposition between nature and culture is thus to be found in distinctions between identity and identification, communication and language, organs and tools, heredity and heritage. Like language, culture thus refers to a system of signs and to the "arbitrary" nature of all symbolic relationships. Beyond these traditions, which we will not have the opportunity to examine in any depth in this book, we need to understand how "culture" has become a *specific object* of sociological analysis. If Durkheim, Weber, and Simmel are viewed as the founders of sociology, then Weber and Simmel can be seen as precursors of the sociology of culture understood in its strictest sense; Durkheim, meanwhile, took no specific interest in the subject.

1. TWO PRECURSORS AMONG THE FOUNDING FATHERS: WEBER AND SIMMEL

While Durkheim effectively placed the crystallized forms of social life to which "culture" belongs at the center of his work, the term itself does not feature in his vocabulary. Nor, indeed, was he interested in the process whereby specific artistic forms were recognized as such. In a functionalist perspective, *The Elementary Forms of Religious Life* (1912) focuses on the beliefs and ritual practices that constitute the symbolic forms guaranteeing the very possibility of social integration underpinning the collective conscience characteristic of life in society. Marcel Mauss, for whom an institution is a symbolic form that creates a world, applies a similar anthropological approach, as exemplified in the idea, developed in *Techniques of the Body* (1934–1936), according to which all day-to-day gestures are informed by culture. But, in Durkheim's work, the question of art occupies a modest place (Menger, 2001). In the rare passages dedicated to it, art appears as an ambivalent field of activity; while the usefulness of artistic education is examined in the last chapter of *Moral Education*, in *The Division of Labor in Society* (1893) it is described in terms of disease, pathology, and the deregulation of social life. In a quasi-Platonic process of devalorization, Durkheim employs the notion of luxury, complete with an explicit, negative value judgment, to describe the ambivalence of art, which has the defect of introducing a risk of anomie, celebrated during the same period by Jean-Marie Guyau as a liberating factor.

1.1 The Question of the Cultural Meaning of Art: Max Weber

The career of Max Weber (1864–1920) is relevant to the early development of the sociology of culture in a number of ways. In *The Rational and Social Foundations of Music* (1910), he characterized that form of artistic expression as an object of research in its own right and as providing a key to an understanding of the processes of rationalization characteristic of Western societies. Weber examined culture, defined in the strict sense of a *differentiated artistic sphere*, in both *The Rational and Social Foundations of Music* and, to a greater degree, in the *Zwischenbetrachtung* (1915)—translated as "Religious Rejections of the World and their Directions" by Hedwig Ida Gerth and C. Wright Mills in 1946—in which he systematically analyzed different spheres of activity. He developed the idea of a competition between the artistic and religious spheres in reference to a function of deliverance that art can provide in the same way as religion.

> [. . .] Art becomes a cosmos of more and more consciously grasped independent values which exist in their own right. Art takes over the function of a this-worldly deliverance (*Erlösung*). It *delivers* us from the routines of daily life, and especially from the increasing pressures of theoretical and practical rationalism. With this claim to a redemptory function, art begins to compete directly with salvation-deliverance (*Erlösung*) religions. Every rational religious ethic must turn against this inner-worldly, irrational form of salvation. For, in religion's eyes, such salvation is a realm of irresponsible indulgence and secret lovelessness (Weber, 1946: 342).

It should be pointed out that the theme of salvation was associated with the *crisis of culture*, a topic of philosophical and sociological debate at the time.

In a broader sense, culture is a central theme of Weber's work (Schroeder, 1992). In a world stricken, according to Nietzsche, by the death of God and the advent of nihilism, Weber referred to the philosopher's viewpoint on Man and modern culture by evoking the coming of the "last men" (" *Die Heraufkunft der 'letzten Menschen' "*). In this regard, a number of Weber's analyses reflect a tone of cultural pessimism. An example is provided in the last pages of *The Protestant Ethic and the Spirit of Capitalism*, in which he mentions, in a discussion of the economic order and modern culture, the "last humans," "mechanized ossification," and the "iron cage" (*stahlhartes Gehaüse*, "a shell as hard as steel") of modern capitalism. The section includes remarks about "that powerful tendency to render styles of life uniform, which today supports the capitalist interest in the 'standardization' of production" (Weber, 2011: 168) and about an economic order based on "mechanized, machine-based production," that determine "the style of life not only of those directly engaged in economically productive activity, but of all born into this grinding mechanism" (Weber, 2011: 177). "Culture criticism" (*Kulturkritik*) and "cultural pessimism" (*Kulturpessimismus*), for which this system is irrational and destructive (a destruction of the simple life, the anarchic unbridling of passions) and for which, in a contrary sense, it introduces a risk of "leveling," a kind of ennui engendered by a loss of the spontaneity and "luxuriance" of life (Grossein, 2003: XII–XII), represent one of Weber's intellectual horizons. Nevertheless, in spite of this reference to a historical horizon marked by decline, the gradual disappearance of religion and the affirmation of capitalist societies characterized by processes of rationalization and intellectualization, Weber never gives in to any form of nostalgia; on the contrary, he maintains that the dissolution of the meaning of the world in no manner corresponds to the disappearance of the question of the meaning of action.

In a broad sense, culture is located at the heart of Weber's exploration of the forms of rationalization developed by major civilizations and in his elaboration of a sociology of culture (Stauth, 1992). Thus, for Weber, culture is a *crucial problematic*. One of his central fields of inquiry is the question of the "cultural meaning" of facts introduced by the problematic of the "disenchantment of the world" (*Entzauberung der Welt*), more exactly translated by the neologism "demagicification"—the disappearance of magical explanations of the world (Weiß, 1991). When he focuses on the practical ways in which religious ideas are appropriated (*The Protestant Ethic and the Spirit of Capitalism*), Weber seeks to understand how Protestantism engendered a type of *ethos*, or, in other words, a rational conduit of life (*Lebensführung*) corresponding to a structured ensemble of behaviors and practices. He explains how Man is fashioned by culture and by the great civilizations. Taking a sociologically comparativist approach, he also examines how Confucianism and Taoism created different *types* of man, as did, in particular contexts and in specific ways, Buddhism and Hinduism, ancient Judaism, Catholicism, and Islam. By positing that each of the great civilizations has produced a specific *type* of man, Weber places the question of culture at the heart of his approach. Thus, when he addresses the issue of capitalism in his epistemological essay on *The "Objectivity" of Knowledge in the Social Sciences* (1904) and his study of *The Protestant Ethic* (1904–1905), he focuses on its "*cultural* meaning," examining the cultural effects of a certain range of religious beliefs in an attempt to understand the formation of entire swathes of modern culture (Scaff, 1994).

Thus, from an attempt to arrive at a sociological understanding of Western *culture*, which is one of the major platforms of his intellectual project, to the more precise question of the cultural meaning of art, examined both in *The Rational and Social Foundations of Music* and in the *Zwischenbetrachtung*, culture, in all its wide-ranging meanings, is a central aspect of Weber's work (Fleury, 2009a; 2011).

1.2 The Theme of the "Tragedy of Culture": Georg Simmel

Georg Simmel (1858–1918), a contemporary of Weber, also placed culture at the heart of his sociology, both in terms of his use of the cultural meanings of money and of his concept of the *tragedy of culture* and his writings on culture and art.

The *cultural* meaning of money is analyzed in *The Philosophy of Money* (1900). Simmel examines the *cultural* ambivalence of a social institution which contributes both to the emergence of the individual and to a leveling of values. Due to its status as a general equivalent of abstract properties, money possesses liberatory effects which encourage the process of individuation by, for example, replacing the personal burden of serfdom with the impersonal constraint of the salariat. However, the monetarization of social relations, which contributes to raising the status of the individual, causes contradictory effects including the decline of the sentiment of the human person, as exemplified by corruption and prostitution. While a factor of liberation for the individual, money also threatens elements that Simmel would have hoped to be saved: human dignity, the body, culture. The use of money also encourages the emergence of various dispositions (cupidity, avarice, and prodigality) and situations (wealth, material deprivation, or poverty). Money, which renders all things comparable, also fashions two types of man, both of them typical, according to the author, of the modern urban metropolis (*GroßStadt*): the cynic, who places all values on the same level; and the blasé, who becomes indifferent to differences. Simmel observed the ambivalence of modernity in his studies on large cities, universes of constraint and freedom, and showed that money contributed to the development of the culture of modern societies, which he characterized by means of three concepts: distance, pace of life and symmetry. A factor in the homogenization of the market through the relative decrease in the price of luxury goods, money increases phenomena of imitation and differentiation, typical, in the view of the author, of social interactions, and accentuates fashion-based effects, characteristic of urbanized societies. Simmel thus bequeathed a central problematic for the sociology of culture: that of the exacerbation of social difference, a notion still referred to as "distinction."

The concept of the *tragedy of culture* highlights another point of ambivalence, namely the tragic opposition between life and form. For Simmel, the founder of sociological traditions focusing on interactions and social forms, life must be mediated by forms in order to express itself, even though those forms stifle its creative élan. Life thus transcends and alienates itself in the cultural forms that it creates. The divorce between *objective culture* and *subjective culture* provides an example of this. The hypertrophy of one goes hand-in-hand with the atrophy of the other. In *The Philosophy of Money*, Simmel took the pessimistic view that the triumph of objective culture is proportional to the defeat of subjective culture:

> If one compares our culture to that of a hundred years ago, then one may surely say—subject to many individual exceptions—that the things that determine and surround our lives [. . .] are extremely refined. Yet individual culture [. . .] has not progressed at all to the same extent; indeed, it has even frequently declined (Simmel, 2004: 486).

The author elaborated a dynamic conception of culture as *Bildung*, the development and realization of the self by means of the assimilation of cultural content. For Simmel, culture is not only the objectivization of the soul in a series of forms ("the subject objectivizing itself"), but also, inversely, the formation of the soul by means of the assimilation of objectivized forms ("the object subjectivizing itself"). Culture is thus defined as the movement of synthesis of the objective spirit and the subjective spirit. To the degree that objective culture (an ensemble of cultural forms pre-existing the individual) becomes autonomous and hypertrophized, "the synthesis becomes a paradox, or even a *tragedy*." Confronted with the hypertrophy of objective culture, the individual is overwhelmed by the magnitude of the accumulated wealth that she is in no way able to assimilate; she is overwhelmed and yet constantly tempted by the mass of cultural contents, even though she is unable to appropriate them. It is in this dichotomy that, according to Simmel, the *tragedy of culture* lies.

A collector of Chinese vases and Japanese ceramics and the owner of two drawings by Rodin which the artist had given to him on his visit to Paris, Simmel also entertained, on the first Monday of every month, Rainer Maria Rilke, Stefan George, Heinrich Rickert, Max and Marianne Weber, Georg Lukacs, and Ernst Bloch in his "salon-museum." Simmel, a philosopher who drew profit from reading the poets and frequenting the painters, sculptors, and architects of his time, was also the author of monographs on Rodin and Michelangelo and of articles on Florence, Venice and Rome and on the landscape, in which he shows that "nature," which we believe to be natural, is in fact cultural, a thing fashioned by man. In his studies on art and culture, Simmel applied to the field of aesthetics epistemological precepts defined in parallel with the historical sciences; indeed, that is where the originality of his contribution to sociology is to be found. Characterized by conceptual borrowing and points of intersection (Deroche-Gurcel, 1997: 9), Simmel's work should be viewed as a whole: reciprocal action, a central category in Simmel's sociology, is to be found at the heart of his aesthetics as is witnessed by his reflections on the relationship between sound and sense in the poems of Stefan George; his critique of epistemological positivism is also echoed in his equally thorough critique of artistic realism. These major themes of the work of Simmel, like that of Weber, mark an initial phase in the process of the emergence of culture as an object of sociological analysis.

2. TWO SOCIOLOGIES OF CULTURE IN INDUSTRIAL SOCIETIES

Weber's sociology of the establishment of forms has influenced numerous intellectual traditions, including the Frankfurt School of Adorno and Horkheimer. Simmel's sociology of modernity inspired the nuanced theses of Walter Benjamin. All these authors share a common concern: cultural developments in industrial societies. In the same way that Weber made a distinction between virtuosos and the masses in the religious dynamic, the issue of the dichotomy between a learned culture reserved to an elite and a mass culture conceded to ordinary individuals began to emerge, with mass culture threatening the very existence of its elite equivalent.

2.1 From Mass Culture to the Culture Industry: The Frankfurt School

Walter Benjamin's *The Work of Art in the Age of Mechanical Reproduction* (1935–1939) proved to be seminal (Benjamin, 2008). He was the first to ask how the photographic reproduction of works of art affected their "aura," which he defined through the dialectic of the near and the far. How did the reproduction of works of art contribute to the loss of uniqueness typical of a classical definition of such works and to the dilution of the cultural or "auratic" value of the work? While Benjamin avoided all proselytism in the matter by skirting clear of the idea that reproduction represented a decline and even focusing on the aesthetic possibilities it offered to a wider public, after the Second World War, Adorno and Horkheimer took Benjamin's thematic in a more pessimistic direction. During and after his period of exile in the United States, Adorno discovered mass culture in the form, among other things, of the power of the radio, the birth of television, the importance of advertising, and the growth of the cinema. Entertainment went hand-in-hand with business; such was Hollywood's mantra. Worse, demanding any form of intellectual effort on the part of the spectator was out of the question: all possibility of critical thought was to be jettisoned in favor of fun and amusement. For Adorno, who had been a student of the Viennese composer Alban Berg, about whom he wrote a monograph, just as he wrote on Mahler, Schönberg, and Stravinsky, the very idea of culture and its ascetic conception of aesthetic experience were under threat. In order to counter these affronts, he drew up, at least in terms of the sociology of culture, a research program.

At a conference held in 1963, Adorno outlined why, in the 1940s, he and Max Horkheimer had preferred the concept of the "culture industry" to that of "mass culture"; the distinction removed all ambiguity from their object of study, which was not the values and cultural practices of the majority, but the ways in which an industrial system capable of delivering cultural products designed for mass consumption was organized (Horkheimer and Adorno, 2000). Upstream of any analysis of aesthetic reception, their project consisted, at that point, in demonstrating how, due to the progress of technology and the concentration of administrative and financial resources, a new industry had emerged, capable of effacing all distinctions between, on the one hand, a culture based on the personal assimilation of a tradition, and, on the other, the promotion of ephemeral, collective entertainment. The focus on efficiency within the framework of a quest for profit, the standardization of products, the preoccupation with special effects, and the rationalization of distribution procedures all pointed to the fact that cultural creations had, in a sense, become commodities (Ducret, 2005). This is Adorno's central theme: the transformation of culture into a commodity affects the very definition of the cultural act by reducing it to an act of consumption, eventually diluting the idea of culture itself. The process of reification highlighted by Marx is thus reflected in the very existence of *cultural* products. Herbert Marcuse developed this critical theory by emphasizing the negative aspects of the reduction of culture to an object of consumerism (Marcuse, 1964). Jürgen Habermas's notion of the "colonization of the lifeworld" by technological society represents another, broader development of Adorno's theme.

The perspectives opened by the Frankfurt School articulated contemporary political affairs and the sociological fecundity at the very heart of the definition of what its practitioners termed a "critical theory." While Adorno's tendency toward normativity was revealed by a few categorical judgments on jazz, his classifications of music listeners (distinguishing *experts* with adequate skills; *good listeners* who lack technical mastery; and *consumers of culture* who do not have the ability to understand music structurally), and his distinction between *superior music* and *light music*, his extremely fecund notion of the *culture industry* nevertheless contributed to founding a sociology of culture. The concept, taken up first by André Malraux and then by a series of French Culture ministers who have since incorporated it into their policies, is central to contemporary thought on the evolution of culture in modern society. Such thought underlines the problem of the meaning of the cultural act in a world which denies it: against a discourse insisting on cultural diversity within the framework of globalization (Mattelart, 2005) and on the rehabilitation of popular cultures, some talk of the disappearance of popular cultures and the emergence of an industrial culture which homogenizes practices and affects processes of individuation and subjectivation (Stiegler, 2004; 2005). According to these observers, the scorn accompanying the "mechanical" turn of sensibility that replaces popular cultures with a single industrial culture leads to the emergence of a form of alienation which, to borrow from a different intellectual tradition (Arendt, 1993), explains the existence of widespread apathy and apoliticization. The place taken by the production of cultural goods and defiance in regard to the industrialization of culture explain the growing importance of Cultural Studies.

2.2 Popular Culture and the "Cultural Turn": Cultural Studies

Willingly associated with a form of pragmatism allergic to theoretical schemas, industrial England nevertheless bore witness to the development of an original debate on culture considered as an instrument with which to reorganize a society that had undergone the upheavals of industrialization, or as an instrument of "civilization" of emerging social groups, or as the cement of a national consciousness. Deeply influenced by the events of the Industrial Revolution, Cultural Studies finds its roots in the cultural critique of the bourgeois society of the nineteenth century. Raymond Williams (1921–1988) elaborated a genealogy of the concept of "culture" in industrial society from the Romantics to Orwell in which he explored the connotations of terms such as *culture, the masses, crowds,* and *art,* while approaching the history of ideas in terms of a historical process of ideological production (Williams, 1958). This debate, which has its equivalent in the intellectual life of most European countries, gave rise, in the post-Second World War period, to an original approach exemplified by the founding works of Richard Hoggart on the lifestyles of the working classes, focusing on the effects of social distance between education and culture (Hoggart, 1957); Raymond Williams's *The Long Revolution* (Williams, 1961); E.P. Thompson's *The Making of the English Working Class* (Thompson, 1963), and the theorizations of Stuart Hall, author of *The Popular Arts* (1964) and coordinator, with Richard Hoggart, of the Center for Contemporary Cultural Studies at the University of Birmingham (Hall, 1992), the focal point of the development of Cultural Studies from 1964 to 1980 (Hall, 1980).

The emergence of Cultural Studies as a paradigm is based on a process of theoretical questioning which gradually crystallized into a coherent approach. Its proponents considered culture in a broad, anthropological sense, overturning a monolithic cultural definition of the nation and introducing an approach based on social groups, the common point remaining a particularist conception of culture. While the proponents of Cultural Studies continued to focus on political aspects, the central issue was to understand how the culture of a group, and, first and foremost, of the working classes, functioned as a protest against the social order, or, on the contrary, as a mode of acceptance of existing power relations.

Indeed, the areas explored by Cultural Studies are consubstantial with the idea of resistance to the industrial cultural order, and popular cultures are examined in terms of their ability to provide resources for resistance. For the culturalist anthropologist, Clifford Geertz, the working classes, far from being passive consumers, mobilize a repertoire of obstacles to domination (Geertz, 1973). Meanwhile, Dick Hebdige points out the ambivalence underpinning a form of resistance based on a purely defensive posture (Hebdige, 1979), alluding to a "celebration of powerlessness" hidden behind an unconvincing attitude of insubordination (Hebdige, 1988). The problematic of the construction of collective identities is also explored in works in which the category of social class is replaced with variables such as generations, gender, sexuality, and ethnicity (Long, 1992).

In France, Cultural Studies are known to a degree inversely proportional to the international recognition received by the field. However, despite this international recognition, it should be pointed out that Cultural Studies' many contributions to the sociology of culture are characterized by a degree of ambivalence. From the return to an emphasis on group sociability and popular cultures which marked the "Birmingham years" to the exploration of themes focusing on gender, the "ethnicization of culture" and the elaboration of problematics oriented toward intertwined processes of domination and resistance, the multiplicity of questions bequeathed to the sociology of culture have revealed themselves to be incommensurable. How do social milieu, age, gender, and "ethnic identity" affect relations to culture? Are the lifestyles of young people linked to forms of resistance? How can we understand the way in which TV programs are received by various publics? (Macé, 2000; 2001). Such questions, posed in England in the 1960s, transformed the definition and status of culture. By according to the experience of the working classes the kind of attention previously reserved to the culture of the highly literate and by taking an interest in design, advertising, audiovisual products, the transmission and exploitation of knowledge, as well as recreational activities, leisure, and tourism, Cultural Studies played a part in promoting the ubiquity of the "cultural" (Passeron, Mayol, Macé, 2003). David Chaney suggests a link between this new positioning of the "cultural" and the notion of the "cultural turn" (Chaney, 1994). From this point of view, culture ceases to be an extraordinary aspect of social life and enters the realm of everyday existence (Silverstone, 1994). The perspectives introduced by Cultural Studies not only touch on the media and its digital manifestations (Scott, 1990) but also inform postcolonial and gender studies and reinstate a dialogue with cultural history and the new sociology of leisure. This omnipresence, which is linked to an anthropological definition of culture, is translated, in France, by the substantive adjective *"le culturel"* ("the cultural"). "The cultural" thus replaces "culture," which, consequently, has begun to connote purely literary culture. Eschewing the broad definition supplied by the "cultural turn" and by the American imperative of "thinking the cultural" (Pfister, 1996), the sociology of culture, as institutionalized in France in the 1960s, focused on what it regarded as "legitimate" culture.

3. THE INSTITUTIONALIZATION OF THE "SOCIOLOGY OF CULTURE" IN FRANCE

The institutionalization of the sociology of culture in France is closely associated with the introduction of public policies on culture which made the country, if not an exception, then at least unusual. The 1960s bore witness to an increasing emphasis on the use of free time, of which there was more and more, providing ordinary people with the opportunity of fulfilling themselves, notably by participating in cultural activities (Dumazedier, 1974; 1976; 1996). However, in its first decade, the sociology of culture had different institutional and intellectual foundations.

3.1 Intellectual and Institutional Foundations

The *institutional* foundations of the sociology of culture are indissociable from the French Ministry of Cultural Affairs, set up by André Malraux in 1959. The Cultural Facilities and Heritage Commission, the first commission specifically responsible for the cultural and artistic sector under the Fourth Plan, was founded in 1961; Jacques Delors accorded its secretary, Augustin Girard, the mission of creating a study and research unit within the newly established Ministry. Shortly after it was set up in 1963, the Study and Research Department requested that Pierre Bourdieu carry out a survey on the frequency of visits to museums in Europe. In 1964, Jean Vilar set up the Rencontres d'Avignon: every year the founder of the Avignon Festival (1947) and director of the National Popular Theater (1951–1963) invited men and women of the theater, cultural professionals, politicians, and researchers in the social sciences to share their thoughts on themes such as "Cultural Development" (1964), "Education" (1965), "Regional Cultural Development" (1966), "Urban Cultural Policy" (1967), and the "Cultural Development of Local Authorities in Europe" (1970). The Bourges Colloquium on Scientific Research and Cultural Development (1964) was based on the same idea. In 1966, the initial results of Pierre Bourdieu's survey of visits to museums in Europe were published.[1] The French National Institute of Statistics and Economic Studies' first survey on leisure dates from 1967.

The *intellectual* foundation of the sociology of culture can be traced to the concomitant elaboration of a theoretical framework by Bourdieu, at the crossroads between a sociology of education, developed with Jean-Claude Passeron—in *Les Héritiers* (1964) and *La Reproduction* (1970)—and an embryonic sociology of cultural legitimacy elaborated in *L'Amour de l'art* (1966 and 1969) and further developed in *La Distinction* (1979). The surveys carried out by Bourdieu showed that cultural practices were socially hierarchized and that the various visitor rates at cultural sites highlighted a hierarchized social distribution of cultural practices. Indeed, this factor, which has remained constant since the mid-1960s, is linked to a particular datum. One of the major contributions of the sociology of culture is to have revealed that factors explaining differentials in the rates of frequentation of cultural venues are symbolic (socialization, cultivated *habitus*) rather than material (geographical distance, price barriers). In 1966, examining the social distribution of cultural practices, Bourdieu suggested that the problem did not reside in an absence of a relation to art, but in an "absence of a feeling of absence." This statement posits desire in reference to a lack and suggests that the absence of awareness of a lack provokes the absence of a desire for culture. The second edition, revised and augmented, of *L'Amour de l'art* ("The Love of Art," 1969), completed the diffusion of these results among the professionals of culture. The publication of *La Distinction* in 1979 completed the conceptual edifice, detailed in chapter 3 of this book, and gave Pierre Bourdieu the status of a founder of the sociology of culture.

3.2 The Developments of an Empirical Sociology of Culture

A Longitudinal Survey of *The Cultural Practices of the French*

The Ministry of Culture's main tool for measuring the evolution of cultural practices is its quantitative survey, first conducted in 1973, which, every eight years, sends a representative sample of the French population a questionnaire about their cultural practices. The five surveys conducted to date (1973, 1981, 1989, 1997, and 2009) shed light on the major trends in the field (Donnat, 1998). A comparison between the most recent survey and the three which preceded it, based on the repeated use of the same protocol, reveals new, even radically new behaviors, as well as a number of more constant aspects. However, the survey is now much broader in scope than it was in 1973, focusing on activities which come under the aegis of the Ministry of Culture, or, in other words, practices essentially linked to various forms of artistic expression but which correspond to a less institutional definition of culture that now includes television, do-it-yourself activities, sewing, and certain kinds of outings. Methods based on polling techniques are used to generate the results, which are detailed in the following chapter. However, polls do not record practices but, instead, declarations of practices, which explains a tendency to overestimate or, on the contrary, to underestimate, as in the case of weak "practitioners" such as, for example, the readers of sentimental novels who, mindful that such works belong to a genre that is often considered minor and, as such, not "legitimate," frequently downplay the number of books they read (Péquignot, 1991). However, in spite of such biases linked to information gathering techniques, *The Cultural Practices of the French* not only provides an accurate reflection of cultural behaviors but also makes it possible to conduct more specific surveys of certain publics and cultural institutions. The survey is thus an indispensable source of statistical information. The sociology of culture, as consolidated by this longitudinal survey, has the merit of generating a positive form of knowledge based on a *description* of cultural practices and a series of concepts applied with a view to *explaining* them. In this regard, cultural practices are implicitly analyzed in Durkheimian terms as social facts demanding explanation.

An increase in the number of empirical studies in the 1990s and 2000s

Following the editions of the survey on *The Cultural Practices of the French* (1973, 1981, 1989, 1998, 2009), the Ministry of Culture's Department of Studies and Forecasts sought to analyze other aspects more familiar to professionals of culture working on a daily basis with the establishment's various publics (Donnat and Octobre, 2001). When it opened in 1977, the Pompidou Center commissioned empirical surveys from Pierre Bourdieu, Jean-Louis Fabiani, and Pierre-Michel Menger on the different kinds of publics that it was attracting. The Pompidou Center's Public Information Library was unique in France; its Studies and Research Department, which focused on building up an empirical database of reading practices, has since become a center for action and observation and has published a substantial number of studies and surveys (Poulain, 1990). The now widespread idea of research units focusing on specific publics derives from the work of this department, from "surveys at the doors of the Center" carried out for a number of years by Nathalie Heinich, and studies led by Claude Fourteau who, while directing the Liaison/Enrollment Department at the Pompidou Center, showed a willingness to borrow from the social sciences by encouraging the practice of gathering empirical data on targeted groups of individuals. *Les Institutions culturelles au plus près du public* (Fourteau, 2002) and *Le(s) Public(s) de la culture* (Donnat and Tolila, 2003) provide an overview of the research carried out in these areas. In spite of their differing approaches and findings, one point these studies have in common is their stable vocabulary. The term "public"—which, due to the accumulation both of actions taken by cultural institutions and reflections developed by sociologists of culture, became "publics"—has always been used to designate the object of research. The choice of the term can be explained in reference to the specific background against which the sociology of culture developed in France, namely the elaboration of a national cultural policy. In conclusion, "culture" has become an object of sociology in its own right and is approached as such by sociologists from various intellectual traditions. This process of academic differentiation, developed over the course of the

20th century, throws light on the evolution of the definition of culture which, initially thought of in terms of an anthropological datum, came to be more specifically seen in terms of a corpus of works especially highly regarded by a given society.

NOTE

1. Bourdieu, Pierre. 1966. *L'amour de l'art. Les musées d'art européens et leurs publics*. Paris: Editions de Minuit. The second edition was published in 1969. For the English translation, see *The Love of Art. European Art Museums and their Publics*, translated by Caroline Beattie. Cambridge: Polity Press, 1997.

TWO
Culture's Publics

There is a historical reason why, in France, people speak of the *publics* of culture. That reason is the existence of public policies on culture. Yet few analyses have been made of the notion of the *public* itself, either in terms of what the word means or of the issues which it raises in the political and artistic discourses which endlessly refer to it. Unthinkingly, the *public* is viewed as something which is not only obvious but also natural. What are we dealing with when we deal with this word, its meanings, and usages? What kinds of communities does it refer to, what kind of destination does it describe? To what symbolic necessities does it respond? What imaginary identities does it permit? And what place does it have in political and sociological discourses?

1. PUBLIC, "NON-PUBLIC," PUBLICS

In the singular, the public is traditionally conceived of as the homogenous and unitary ensemble of readers, listeners, or spectators of a piece of literature or music, or a film or theatrical production. Because there is no such thing as a monolithic public, sociologists regard the use of the term in the singular as an example of common sense naivety: there is not one public, there are many, and the same is true of existing artistic genres and the affective and intellectual "expectations" of individuals. Nevertheless, for subscribers to and members of cultural institutions, the category known as "the public" often provides a useful way of identifying people. Metaphors used to crystallize the notion of "the" or "a" public have an important role to play. For sociologists, metaphors are often traps for thought, sedimented "truths" acting as illusions whose illusory nature has been forgotten, used up rhetorical figures which have lost any real meaning they might once have had. These remarks are intended to highlight the negative impact of the *uncontrolled* use of metaphors and underline the fact that representations of reality influence reality itself. Various ways of thinking of the public have emerged, the effects of which, judging by the identifications they provoke, can be very real.

1.1 The double metaphor of the "public"

A synecdoche of the *people*—a part representing the whole—"the public" corresponds first and foremost to the ontological metaphor of the unified political body, a single, indivisible Republic. A number of examples of this idea of the public are to be found in the history of popular education (for example, *Peuple et Culture*, a large federation set up in 1945, at the end of the war) and of the popular theater. Jean Vilar, director of the National Popular Theater (TNP), thought of the organization's public in this way, defining it in terms of the *populus*, people living free of any form of exclusion in the unified city, rather than in terms of the *plebs*, a designation applied to the "lower orders," informed by ideas of differentiation and hierarchy. For Vilar, the meaning of the word "people" varied according to the type of theater involved; to the bourgeois theater which disparaged the people, regarding them as *plebs*, he opposed the popular theater which valorized them as members of the *populus*.

The idea of the public is described by another metaphor, that of the literary public sphere, closer to the traditional definition of the public, or, in other words, readers, spectators, and listeners considered as recipients, consumers, and critics of art and literature. The public space, or the bourgeois public sphere, was born of the *egalitarian* practices of conversation and literary criticism that emerged as court society declined. For Jürgen Habermas, public opinion affirms and asserts itself in literary debates, where, in sharing aesthetic sentiment, it first became conscious of itself, whence his well-known distinction between a *culture-debating public* and a *culture-consuming public* (Habermas, 1989: 159–175) which coincides with another dichotomy, this one between the *(literary) bourgeois public sphere*, characteristic of the eighteenth century, and *(post-literary) plebiscitary public opinion*, typical of media societies.

The category of "the public" in the singular is thus actualized as a *myth*. This event highlights the fact that reality is not only real but also imagined. "The public" is a category that provides metaphorical support for an imaginary sphere linked to politics, which betrays a political will to *conquer* and *encourage public loyalty* in the well-known style of the civilizing mission. The category is therefore an important one. The idea of the popular public has encouraged the emergence of a series of definitions that have been analyzed by means of an approach based on the sociology of uses. Rather than accepting a conception of the symbolic order that reduces representations to pure illusions and ideologies to mere instruments of dissimulation, we should examine the social and political efficiency of myths in which reality and imagination are consubstantial.

Surveys on publics attending festivals have demonstrated that processes of "becoming a spectator" or "a public" are underpinned by processes of formation of individual and collective identities (Ethis, 2005: 21). Public action engages the imagination. Beyond the category of recipients that they outline, policies concerning the public provide the potential for individuals to identify with larger social groups. Without wanting to "de-metaphorize" the use of such language, we should be aware of its highly metaphorical content and, above all, be wary of the ramifications of another notion, that of the "non-public."

1.2 The Invention of the Concept of the "Non-Public"

Amid the upheavals of May 1968, Roger Planchon invited forty theater directors to the Théâtre de la Cité to sign the Declaration of Villeurbanne, a document which introduced the notion of the "non-public." The idea emerged from two meetings, the first between the directors, and the second between theater professionals and academics working in the social sciences.

Perceived by the population as an ensemble of apparatuses destined to deliver high culture to a privileged public, cultural policy seems to suffer from a degree of redundancy in that the spectators targeted are always those who possess the means necessary to cultivate themselves, namely the upper classes and the most educated section of the middle classes. According to Francis Jeanson, author of the Declaration, this is where the notion of "public," as opposed to the concept of "non-public," came into play. "*On one side, there is the public*, our public, and it doesn't matter whether it is actual or potential; and *on the other side*, there is the 'non-public', a mass of humanity who do not have access to *and who have no chance of accessing culture any time soon* in the forms which it takes in almost all cases" (Jeanson, 1972: 119–120, my italics). By positing a separation between the "cultivated" and the "non-cultivated," the Declaration of Villeurbanne postulated that different people have different cultural aptitudes. Apparently neutral and applied by a number of theaters and museums, the notion nevertheless introduced an original dimension. Beyond the various ways in which it was appropriated by different cultural institutions, it is important to think about the ramifications of such an idea (Fleury, 2004b). When Francis Jeanson used it in the Declaration of Villeurbanne, was he aware of creating a radical exteriority? The scorn that the notion implies already signals a process of marginalization, or even exclusion.

For the first time since the sixteenth century, the period during which the literary public came into being, a part of the population was implicitly denied the formal possibility of becoming a part of that public. The

Villeurbanne directors claimed that they wanted to encourage members of what they described as the "non-public" to go to the theater, but this declaration of intent was an affront, since it was unlikely that these last would ever emerge from the metaphorical prison-house of the identity assigned to them, an identity based on a form of institutionalization. While the notion has the appearance of objectivity, we should not forget the arbitrary character of a judgment that introduces an artificial frontier into a reality which is largely characterized by the continuity or contiguity of various situations. More than a description of reality, it is a representation of reality informed by a number of rarely defined presuppositions. The invention of the notion of the "non-public" contributes to the naturalization of a social construct. The kind of discrimination thus introduced is not so much sociological as ideological. The word is reduced here to a label with no value as an instrument for perceiving reality. Indeed, our usual perspective needs to be reversed: it is not because the "non-public" is different from us that it should be politically excluded from the, albeit imaginary, community of the public. It is, rather, because it is institutionally and politically constituted as a "non-public" that it appears as the Other and that its cultural and social differences are so visible. By introducing this irreducible separation, the discourse partially realizes what it announces.

The "non-public" is thus revealed as a negative and exclusive category. With the transition from the notion of a *potential public* to that of a "non-public," we move, almost imperceptibly, from a probabilistic universe to a universe of certainty. The doubtless involuntary effect of the Villeurbanne Declaration was to ostracize a substantial percentage of the potential public by relegating it to oblivion and exiling it from the cultural sphere. A process of disqualification and marginalization came into view. The "non-public" referred to the ne'er-do-wells, the "excluded," the "paupers" of culture. The notion of poverty referred first and foremost to a lack of income: the poor man does not have enough or has only just enough. But this poverty, which often leads to those suffering it to be viewed not just as poor but also as stupid, is not the integral poverty of the nineteenth century in which members of the bourgeoisie, *flâneurs*, Napoleonic soldiers, and beggars could be seen together in the corridors of the Louvre. It is, rather, the poverty of the marginalized and the disqualified, as described by Simmel.

The notion negates the *temporality* of cultural practices by redefining a potentially transitory exclusion as a chronic prohibition. The notion also negates the *sociality* of cultural practices by debarring a certain group of people from culture. Indeed, the absence of sociability exacerbates exclusion: "the excluded individual is surrounded by other excluded individuals." Assigning people to a negative category has the effect of reifying a statistical regularity, leading to its essentialization and substantialization. In this sense, the rigidity of the notion of the "non-public" promotes a form of class ethnocentrism: the imposition of a symbolic violence that arouses feelings of indignation. The "non-public" represents the Lacanian "Other," a synthesis of all the counter-qualities constituting the idealized collective image of what it is to be "Us." What we witness is the construction of an irreducible alterity, the formation of a radical exteriority, the elaboration of a naturalized category. This process of naturalization of the "cultivated" and the "non-cultivated" is underpinned by an identity-based discourse founded on a denial of the identity of the Other, to whom the very possibility of acquiring a capacity to appreciate or understand culture is denied. Because identity is constantly constructed and reconstructed in social exchanges, because it develops within the framework of a relationship with the Other, there is no identity *per se*. There are fewer differences than there are enterprises of differentiation. Phenomena of social reproduction develop, offering spaces of negative identification which encourage an interiorization of feelings of indignation which are at the origin of the self-censorship experienced by some in regard to cultural facilities and venues.

In conclusion, the transition from the *event* of Villeurbanne to the *advent* of a category, the ideological character of which should be underlined if we want to understand its pretention to constitute a sociological category, inspires at least two remarks.

The first concerns the effects of the diffusion of knowledge from the social sciences. Far from being emancipatory, the notion of the "non-public" serves as the vehicle of an ideological effect. By interiorizing the negative definition foisted upon them, members of the so-called non-public may suffer feelings of guilt. Behind the semantic disagreements concerning the correct definition of words lurk social and political disagreements. Perhaps, in the discursive creation of such a radical alterity, the young working class theater directors said as much about themselves as they did about the "non-public." They were responsible for an ideology which essentializes social traits and generates political effects. Thus, struggles over the definition of words hide social struggles.

A remark should also be made about the nominalist trap inherent in all taxonomic enterprises. On the one hand, in the case of the Villeurbanne Declaration, the power of naming is very much in evidence. Words are not neutral: by acting on reality, they appropriate the power to realize what they *state* (Merton, 1948), as well as what they *enunciate* (Austin, 1962). To name is simultaneously to pose a problem and, in a certain sense, to resolve it. Words produce political effects and provide a vehicle for social norms. That is why all attempts to produce a taxonomic framework are liable to come up against the problem of nominalism. Furthermore, words can cultivate the illusion of change. For, in spite of what is often imagined, the introduction of the notion of the "non-public" in 1968 did not lead to any real change in approaches to *cultural action, cultural development,* or *cultural mediation*. In spite of the fact that nothing had changed, there was a belief that change had been effected. But while the idea that approaches to public intervention had shifted was illusory, the way in which a certain section of the public was represented really was new. The effect of reification inherent in the process of developing classifications raises the problem of usage; the category of the "non-public" produces a negative identity that triggers three processes: the marginalization, disqualification, and exclusion of part of the public. The meanings assigned to words hide fundamental issues. Words possess the power to institute frontiers, which are, by definition, arbitrary.

1.3 The Advent of a Plurality of "Publics"

In order to describe the "publics of culture," we should bear in mind the distinction between the "invented public" and the "observed public." Jean-Louis Fabiani recalls that the *observed public* is more reticent than might be imagined and also, perhaps, more intermittent and reflexive than sociological theory might lead us to believe. Our perception is often obscured by an excessively "communitarian" view of the public. But far from corresponding to the definition of a public won over to the cultural cause by public action, the users of cultural facilities observed either from a learned point of view (sociological analyses) or a practical viewpoint (observations made by the staff) "do not present well." This is particularly true of libraries in which the observed public does not exactly correspond to the invented public, or, in other words, the "good" public (the people in its studious form, full of cultural goodwill and always ready to listen to the right mediators), who hardly ever visit libraries (Bertrand, 2003). It is another public that librarians meet, a different kind of people: noisy groups of individuals eating sandwiches and drinking cans of beer, or worse, who have nothing to do with the ideal type that the national education system and cultural militants have defined as their target public (Fabiani, 2003). Indeed, *the gap between the observed public and the invented public* is at the origin of the highly varied range of positions on culture in general.

To these two types of public, Jean-Louis Fabiani adds a third, which he refers to as a *denied public*, created by a mechanism "that produces various procedures designed to domesticate audiences with a view to transforming them into a pure receptacle, and that also denies the legitimacy of the expectations and demands of ephemeral groups interested in specific artists and works" (Fabiani, 2004). In effect, according to the author, there is:

> an inherent contradiction in artistic life, since the history of culture is also the history of the process by which artists gradually became autonomous, of the imposition of their legitimacy, with no other foundation than the affirmation of the self that constitutes them. The artist's project of absolute autonomy, every bit as utopian as the fantasy of a commu-

nity of audiences, doubtless implies an implicit project designed to make the audience disappear, or to create an entirely domesticated, or, to be more generous, educated public. (Fabiani, 2007)

An analysis of the emergence of a particular public, paradoxically transformed into an excluded third party, presupposes a sociology of the political economy of cultural production. The project thus involves deconstructing the unitary notion of the public by applying an analysis of forms of relationship between works of art, cultural agents and "spectators."

Analyzing various kinds of relationships from a sociological point of view affords a degree of protection against the risk of essentializing a collective body such as "the public" and guards against the notion, encouraged by everyday linguistic usage, of the public as a unified entity. There is no public in general: there are only ephemeral coalitions or groupings that modern individualism has rendered more precarious than ever before. The world of multiple publics is, in spite of the sociological observation of cultural regularities characterizing relations between social classes, one of permanent change and realignment. The notion of the public needs to be placed in a historical context, and situated observation must always be applied: a relationship between a public and a cultural object only exists if it can be observed at a local or regional level, which obliges us to reappraise the forms we use to generalize our observations (Passeron and Revel, 2005).

In conclusion, just as Weber rejected, from a methodological point of view, the use of collective concepts (state, society, group), while recognizing, theoretically, their value in terms of explaining the orientation of social action, we too should be careful not to substantialize the public but, instead, focus on how such a category contributes to "instituting" the individual who goes to the theater or the museum as a spectator. *Instituted* by the policy, the category of the public in turn provides a vehicle for schemas of action *instituting* the social actor; in this sense, it must be taken into account by sociologists.

2. A SOCIOLOGY OF THE PUBLICS OF CULTURE

A detailed description of quantitative data on the cultural behaviors of the French, accompanied by a number of tools for interpreting evolutions in those behaviors can be found in the successive published editions of the survey on *Les Pratiques culturelles des Français* ("The Cultural Practices of the French") (1974, 1981, 1989, 1998). INSEE's 2003 survey is the latest in the series (Muller, 2005).[1] Rather than indulging in another fastidious recapitulation of known results, it would be useful in this context to examine a number of contrasting evolutions characterizing two major changes, one an increase, the other a decrease. The description of cultural practices is informed by a paradox: the relative permanence of differences in the number of visits to cultural facilities and upheavals in the world of cultural practices over the last thirty years. Those differences should be examined before moving on to an explanation of the persistence of inequalities (chapter 3).

2.1 An Upward Trend: "Screen Culture"

Information on cultural behaviors derives from three main sources: surveys on the use of time ("how much time do you spend on . . . ?"), on expenditure ("how much money do you spend on . . . ?"), and, lastly, on activities ("how many times do you go to . . . ?").

The irresistible rise of TV and radio between 1973 and 1997 suggests just how great was the renewal of interest in culture and the arts during that period. An increasing number of households equipped themselves with TVs, radios, and record and DVD players, spending more time (and/or money) on TV programs, discs, audio-cassettes, software, and CD-ROMs, the first and most visible expression, because the most easily measurable, of a massive expansion of "screen culture."

The development of "screen culture" was among the major factors highlighted by the survey. As Olivier Donnat (2009) points out, due to the combined effects of the dematerialization of content, the spread of broadband Internet and the number of computers, computer games, and smartphones purchased by members of the public, conditions of access to art and culture changed profoundly. Everything could now potentially be viewed on a screen or accessed via the Web. The author underlines the profound originality of his survey by observing the following paradox: "although very widely used in households, it seems that the new media is linked to the culture of going out characteristic of young people and graduates, whose leisure activities tend to take place outside the home and whose cultural life is more intense than that of other categories" (Donnat, 2009: 2). The current situation is substantially different from the one that pertained in the 1980s and 1990s when screen culture was essentially limited to TV viewing. Watching television for long periods of time was generally associated with a low level of participation in cultural life. However, as Donnat points out, the Internet is primarily used by those most involved with culture.[2] This explains another evolution; the amount of time spent watching television or using the new screens varies inversely from one category to the other: if one is below average, the other is generally above. Thus, the amount of time spent watching television tends to diminish with the level of academic qualifications of the viewer, while the amount of time watching new media indicates a higher level of education.

Another important development came in the form of the "music boom." The 1970s were characterized by a substantial rise in record and cassette sales at a time when most households did not have record or cassette players. In fact, it is interesting to note that, more than causing the boom, the spread of hi-fi systems, compact disk players, and Walkmans, actually accompanied it. The increase in the amount of time spent watching television, associated with a diversification in the offer of TV programs, was more marked in the 1980s and continued on an upward curve in the 1990s. Between 1997 and 2008, interest in music continued to progress (in 2008, 34 percent of French people listened to music—other than on the radio—on an almost daily basis, as opposed to 27 percent eleven years earlier). The music boom which began in the 1970s continued, spreading shock waves throughout French society as the generations which started it grew older (Donnat, 2009). When it went digital, music became even more accessible: new ways of storing, exchanging, and transferring it from one medium to another, as well as the increase in the number of ways to listening to it—mobile phones, computers, MP3s—meant that music was becoming increasingly more a part of daily life, not only in the home but also while traveling and, for some, at work. The survey also records a number of other phenomena, including a decrease in TV watching and radio listening among younger people, as well as a continued decline in book reading. Similarly, while the link between watching television and other cultural practices is not strong, in that it cannot be maintained that television has the effect of reducing time spent reading, an inverse symmetrical evolution can nevertheless be observed, namely a decline in the number of books read.

2.2 A Downward Trend: A Decline in the Number of Books Read

While book sales increased (63 percent of French people bought at least one book in the last twelve months, i.e., 1997, as against 51 percent in 1973), and libraries were busier than ever (membership in municipal libraries has more than doubled since 1973), reading declined overall. The percentage of people who do not read books has remained stable. As generations age, the number of readers drops. Furthermore, the quantity of books read declined regularly between 1973 and 1997; the practice of reading a large number of books became less frequent than it was in the early 1970s, notably among younger people, as is exemplified by the continued decline in the number of those who read widely (in 1997, 14 percent of French people read twenty-five books or more during the course of the last twelve months, as against 22 percent in 1973). The trend is mirrored in the daily press: since 1973 there has been a regular and spectacular fall in readership figures, while figures for magazines have remained stable and actually increased among younger people. The evolution of reading practices is characterized by a fall in the number of books read, a decline in reading in people between fifteen and twenty-four years of age, a feminization of the readership, an increase in the number of readers aged over sixty, and a decline in reading among the middle classes and people living in medium-sized cities. How can this general decline in the number of books read be interpreted?

There are a number of explanations for the decline in reading, primary among which is competition in terms of both space and time (more people are joining associations and indulging in amateur artistic activities, and there has been a slight increase in visits to cultural facilities). There has been a spectacular diversification of leisure activities: the logic of a wider spectrum of cultural practices has become the norm and the development of new activities in the fields of sport, holidays, and micro-computing have had a negative impact on the level of reading. In regard to the recurrent theme of competition between books and television, while television is not the only factor responsible for the fall in the number of books read, it nevertheless plays a major role. In conclusion, the conjunction between the diversification of leisure activities and the spectacular growth in the consumption of screen content makes it more difficult to find a slot for reading in the time and space allocated to leisure.

The decline can also be interpreted as a consequence of a *transformation in approaches to reading*. The idea is that the French do not read less, but, instead, are developing new uses of the book and of printed matter. An initial transformation: even if different forms of reading are generally cumulative and do not compete against one another, it should be noted that newspapers have less and magazines more readers than used to be the case. Due to growing requirements for information in daily life, and to the increasingly technical and scientific character of education, disinterested reading tends to give way to reading of a more fragmented and utilitarian kind. Most people questioned in surveys do not regard this kind of material as genuine reading matter and therefore often fail to mention it. Last, a decline in reading among young people is interpreted as a perverse effect of the excessive emphasis placed on books in the education system. Perhaps, in this context, it would be more useful to think in terms of a reduction in the time available for reading for pleasure and an increase in reading as a pragmatic, educational activity which makes it more difficult to find time for reading as a leisure activity. French people might read less, but it is also true that they read differently (de Certeau, 1990). This second interpretation of the act of reading at least has the merit of not being unduly pessimistic.

A third possible explanation for the fact that French people are reading fewer books, linked to the two preceding interpretations, is that books have, to a degree, lost their symbolic value and that, consequently, reading is no longer as attractive to adolescents as it once was (Dumontier, de Singly, and Thélot, 1990). Books no longer play a major role in the kind of strategies of differentiation practiced by younger people. Indeed, they are increasingly associated with a time before the advent of the new technologies and the popularization of values such as speed, conviviality, and hedonism. There is nothing unusual about this evolution, which is part of a long-term process already highlighted in earlier *Cultural Practices* surveys. For many decades, every new generation has arrived at adulthood with less commitment to reading than the previous one, so much so that not only has there been a fall in the number of newspaper and book readers, but, on average, the readership is getting older (Donnat, 2009).

2.3 An Increase in the Number of Surveys on Specific Publics

The theater discovers its publics either by means of surveys on one institution in particular (Guy, 1991), or research on festivals. The surveys carried out on the Avignon Festival since 1996 focus on concrete socio-morphological effects on the construction and transformation of publics participating in the kind of non-traditional cultural practice represented by the festival. What the surveys conducted by Emmanuel Ethis, Jean-Louis Fabiani, and Damien Malinas reveal is, above all, how the cultural dynamics of spectators culminate in visits to festivals, which are, *de facto*, constitutive of their cultural experience and personality (Ethis, 2002). A previous survey, conducted at the Cannes Film Festival, had already shown how the *function of participating* in a cultural event of that kind emphasized the fact that the construction of a cultural experience involves a good deal more than an encounter between the public and the work (Ethis, 2001).

The sociology of the cinema was initially developed in France by Edgar Morin, Pierre Sorlin, and Jean-Pierre Esquenazi who, following in the footsteps of Siegfried Kracaurer, examined the ways in which the cinema "expresses" society. More recently, researchers have focused on the cinema's various publics and the ecology of their practices: how has moviegoing become the most important cultural practice in terms of visits, audience numbers, and influence? How do people create a narrative for themselves thanks to the movies, actors, and stars that play such an important role in their lives? What is the position of the cinema, with its rites and codes, within the *polis*? All these questions are clearly associated with the task of defining contemporary cinema culture (Ethis, 2005).

Emmanuel Pedler's work on the opera shows that only a very small percentage of people, all of them in the upper classes, are likely to base their social identity on their knowledge of operatic productions. Insisting on the traits by which it is characterized (a relatively tiny number of productions, all of them put on in cities), Pedler demonstrates that the study of opera constitutes a blind spot for traditional sociology, which emphasizes the notions of "dominant classes," "cultivated practices," and the "social milieu." The opera is more clearly correlated with academic qualifications and belonging to a family milieu marked by its cultural practices (Pedler, 2003: 14). Another specific public from another area of legitimate culture—contemporary music—is largely made up of professionals (Menger, 1986).

Highly uneven within the French population, figures on the attendance of professional dance productions indicate that it is an occasional leisure activity rarely motivated by a love of the art form itself. Indeed, few spectators have ever danced themselves. Dependent on the offer and its proximity, dance is of interest to a relatively small number of French people and is subject to the image that individuals have of cultural outings, dance in general, and specific genres of dance in particular (Guy, 1991). Concerning the performing arts, it should be noted that the rate of visits to cultural venues has remained relatively stable. Cultural outings and visits have been much less negatively influenced by the growth of cultural practices linked to digital technology than ordinary leisure activities such as watching television or reading magazines (Donnat, 2009).

One point that these surveys have in common is that they all highlight both diversity and differentiation within single fields of activity, as is witnessed by typologies traditionally presented in books in which the results of surveys are published. Insofar as reading is concerned, the intersection of the social structure of the readership and of different kinds of reading makes it possible to establish four types of relation to reading: "reading for amusement," "didactic reading," "reading for health," and "aesthetic reading" (Mauger, Poliak, and Pudal, 1999).

In this context, criticizing the behaviors of the elite in the manner of Pierre Bourdieu in *La Distinction* is all the more likely to be misleading in that the surveys on which such analyses are based themselves date from the 1960s. As Richard Peterson remarked of the United States, the dominant actor in the cultural game is no longer the purist, the snob, or the pedant, a *univore* consuming an exclusive repertoire, but an eclectic and inclusive *omnivore* little concerned with traditional borders between legitimate, learned culture and popular, illegitimate culture (Peterson and Kern, 1996).

3. BUILDING CULTURAL WORLDS

Starting with the observation that there is a growing hybridization of cultural universes and an increased porosity between learned and popular culture, and between classical tradition and the most wide-ranging definitions of the cultural, Olivier Donnat, responsible for the Ministy's *Cultural Practices* survey, sought to relate the field of *areas of knowledge* to that of behaviors, proposing an initial transition from the "three cultures" model (legitimate, average, popular) to a model based on "seven cultural universes" (Donnat, 1994).

3.1 Two Variables: One Behavioral, the Other Cognitive

In order to "surpass the limits of approaches which focus on cultural practices" and address the theme of culture from the cognitive point of view, a questionnaire containing a list of sixty-five personalities selected with a view to covering all forms of artistic expression "from the most avant-garde and elitist to the most popular, from the most ambitious in terms of cultural content, to the most modest" (Donnat, 1994: 17) was used to compare the "competence and taste of French people in the artistic field" and the "level of notoriety and the 'image' of artists" (Donnat, 1994: 18), as well as to examine the categories of the vulgar and the distinguished, and the modern and the classical, which, more or less explicitly, govern debate about artistic taste (Donnat, 1994: 18).

However, although Donnat adds an extra layer of complexity to his analysis of cultural behaviors by introducing a cognitive dimension, his work is still characterized by the issue of legitimacy. The categories that he suggests in terms of both his classification of artists and of French people bear witness to this. He not only distinguishes five groups of artists that he defines as "patrimonial," "popular," or "famous," or "belonging to the first circle of high culture" or the "second circle of high culture" (Donnat, 1994: 44–49), but also distinguishes, conjointly, two sub-lists, one of "consecrated artists," the other of "consecratable" artists, on which he builds an indicator of "traditionalism" or "modernism" (Donnat, 1994: 37–38).

The five groups of French people identified in the survey are as follows: first, the "Excluded" (15 percent) who are only familiar with "patrimonial" and "popular" artists (quoting an average of fifteen names out of the sixty-five on the list) and who are "extremely marginal in terms of symbolic struggles" (Donnat, 1994: 57); second, the "Deprived" (31 percent) display (with an average of twenty-six names with which they are familiar) a significant tendency to contest established values (notably in rejecting "patrimonial" names); third, the "Crossroads of the Average" (23 percent), with individuals (who recognize an average of thirty-seven artists) at the center of symbolic struggles in the artistic field; fourth, the "Informed" (23 percent) who (recognizing an average of forty-five names on the list) globally share the tastes of the minority of those who are more competent in the field; and, last, the fifth group, the "Voguish" (8 percent) who, disposing of the most far-reaching and diversified capital of information (with an average of fifty-six names recognized) judge in an undogmatic fashion, "integrating alongside the best known artists [. . .] artists working in genres adjudged to be minor or infra-cultural" (Donnat, 1994: 124).

3.2 The Seven Cultural Universes of the French

Visiting theaters and galleries, listening to music, and reading are the three fields on which Olivier Donnat focused when he developed a typology of attitudes to culture and the behaviors associated with it. He also described seven different cultural universes.

The universe of exclusion is essentially made up of elderly, rural former farmers and laborers with no academic qualifications, who do not visit cultural facilities and who ignore cultural markets and policies. The "Excluded" are characterized by their almost total lack of interest in the world of culture and the arts.

Those inhabiting *the universe of deprivation* have relatively little knowledge of the world of arts and culture and only rarely visit cultural facilities. However, the break with cultural life is less radical due to a greater degree of social insertion and sociability. According to Donnat, this configuration is typical of working class milieus.

Juvenile culture encompasses everyone aged between fifteen and twenty. Even if young people's reaction to the media and its influence is largely dependent on their social background, their gender, where they live, the kind of schools they go to, and the subjects they study, daily contact with it tends to structure their extracurricular activities. They also tend to listen to a lot of music and to be somewhat defiant in regard to the most consecrated forms of culture.

The universe of the average French person is, broadly speaking, organized around television, music, and film. The average French person is familiar with the most "mediatized" aspects of cultivated culture, but has very little knowledge of the performing arts (theater, concerts, etc.). Covering most people occupying a median position in regard to normal socio-demographic variables (age, educational qualifications, place of residence), the "average French person" is a term also applied to large fractions of young urban workers and employees, as well as to newly promoted middle managers.

Three other universes, characterized by a "cultivated relationship" to culture, have closer links to cultural life. Their relations to art and culture take different forms. Organized around the regular reading of books, visits to museums and theaters, and, especially, outings to classical music concerts, *the universe of the "traditionalists"* is largely inhabited by graduates of over forty-five years of age, most of whom are members of the middle classes born before the War, whose "cultural goodwill" also extends to the field of television (cultural channels and programs). Since many of them missed the "music boom" of the last thirty years, these individuals have kept their distance from new forms of artistic expression and are frequently distrustful of the audiovisual milieu, even if they do watch a good deal of television.

Constructed around recently developed forms of expression to which there are relatively fewer symbolic barriers, *the modern cultivated universe* primarily involves listening to music and going to jazz and rock concerts, dance productions, and the movies. Although the practice of reading books still plays an important role here, it has lost much of its power as a social marker. Practices typical of this category are dominant among young urban graduates with an open attitude to the world in general, who are sensitive to changing fashions, who tend to focus on current affairs and cultural developments, and who cultivate a certain reserve in regard to forms of expression adjudged to be overly intellectual.

Lastly, *the universe of the "Voguish"* designates those bulimic and eclectic individuals who have a propensity to accumulate sources of information and to get the best out of the most effective of those sources, namely word-of-mouth. This minority, on whom a good deal of cultural life is based, includes the most assiduous users of cultural facilities and venues. Their tastes are organized around the principle of eclecticism understood as the "property of associating activities with genres of books, music and shows [. . .] and distinguishing themselves by being equally familiar with classical culture and modern forms of artistic expression; equipped with numerous advantages (cultural capital, availability, proximity of the cultural offer), the *Voguish* are composed of often unmarried, middle-aged university graduates living in large cities, principally Paris" (Donnat, 1994: 343).

3.3 The Limits of a Typological Construction

Donnat's typology is characterized by three limitations. It involves a risk of *reification*, since such categories tend to freeze-frame the representation of attitudes and behaviors that, in terms of culture, are neither univocal nor static. However, defining particular "universes" in this way can obscure the dynamic trajectories described by attitudes to culture and by cultural behaviors. The objectivization of such attitudes and behaviors runs the risk of rendering any form of movement invisible. While typologies make it possible to substitute an increased intelligibility of social phenomena for the infinite diversity of the real, their limited status should nevertheless be borne in mind: necessary interpretative tools, typologies can never entirely explain the categories proposed. Weber, for example, considered "ideal types" as no more than utilitarian constructs designed to aid research.

Furthermore, Donnat's insistence on the idea that the "average French person" is concerned with conforming to preexisting norms implies a risk of *stigmatization*. He defines members of the category as follows: "anxious to master the most elementary mechanisms of distinction, most of their choices are based on a desire to conform to what they regard as the most appropriate values (the values shared by the largest number of people), and are thus informed by a desire for the 'happy medium'" (Donnat, 1994). The category of the "average French person," employed as a synonym for the "Crossroads of the Average," expresses the ambivalence inherent in declining to choose between the descriptive sense of the term "average," associated with statistics, and a more normative sense characterized by depreciative connotations or even betraying a form of ethnocentric disdain.

Typologies can also betray a form of *theoretical denial*. By developing his categories hierarchically, Donnat consolidates the model that he furtively criticizes. Examples of this are his idea of "absolute exclusion," which ignores the biases associated with polling, and his description of the last three universes of which it is said that their relationship to culture is "cultivated," which implicitly disqualifies the first four universes. Framing the problem in terms of hierarchy and legitimacy is a ploy typical of the theory of distinction which Donnat's theory claims to criticize (Donnat, 1994: 129). Furthermore, the eclecticism of the Voguish is central to the "omnivore/univore" model suggested by the American sociologist Richard Peterson (Peterson and Simkus, 1992), according to whom the upper classes are today distinguished less by their penchant for learned music than by the eclecticism of their tastes (rock, hip-hop, and pop, as well as classical), while the popular classes have more exclusive tastes. This eclecticism is a sign of symbolic domination in that it translates a power of cultural rehabilitation characteristic of the dominant classes.

In conclusion, and in spite of these limitations, the publics of culture are now known. Data on cultural practices from surveys carried out by the French Ministry of Culture and the French National Institute of Statistics and Economic Studies (INSEE) show that the consumption of cultural goods and services continues, in spite of certain changes, to reflect the characteristics of social stratification. In other words, all approaches should be nuanced by simultaneously recognizing a diversification of the ways in which cultural products are consumed and by continuing to apply the notion of cultural legitimacy. In effect, statistical descriptions of cultural behaviors and their evolution reveal a social distribution of those practices strongly marked by inequalities. It therefore remains to be explained why the most "noble" of these practices continue to be confined to the upper classes. In the next chapter, this issue will be addressed by means of a sociological explanation of social and cultural hierarchies.

NOTES

1. Muller, Lara. 2005. *Participation culturelle et sportive : tableaux issus de l'enquête permanente sur les conditions de vie de mai 2003*. Paris: Insee. The survey deals with the following subjects: cultural activities and practices concerning reading, visiting libraries, going to the movies, to the theater, to concerts, visiting museums, historical monuments and exhibitions, going to festivals, and listening to music.

2. The probability of having gone to the movies or the theater, visited a museum, or read a substantial number of books in the last twelve months regularly increases in function of internet usage (Donnat, 2009).

THREE
Explaining Social and Cultural Hierarchies

In contradistinction to the contemporary view of aesthetic taste as a gift of nature, Pierre Bourdieu developed a scientific perspective according to which it is, instead, determined and organized by the position occupied by individuals within the social hierarchy. Having revealed that judgment and taste are socially distributed, the author of *The Love of Art* advanced the idea that there is a correlation between aesthetic skills and the propensity to appreciate art. For Bourdieu, the judgment of taste is dependent on an individual's level of aesthetic "competence," which he defines as the capacity to recognize the stylistic traits of a work of art and situate it in his or her world, while at the same time understanding the differences between individual works. Consequently, in order to explain taste, we need to examine the conditions in which aesthetic competence is acquired. Defining the instances of socialization that exert the most influence on cultural practices with a view to describing the conditions of acquisition of aesthetic competence thus becomes vital, as does an analysis of the way in which socialization and aesthetic taste are articulated. In this sense, cultural socialization is located at the crossroads between the sociology of education and the sociology of culture.

1. TASTE: A PRODUCT OF SOCIALIZATION

Judgments of taste are *synthetic* judgments based on the valorization of codes already internalized in previously existing regimes of socialization. Of the traditional instances of socialization (school, family, peer groups, television), school and family in particular have been the object of thoroughgoing and complementary investigations.

1.1 Using Cultural Socialization to Explain Inequalities

School: A Crucial Instance of Cultural Socialization

Since level of education is the most powerful determinant in terms of "European art museums and their publics"—to borrow the subtitle of *The Love of Art*—it would appear that the secondary education system plays a fundamental role in explaining and understanding the individual's relation to culture. Students embarking on their careers in tertiary education are generally extremely enthusiastic about all things cultural. Providing the opportunity to access culture by means of classifications of authors, genres, schools, movements, and époques (the study of literature in particular provides a certain number of tools and concepts with which to approach works of art), the educational system seeks to inseminate the "cult" of culture, or, in other words, "the duty to like" certain works, regardless of the oxymoron constituted by the juxtaposition of the words "duty" and "like." Last, the role of education is all the more paradoxical in terms of this process of cultural socialization in that it reserves a marginal place for the teaching of art.

The Family: A Privileged Instance of Cultural Socialization

Another instance of socialization, the family, traditionally occupies a privileged place in terms of the acquisition of the norms and values of a given social group due to its chronologically primordial character, the continuous nature of the learning process which takes place within its parameters, and, last, the affective climate that it provides, which often favors the interiorization of specific standards and behaviors. When parents introduce their children to culture from a very early age, those children are able to acquire and appropriate the tools enabling them to develop a degree of familiarity with works of art over a longer, more continuous period and in a more diffuse manner than would otherwise be the case. Through these imperceptible and unconscious processes of learning, families are able to instill in their children a precocious relationship with culture.

These two very different types of learning generate specific and differentiated behaviors and attitudes in regard to relations to culture. Families with the highest degree of "cultural capital" consider it a kind of "family treasure" to which their children regard themselves as legitimate heirs. Their relation to culture is thus characterized by a sense of ease and familiarity. In such cases, culture seems to belong "as of right," whereas, in cases in which it has been acquired by dint of often strenuous effort, it is regarded with reverence and respect and held in a degree of awe. The education system sanctions and reinforces initial inequalities by judging pupils by what they have learned outside school; this, at least, was true at the time of publication of the surveys providing the source material for the two books by Pierre Bourdieu and Jean-Claude Passeron, *The Inheritors* (1979), first published in 1964, and *Reproduction* (1977), which originally appeared in 1970, in which the authors distinguished exclusively school-based learning—late, methodical, and accelerated—from precocious, latent, almost invisible, or unsuspected learning in the family milieu. Bourdieu distinguishes "scholarly culture," acquired in the education system, from "free culture," liberated from its scholarly origins.

The Interaction Between Family and School as Instances of Socialization

Is the role of the family in the socialization of children becoming less important, as Talcott Parsons claimed in the 1950s, or is it reinforced by schooling, as Durkheim and the historian Philippe Ariès (de Singly, 2007: 16–33) believed? In *Reproduction*, Pierre Bourdieu and Jean-Claude Passeron demonstrated that, in France, the culture of the educational system functioned as a *class culture* in that it contributed to the reproduction of cultural inequalities by *legitimizing* their role in social selection.

In the early 1960s, the English sociolinguist, Basil Bernstein, established a link between social class, modes of socialization, and linguistic competence by making the distinction between the "restricted linguistic code" of the working classes and the "elaborated" code of their socially superior counterparts (Bernstein, 1971). The author focused on the ways in which modes of communication are structured with a view to explaining the varying levels of linguistic ability of members of different social classes. He maintained that those differences were reinforced by the education system in which children from the higher social classes were favored by an emphasis on clear, grammatically correct language. In spite of the democratization of the education system, a process attested to by a slew of statistical data, children from so-called advantaged backgrounds had more chance of succeeding in school than their comrades from the working classes. Different levels of linguistic skill partially explain differentials in rates of success and failure in examinations, a phenomenon particularly marked in French *concours*. Pierre Bourdieu and Jean-Claude Passeron describe this process as one of "symbolic violence," implying an ontological complicity on the part of the dominated class. Passeron points to the examination or, more precisely, the tripartite structure of the dissertation of the literary *concours* in France and the four-part dissertation of the Ecole Nationale d'Administration (ENA), as techniques for highlighting the linguistic superiority of the country's elites. There are other, equally convincing examples of the social role of examinations in the process of selection based on the simultaneous inculcation of a code of cultural manners and a strict definition of socially empowering linguistic competence. The top-ranked British and American universities, intellectually selective in terms of their specialist areas of education, are in fact reserved, in terms of recruitment, to the social elites, while Japanese universities exert a huge amount of pressure on their students in terms of the number of selective examinations that they are obliged to sit (Passeron, 2004).[1]

1.2 Understanding Exceptions to the Rule from a Sociological Point of View

Research on exceptions to the "rule of reproduction," including both *heirs* and the *disinherited*, has proved to be of great value. François de Singly has demonstrated that cultural "heritage" is a fruitful field of inquiry. Merely being an *heir* does not guarantee the appropriation of a cultural heritage; unlike economic capital, cultural capital cannot be appropriated without work (de Singly, 1996). Furthermore, it is always possible to renounce a legacy that has been appropriated or to reject one after it has been acquired; indeed, cultural capital is not automatically and of necessity handed down to the next generation (de Singly, 2003). Meanwhile, focusing on the *disinherited* and the *untalented*, Bernard Lahire analyzed establishments in Priority Educational Zones (ZEPs) in the Lyon suburbs and families of North African origin whose heads of household had a low level of cultural capital. He examined the differences between the academic careers of children from the same social milieu by focusing on several areas, including their familial context (oldest, youngest, or middle child, parental authority, economic and educational capital), their behavioral norms and values, and the resulting relationship with the educational establishment viewed as a source of tensions and contradictions leading either to academic success or failure. Avoiding an overly mechanistic approach to the transmission of cultural capital, Lahire emphasized the need to take into account the social and relational conditions on which the process, at least to some extent, depends.

1.3 Contemporary Evolutions in Spheres of Socialization

A symmetrically inverse evolution can be observed with, on the one hand, the decline of familial authority and that of the education system, and, on the other, the growing influence of peer groups and television.

The Decline of the Educational Institution?

The education system encourages individuation by emancipating the subject from communitarian constraints (tribe, family, church) and universalizing it within a public space, furnishing it with an impersonal, universal, and abstract status which provides the foundation of its quality as a "citizen-individual" (de Singly, 2003a). This process of subjectivation liberates the subject and helps it to achieve autonomy. Representing an encounter with the impersonal rule, referred to by Durkheim as "the nature of things," the process is part of the construction of the social subject, at once abstract and universal, through the notion of *science*: "schooling communicates to all the idea of science, the idea of objective knowledge and universal reason" (de Querioz, 2005: 19). François Dubet emphasizes the fact that socialization in school helps the individual to acquire an autonomous conscience (Dubet, 2002). This was the original sense of the secular school system: to fashion the kind of individual typical of modern societies. But doesn't, by definition, the modernity which promotes autonomy as the right and the capacity to construct one's own convictions and authenticity negatively affect cultural transmission by breaking the magic chain of communitarian solidarities ? Dominique Pasquier develops this question when she observes that the juvenile world is characterized by numerous tensions born of a clear-cut desire to acquire autonomy on the part of young people by conforming to the behaviors of their peer groups (Pasquier, 2005). Her survey undermines several stereotypes about relations between young people and cultural practices and the way in which they communicate with each other and with the wider world.

Against all expectations, the peer group constitutes the most important instance of socialization for *lycée* (high school) students in France due to the superior constraint that it represents in comparison to the family or the education system. This situation has a negative influence on the transmission of culture between parents and children. Younes Amrani is worried about the risk of a Tocquevillian "tyranny of the majority" inherent in all democratic regimes:

> I've always told myself that living in the projects was a serious handicap, but I also told myself that it was an advantage, albeit a double-edged one. On the one hand, we're protected; we take refuge with people like ourselves. But, on the other, we know nothing except our own culture, if you could call it a culture (Amrani and Beaud, 2005: 127).

Dominique Pasquier contributes to the debate on individualism with a critique of Anthony Giddens's ideas on the undifferentiated character of the rise of individualism. An attentive reading of sociological analyses of the lifestyles of the working classes, particularly surveys conducted in peri-urban developments in which a high proportion of residents are immigrants, highlights the distance separating this social world, marked by the difficulties that individuals find in expressing themselves when confronted by group solidarities, from that of the middle and upper classes, in which a psychological culture encouraging the authentic development of the self is more widespread. Stéphane Beaud's study (Beaud, 2002) on the reasons for the failure of young students from such neighborhoods at university corroborates this idea by demonstrating that they find it difficult to complete university courses due to problems with mastering the "individual-subject" code dominant within such establishments.

However, in a survey based on ninety young people from "difficult neighborhoods," Michèle Petit shows how their career trajectories were changed by frequenting a public library (Petit, 1997; Bourdieu, 1990). Distinguishing between shared space (at the basis of the individual as a *particular* being) and public space (at the basis of the individual as a *universal* being), she suggests that cultural institutions provide a way out of the suffocating sense of "solidarity" characteristic of the shared social space of difficult neighborhoods and an opportunity to discover the universal qualities associated with the status of the citizen-individual. The lesson to be drawn from the processes of the "construction of the self" outlined in Petit's *Éloge de la lecture* (2002) seems to concern the value of removing the communitarian constraints characteristic of working class life with a view to developing one's autonomy as an individual.

2. TASTE: THE EXPRESSION OF A *HABITUS*

The *habitus* is the second analytical variable applied to explaining the social determination of taste. One of the definitions of the *habitus* suggested by Pierre Bourdieu is expressed in the following way: the *habitus* is "the exteriorization of an internalized exterior," or, which is the same thing, "the exteriorization of the internalization of the exterior." These two articulated aspects are a result of cultural socialization. The *habitus* is *produced* by significant past practices and *produces* significant future practices. The concept is informed by this duality.

2.1 The Habitus: *Catalyst of Social and Cultural Practices*

A product of significant past practices, the *habitus* derives from an accumulation of past experiences and becomes, reciprocally, a producer of significant future practices. Like a catalyst activating a previously passive element, the *habitus* actualizes the past and places something new at the disposition of the future. According to Bourdieu, the word *disposition* is particularly appropriate to the structure of the *habitus*, a form of organizational action which defines a habitual state and constitutes a predisposition, or, again, an "ensemble of incorporated dispositions *and* a generating principle of practices" (Lahire, 2001). According to Bourdieu, "the *habitus*, a product of history, produces individual and collective practices—more history—in accordance with the schemes generated by history" (Bourdieu, 1990: 54). Powerfully generative, the *habitus* is capable of engendering an infinite number of practices.

The idea of *"capacities for generating acquired dispositions* that are socially constituted" (Bourdieu, 1987: 23) is derived from the "generative grammar" developed by the American linguist Noam Chomsky. Indeed, the notion also implicitly refers to the idea of the generative character of the *habitus* developed by Weber. The notion of *habitus*, applied, among other things, to define the innerworldly asceticism derived from the Calvinist vision of salvation, effectively coincides with the question of "how life should be lived." For Weber, religions produce an *ethos*, or, in other words, a system of consecrated dispositions which determine particular orientations in terms of action. They are capable of fashioning social relations to the degree that they provide an order of life (*Lebensordnung*) which informs the way of life (*Lebensführung*) of the individual. Weber analyzes the interior *habitus*, the internalized normative order, the incorporation (*Verkörperung*) by individuals of a rational way of life.

2.2 The Impasse of a Univocal Interpretation of the Habitus

In his appraisal of culture, Bourdieu makes systematic use of the concept of *habitus*, which he associates with the notion of a profoundly internalized schema which does not rely on individual consciousness in order to be effective. He explains that members of the same class generally act in the same way without having to consult one another. This interpretation presupposes that individuals should be considered in reference to the social class to which they belong. Thus, if we accept the validity of Weber's approach, the individual should be studied within the framework of three hierarchies, corresponding to the economic, social, and political orders, themselves dependent on the values of wealth, prestige, and power: classes, status groups, and parties. Weber emphasizes the importance of the status group which, he says, possesses a decisive consistency because it differentiates itself from other groups by applying specific hierarchical social values (prestige and honor), or, in other words, cultural practices. It seems, as Bernard Lahire observes (Lahire, 1999), that Bourdieu was unaware of this multiplicity of spheres of socialization.

This reduction to a class *habitus* has consequences on ways of thinking about exchange. When Bourdieu reduces the "gift" to an elevated and cunning form of domination, he effectively dismisses the implications of the process of civilization that thinkers like Freud and Elias understood so well. Jeffrey Alexander suggests that Bourdieu was incapable of appreciating the positive elements of the abstract obligation that Marcel Mauss presented in *The Gift*, underlining that all exchanges are regulated by real mutual obligations and by cultural forms (Alexander, 2000: 69–70). In conclusion, the fact that the *habitus* is unstable and lacking in any form of uniqueness or systematic scope calls into question its predictive power and renders it more difficult to use as an explanatory tool.

2.3 The Basis of the Existence of "Class Culture"

Bourdieu combines Marx's perspectives on the dominant culture of the bourgeoisie and the class consciousness of the proletariat (outlined in *Das Kapital* and *The Class Struggles in France, 1848–1850*, *The Eighteenth Brumaire of Louis Bonaparte*, and *The Civil War in France*) with those of Weber on the symbolic dimensions of legitimacy associated with the prestige of status groups, developed in his analyses of the emergence of the entrepreneurial capitalist class and the Western bourgeoisie (*The Protestant Ethic and the Spirit of Capitalism*, 1904–1905). Bourdieu thus introduces the notion of the "way of life," defined by cultural capital and its influence on the representation of the social space, and adds a degree of complexity to the notion of *standard of living* that Marx associated exclusively with economic conditions. Sociological approaches to the bourgeoisie and/or the proletariat have been developed in a number of different ways, notably from the cultural point of view (Le Wita, 1988; Pinçon and Pinçon-Chariot, 2000). "Working class culture," the analysis of which owes a good deal to Maurice Halbwachs's *La Classe ouvrière et les niveaux de vie* ("The Working Classes and Standards of Living," 1912) was also examined by Richard Hoggart in his work on the "lifestyle of the working classes in England" in *The Uses of Literacy* (1957) and in later monographic studies (Verret, 1996; Beaud and Pialoux, 2005). Halbwachs, who defined the working man as the "man of matter" (Halbwachs, 1912: 74–75), was influenced by both Marx and Weber.

In *Distinction* (1984) — originally published in French in 1979 as *La Distinction* — and again in *The Logic of Practice* (1990) — originally *Le Sens pratique* (1980) — Bourdieu develops the idea of the homogeneity of the *habitus* of groups and classes which, in his view, leads to a homogeneity of aesthetic taste in which preferences and practices are predictable and "perceived as obvious and self-evident" (1990: 58), and in which, "each individual system of dispositions is a structural variant of the others, expressing the singularity of its position within the class and its trajectory" (1990: 60). He opposes the legitimate culture of the dominant classes to mere popular culture, and the *choices of freedom* of the dominant social classes to the *choices of necessity* — associated with the demands of day-to-day existence — of the working classes. According to the author, relations between the working classes and legitimate culture are characterized by dispossession, resignation, imitation, and exclusion. He maintains that respect for the principle of conformity is typical of the working classes and antithetical to the kind of singularity sought by the dominant classes as a vector of distinction. Moreover, in defining the components of *"petit bourgeois* taste," he characterizes the new middle classes in terms of their "cultural goodwill."

3. TASTE: THE PRACTICAL MANIFESTATION OF SOCIAL DIFFERENCE

In *Distinction*, Bourdieu describes cultural practices as socially determined and inscribed in a symbolic system of power and self-representation. Bourdieu's book, which has become a classic, is a summation of works on the sociology of education and culture. The logic of distinction, which he observes in the routine of day-to-day living (clothes, food, accommodation, leisure), and more unusual events (celebrations, religious ceremonies), highlights tastes which, in turn, are mirrored in both lifestyles and the "unconscious strategies" of distinction applied, in his view, by all social classes. Here again, Bourdieu appropriates and systematizes a logic of differentiation that the precursors and founders of sociology had already observed and theorized and applies it to the logic underlying the ascension of the bourgeoisie and its opposition to the nobility.

3.1 Distinction in the Bourgeoisie and the Aristocracy: From Tocqueville to Norbert Elias

Tocqueville emphasized the tensions between a nobility whose pauperization obliged it to live at the court of the king, where it inevitably lost its traditional function of governing the peasantry, and consequently, of protecting it from the arbitrary use of royal power (Tocqueville, [1856]; 1986), and the bourgeoisie, which, as it grew richer, was able to move to the cities, obtain functions in the civil service, and avoid paying taxes, thereby abandoning the peasantry to shoulder the crushing burden of taxation on its own. Tocqueville's opinion of social progress as a force that, while enriching all other classes, left the peasantry in a state of desperation, as if it were the sole prey of civilization as a whole, encapsulated his view of the devastating effects of state centralization in the *Ancien Régime*, which, he believed, destroyed social bonds and led to the collapse of the aristocratic order.

Meanwhile, Norbert Elias examined the logics of distinction at work in court society (Elias, [1969]; 2006). Etiquette fulfilled two primordial functions: a function of domination for the king, and one of prestige and social distinction for the members of the court as a whole. In court society, the logics of distinction constitute an end in themselves and opinion is the very foundation of social existence. In the court, the spontaneous use of physical force characteristic of chivalrous society is replaced by the arts of foresight, observation, and manipulation. Leading the other, without him realizing, to think according to one's own desires becomes one of the central tenets of court society. In such a context, a mastery of oral and corporeal language is the most powerful of arms. The *ethos* of the court implies a regulation of the passions, a mastery of form, and a control of the emotions. Elias insists on the duality of the process: to a given social configuration corresponds a specific *ethos* which contributes to the social reproduction of that configuration and vice-versa. A prime example of this process of distinction is to be found in eighteenth-century Germany where it contributed to the development of *Kultur*, beloved of the bourgeoisie and of *Zivilisation*, characterizing the German nobility; the bourgeoisie laid claim to intellectual values, conceding courtly values to the German princely aristocracy in the era in which it was marginalized (Elias [1969]; 2000).

3.2 The Distinction Between the Bourgeoisie and the Proletariat: The Figure of the Heir in Sartre

In his *Critique of Dialectical Reason* (1960), Jean-Paul Sartre examined the principles governing the distinction established by the bourgeoisie in the late nineteenth century in its relationship with the proletariat, developing an analysis of the kind of distinction associated with and promoted by the *heir*. According to Sartre, distinction is the mode of being in the world of the bourgeois, who inherit what their fathers have instituted. The French Revolution abolished the order-based society of the *Ancien Régime*, which distinguished the privileges of those born into the nobility ("you took the trouble to be born," as Beaumarchais has Figaro say) and established the idea of natural equality between men, enshrined in law in the *Declaration of the Rights of Man and the Citizen*, published on August 26, 1789. But while the bourgeoisie put an end to the dominance of the aristocracy, whose equal, as a social class, it became, its members did not accept that the principle of strict equality contained in the political assertion of the universal nature of human rights should be applied to the proletariat.

To counter the idea of a natural equality between men, the bourgeoisie developed new strategies to distinguish itself from the proletariat by attempting to deny the natural universality of man. Radically, it attempted to kill both the idea and reality of need by exercising a dictatorship over the body. Distinction functioned as a kind of anti-nature: it denied the natural universality of men. As Dominique Colas remarks:

> The bourgeoisie of the second half of the century adopted a lay puritanical attitude to life, the signification of which revealed itself to be oppressive: distinction (Colas, 2006: 48).

The bourgeois thus wore a stiff collar and a bib, dressed in black, the color of mourning, and ensured that he practiced sobriety and his wife frigidity. The body, as a biological universal, had to be repressed, domesticated, disciplined. The body of the master, insofar as it was a human body, had itself to be mastered. The bourgeois affirmed himself vis-à-vis the worker, defining himself in terms of "culture without nature." This precocious attitude enabled him not only to justify his prerogatives but also to justify his exploitation of the proletarian. Underpinned by violence, this form of distinction was all the more powerful in that it was focused exclusively on the proletariat. Bourdieu borrowed these three key notions—*distinction*, the position of the *heir*, and *violence*—from Jean-Paul Sartre, without quoting his sources. An excess of admiration, perhaps?

3.3 Inter-Group Distinction and Intra-GroupDistinction: Goblot, Veblen, Milner, Elias

In the *La Barrière et le niveau* (1925), Edmond Goblot characterized the bourgeoisie in terms of the "spirit" which guaranteed its class cohesion and the "code of life" which defined its behavior. For Goblot, professions and levels of income were not enough to identify social classes. He focused on the image which the bourgeoisie created for itself, an image which it portrayed to the wider world. Unlike societies based on orders, class-based societies are characterized by social mobility. Unlike castes, which are enshrined in law (Dumont, 1990), classes are *de facto* groups open to change, never definitively stabilized or recognized. By building a *barrier* visible to other social classes, what Goblot terms "distinction" enables groups to carve out a place for themselves in the social structure. By underlining the artificial nature of that *barrier*, he inscribes the bourgeoisie in the world of facticity. He develops the analysis of processes of imitation and differentiation initiated by Simmel (1997b) by choosing, like the German sociologist, the example of fashion to illustrate his thesis. Fashion provides an ideal sphere of distinction: we choose our clothes above all to show people who we are. In effect, clothes fulfill two functions; first, as a *barrier* when, for a specific social group, they are used as a means of distinction from other groups: in this sense, fashion acts as an ever-moving *barrier* thanks to the processes of imitation that it provokes in the lower classes, tempted, according to Goblot, to copy the trends originated by the bourgeoisie. Second, fashion serves a *leveling* function governed, on the contrary, by the principle of conformity to the group; in this context, individuals are assumed not to want to distinguish themselves from other members of their social class, but, instead to focus on resembling them in order to avoid the awful fate of being banished from that class.

In *The Theory of the Leisure Class* (1899), Thorstein Veblen examined the kind of rivalries which lead men to indulge in processes of distinction in which they attempt to display their superiority. Veblen was interested in the modes of consumption of the bourgeoisie in the late nineteenth century. At the time, the best way of distinguishing oneself was to make it known that one did not work, or, more precisely, that one did not need to work in order to live. It was therefore a matter of some importance to display the fact that one had leisure time at one's disposal. Morally forbidden to the noble, free man, work was incompatible with a virtuous life. In contrast to the vast majority of people who were obliged to live by their industry, or in other words, by their labor and the sweat of their brow, the fortunate few were able to live off the efforts of the majority. This extorted wealth made it possible to create an "idle class" which demonstrated, in an *ostentatious* way, that it did not need to work to live. Leisure, idleness, the "so-called arts of pleasure, knowledge of operations and events which do not contribute directly to the progress of human life" ([1899] 1970: 32), useless occupations in the economic sense of the term, require domestics and household staff to provide external services, because it is not enough to be idle, it is also necessary to demonstrate *ostensibly* that one has the means to be so. Thus, *ostentatious consumption* had a social value. White hands were one of the clearest proofs of "not working" in a world which was still largely agricultural. In the end, if idleness and *ostentatious consumption* serve one and the same purpose, the second is more visible in a mass society. This logic of distinction causes important social effects including the injunction "not to break rank." The fact that, according to Veblen, everyone tries to climb the social ladder and identify with the reference group immediately above them triggers endless competition between social groups.

Analyses of the rise of the salaried bourgeoisie in the twentieth century have shown that, in order to remain distinct from the proletariat, members of the class sought additional money and time as a material support for *culture* and *effective freedoms* constituting the idea of *otium* (Milner, 1997). This form of distinction mirrored the one which once separated the salaried bourgeoisie, which did not live off rents and which in fact had to work to live, from the *rentier* bourgeoisie, the idle class described by Veblen. Jean-Claude Milner insists on the fact that, in spite of its fall from grace, the figure of the *rentier* remained highly attractive:

> The bourgeois themselves recognize it as their *ideal*, the position that they should occupy in law, even though they do not occupy it in fact: the position that they hope to attain by the end of their earthly existence or, at least, ensure that their children attain thanks to inheritance laws (Milner, 1997: 9).

Once in the minority, non-*rentier* members of the bourgeoisie are now in the majority. In this regard, statistical change reflects structural change. Belonging to the bourgeoisie is now defined by different criteria. The attribution is no longer based on property but on a certain level of income and, above all, on the *way of life* it makes possible. Because the salaried bourgeois is now the fundamental type on which the entire class is based, the *ideal* pursued by all members of the class both for themselves and their children is no longer property or rental income, but a high-paying job. The *rentier*, once a shadowy figure, is now clothed in the discrete charms of nostalgia: "the dreamy bourgeoisie," wrote Drieu La Rochelle;

"dreaming of rental income," according to Milner, for whom "the bourgeoisie still enjoys the images of the old *rentier* existence and cultivates the tender memory of its emblematic figures (the Belle Époque and Sacha Guitry, Forsythe, and Agatha Christie), and likes to picture their decline and their heroic resistance to the modern world . . . the genteel world of the 1970s French TV series, *Les Dames de la Côte*, the microcosm of Miss Marple . . . the property-owning bourgeoisie is to the salaried bourgeoisie of today what the aristocracy once was to the property-owning bourgeoisie" (Milner, 1997: 11).

Processes of distinction can also be observed within the working classes. Norbert Elias suggests as much in *The Established and the Outsiders* a study of the logics of exclusion characterizing two working class neighborhoods (Elias, [1965]; 1997). Thanks to his Jewish origins, the author was well aware of the implications of the insider/outsider dichotomy. Since he experienced this relationship directly, Elias was familiar with the singular experience of belonging to a stigmatized minority group and, at the same time, feeling completely at ease with the cultural milieu and social and political belief-systems of the majority by which it was being denigrated. A German Jew, he knew on a practical level what scorn meant. He considered it *probable* that his interest in sociology, which first developed in early childhood, was due to his experiences as a Jew in Germany. In *The Established and the Outsiders*, a study first published in 1965, the small working class town of "Winston Parva"—in fact an unnamed community near Leicester in the English midlands—is described in detail. The town was divided into three communities, one middle class, one working class, and the third made of up working class newcomers. For the established working class community, the act of excluding the newcomers, who were seen as intruders, was a powerful weapon, used to perpetuate its own identity, assert their superiority, and keep the newcomers in their place (Elias, 1997: xv). Elias suggests that one group can only stigmatize another as long as it maintains a position of power to which its rivals are denied access. The original working class residents had developed a shared way of living and a series of norms; they were happy to respect certain rules. Consequently, they experienced the arrival of newcomers in the neighborhood as a threat to their way of life, even when those newcomers were of the same nationality and ethnicity. The superiority (group charisma) the original residents attributed to themselves was mirrored by the *negative* characteristics (the group disgrace) that they attributed to the newcomers. As the intruders (newcomers and strangers vis-à-vis not only the original working class residents but also each other) lacked cohesion, they were incapable of striking alliances with each other and fighting back (Elias, 1994: xxii). Because any contact with the newcomers implied the risk of diminishing one's status within the established group, no one was willing to lose the consideration of their peers and the imagined superiority associated with belonging to the group made up of the neighborhood's original working class community (Elias, 1994: xxiv). As the author concludes: "The whole drama was played out by the two sides as if they were puppets on a string" (Elias, 1994: lii).

Often considered to be of central importance in Pierre Bourdieu's *œuvre*, *Distinction* vigorously explores mechanisms of access to certain cultural practices without, however, innovating in terms of problematics, as is witnessed by the history of the concept outlined above. While the author suggests a reversal of perspective by reinterpreting the judgment of taste not as an individual phenomenon—the meaning generally applied to the concept—but as a socially *determined* phenomenon which, in turn, *determines* the place occupied by an agent in the social space, he is nevertheless profoundly reliant on the sociological tradition to which he ceaselessly appeals in order to develop his theory. In conclusion, contemporary critiques of the theory of distinction, which Bourdieu in fact merely systematized and applied to the field of culture, suggest that the explicative scheme it proposes could be applied within the framework of a historical sociology to take into account processes of differentiation in *societies of orders*—the Ancien Régime analyzed by Tocqueville and Elias—and in the kind of *class society* with which Jean-Paul Sartre and, later, Bourdieu himself, were familiar. But a question remains unanswered: does *mass society*, characterized by contemporary individualism and the hybridization of cultural practices, oblige us to take a new approach to the problematic of *distinction*?

NOTE

1. Jean-Claude Passeron. 2004. « À propos de l'écriture et des lectures de La Reproduction », interview with Natalia Chmatko. Afterword to the Russian translation of *La Reproduction* by Bourdieu and Passeron. My thanks to Jean-Claude Passeron for providing me with a copy of the interview.

FOUR

The Question of the Democratization of Culture

The *sociological* question, "What are the cultural practices of the French?" is often followed by the *political* question, "Has access to culture been democratized?" or by a more prophetic question: "Will we one day realize the ideal of the democratization of culture?" Posed in such broad terms, these questions can be discouraging, especially in that, today, it is fashionable to take the view that "the failure of democratization" is a given. In fact, some commentators are only too happy to present the social *determinants* of cultural practices highlighted by the sociology of culture described in the preceding chapter as purely *deterministic*. In this chapter, a more sophisticated approach will be taken to the question. An attempt will be made to demonstrate that, in contrast to received ideas, the democratization of culture has enjoyed unarguable successes, as is attested in surveys on cultural institutions. In effect, such institutions are places in which collective identities are expressed and crystallized. Making a major contribution to structuring cultural experiences, social practices, and ways of experiencing relations to art, cultural institutions help to make the ideal of the democratization of culture a real possibility.

1. THE DEMOCRATIZATION OF CULTURE: THE HISTORICAL DEVELOPMENT OF AN IDEAL

"Equal access to culture for all." This apparently straightforward ideal, which in a democracy, is clearly beyond reproach, is based on a striking contradiction between two orders of values, which, in spite of being equally legitimate, are nevertheless difficult to reconcile (Heinich, 2004). The egalitarian ideal promotes the notion of universal access to a universal good, with it being implicitly understood that access, which is not automatic, must be organized. Because universal access to culture is in the general interest, it is organized by the public authorities and cultural institutions. On the other hand, what traditionally attracts people to culture is the idea of a personalized relationship with works of art which helps to develop what might be termed an aristocracy of the spirit, which in turn adds to the sophistication of the process of elite selection. According to Simmel:

> [. . .] just as the substance of education—in spite of, or because of its general availability—can ultimately be acquired only through individual activity, so it gives rise to the most intangible and thus the most unassailable aristocracy, to a distinction between high and low which can be abolished neither (as can socioeconomic differences) by a decree or a revolution, nor by the goodwill of those concerned. (Simmel, 2004: 477)

On the one hand, sharing; on the other, distinction. A fundamental antimony between what, in theory, is a right, and what is experienced in practice as a *privilege*. The Nietzschean conception of the aristocratic morality of distinction (*Vornehmheit*) that Simmel liked to contrast with the leveling of values characteristic of modern societies is echoed to some degree in the work of Weber. However, Weber goes beyond this dichotomy by pointing out that the ideal of distinction is not necessarily expressed as an opposition to mass democratic societies in all aristocracies (Fleury: 2005b). This tension is nevertheless to be found in public policies on culture and informs the sociology of culture itself.

1.1 The intimate relationship between politics and culture: a political question

Formulated in anachronistic terms, the question of the democratization of culture can be traced back two thousand years. Paul Veyne posed it in his discussion of "euergetism" in his *Bread and Circuses* (1990), a book originally published in French in 1976. Recalling that politics poses the tragic question—tragic because insoluble—of the art of living in society, he examined the reasons why the elite organized games and celebrations for the people. The issue, as Veyne sees it, was to transform an infinite diversity of individual desires and interests into a civic and political unity, translated, with the advent of the nation-state, into a national cultural identity. Since the *Ancien Régime*, French cultural policy has addressed the issue by setting up academies (the Académie française in 1635, the Royal Academy of Painting and Sculpture in 1648, the Royal Academy of Music in 1669) and creating patronage organizations (the Royal Private or Princely Mecenat and the Royal Public Mecenat, the Royal Library, the Royal College and the Superintendency of the King's Buildings). This approach was reflected in the education policies of the late nineteenth century to which Jules Ferry lent his name, and the cultural policies of the second half of the twentieth century associated with André Malraux.

In France, the construction of a sense of nationhood was based on political voluntarism. The Ordinance of Villers-Cotterêts (1539) made it obligatory to publish all legal and notary acts in French; the Académie française stabilized syntax, grammar, and orthography, founding the "bel usage" of the language (1635); and the Jules Ferry laws on public, free, and secular education in which French was chosen as the exclusive language, thus eradicating vernacular languages, were all milestones on the road to the linguistic unification of France. Germany presents the inverse configuration since a linguistic community preceded the unification of the state. Luther's translation of the Bible against the background of printing and the rise of the book provided Germany with its own "book" and, consequently its own national language, some four hundred years before the country's political unification, which occurred between 1866 and 1871.

These two historical examples share a linguistic conception of the nation-state, a notion that the British anthropologist Ernest Gellner defined as an organization that successfully lays claim to a monopoly of *legitimate* culture in a given territory (Gellner, 1983). Reminiscent of Weber, this definition insists on the cultural basis of identification with the nation. The particularist conception of culture expressed by the idea of the *Volksgeist*—literally, the spirit of the people—is reflected in Germany in the work of Johann Gottfried Herder. The term "nationality" first appeared in French in the nineteenth century, when it had two meanings: on the one hand, it referred to a group of individuals sharing a common origin, history, and tradition, and, on the other, to a *link* between the people and the state. In this second meaning, nationality does not refer to a *given* community, but to the idea of a *potential* or elective community. It is this last, properly political link, instituting a community in the *polis*, that the ideal of the democratization of education and culture was designed to establish. Because, in a functionalist perspective, atomized industrial societies, anonymous and fluid, are bereft of collective beliefs; it is up to the state to constitute a common culture. In France, the cultural definition of the nation-state is intimately linked to the development of educational and cultural policies. For centuries, the state has played a leading role in the diffusion of a *literary culture*, first through the academies and then through the education system. While the democratization of culture is a part of the state's project to invent the nation and create its culture *ab initio*, the issue of cultural democratization can be viewed in terms of the production of symbols instituting a social order, or, in other words, as a *political question*.

1.2 The Institution of a Republican Order: A Historical Question

The ideal of democratization is indissociable from the French Revolution and the Republican affirmation of the principle of equality between citizens. With the abolition of privileges, the political revolution of the eighteenth century undermined the previous social configuration based on orders. The *Universal Declaration of the Rights of Man and the Citizen* of August 26, 1789, instituted a society of individuals by proclaiming the principle of equality and sparking the transition from a society that was unequal in law to a society that was equal in law. The coexistence of legal equality and *de facto* social inequality prompted Marx to criticize the contradiction between "formal rights" and "real rights." The ideal of the democratization of culture seeks to overcome this contradiction. Democracy presupposes that all citizens are able to exercise functions of power. This capacity, which is largely dependent on the cultural tools and knowledge of which citizens dispose, demands, in particular, a knowledge of reading and writing. From Condorcet's *Report on the General Organization of Public Instruction* (1792) to the Preamble to the French Constitution of 1946 asserting "the right to culture" and the Decree of July 24, 1959, founding the French Ministry of Cultural Affairs, the milestones of a history of cultural policy point again and again to the ideal of the democratization of culture. This ideal, which informs the development of associations of popular education, is echoed in the cultural policies developed by the Popular Front (1936), in the organization of Youth and Popular Education Movements by Jean Guéhenno (1945), and in the decentralization of the national theater affected between 1946 and 1952 by Jeanne Laurent (Denizot, 2005).

The political issue underlying this historical development can be expressed in the following question: What does being partially, if not "democratized," then at least institutionalized mean for art and culture understood as a corpus of consecrated works? How can a form of culture, proposed by institutions, be consonant with the demands of free individuals? Otherwise expressed, the question is whether the cultural institution plays a role in the creation of a "positivity," or, in other words, promotes an approach which, due to its dogmatic, institutional character, is liable to transform art into a form alien to the community, an ideology foreign to a people made up of free individuals or, conversely, whether it contributes to the elaboration of a culture shared within a critical public space. The very fact that such a question can be asked suggests that the issue of the legitimacy of our aesthetic values is a political problem. Even today, in order to distinguish themselves from the market, politicians often use culture and attempts to democratize access to culture as a symbolic pretext to safeguard their interests. Politicians are aware of the principle according to which the symbolic orientations and mechanisms of human action have practical consequences for action, consumption, and production in terms of the way in which actors "construct the social." The accusation according to which the democratization of culture is a utopian ideal is linked to the fact that, in France, the ideal of founding a public space has existed for just a little over two hundred years. Indissociable from the political foundation of a Republican order, the democratization of culture is therefore also defined in terms of a *historical utopia*.

1.3 Evaluating Cultural Policies:
A Technical Question

Because, at least since 1959, the ideal of democratization has provided the political basis of public intervention in the field of culture, cultural policies have regularly been judged in the light of this ideal. Against the background of the institutionalization of a cultural administration, of the professionalization of the artistic field, and of the elaboration of successive definitions of public action (cultural action in the 1960s, cultural development in the 1970s, cultural mediation in the 1990s), a largely symbolic conception of cultural policy was replaced by a more technocratic approach. In fact, an interdependence between culture and politics gave way to an articulation between the *sociology of culture* and *public policy*. For forty years, the sociological concern with examining the cultural practices of the French has been accompanied by the political question as to whether access to culture had or had not been democratized. The lack of distinction between the two discursive registers, one descriptive, the other normative, has produced ideological effects on knowledge generated and diffused by the social sciences.

If we agree that the evaluation of public policies can be defined as the formation of a judgment about the value of those policies, then it must be admitted that the democratization of culture has provided a standard by which the success of cultural policies can be judged. This conception of policy insists on its instrumental aspects, rather than on its role in constituting a political and social order, and thus tends to cast the issue in terms of costs and accessibility. Consequently, the question of the democratization of culture is posed as a *technical question*. The paradigm of efficiency thus only partially obscures the transformation of the very status of public policy, often praised for its social and economic functions more than for its artistic and political aspects. The transformation of the political economy of culture in France runs the risk of reducing democratic aspects in the evaluation of policy choices to technical considerations about how their effects can best be measured.

The ideal of the democratization of culture has been compared, on the one hand, to a utopia, and, on the other, to an ideology. Utopia in the sense of achieving the formal equality between citizens proclaimed in 1789 and laid out in terms of culture in the *Preamble to the Constitution* of

1946. Ideology in the broad sense of the term, as an ensemble of representations which have provided structure to the French government's cultural policy since the end of the Second World War and which were reaffirmed in the Decree of July 24, 1956 setting up the Ministry of Cultural Affairs. Due to inequalities in standards of living between social classes and differences in lifestyle between social groups, this body of cultural policy might, at first sight, appear to be no more than an unrealizable phantasmagoria. Highlighting differences in the number of visits to cultural facilities has made the likelihood of achieving the democratization of culture seem even more far-fetched due to the popularization of a discourse comprised of observations about the social distribution of cultural practices and the sociological explanations for them mentioned in the previous chapter.

2. "THE FAILURE OF DEMOCRATIZATION": A POLITICAL DISCOURSE

The sociology of culture can be credited with having produced a positive body of knowledge deriving from the description of cultural practices and the series of enlightening concepts designed to interpret them. However, the use of the results produced by the sociology of culture poses a problem in that the discourse of the "failure" of democratization has acquired the status of a self-evident truth, a status all the more unassailable in that it is underpinned by the sociology of culture. The fact that social *determinants* have been treated as *determinisms* raises another problem for the reception of the sociology of culture. A critical approach presupposes an examination of the theory's social implications. Such an approach is required if we are to avoid the normative effects characteristic of the social sciences, normative effects that, sometimes unbeknownst to their practitioners, often accompany the diffusion of knowledge generated by the social sciences in society at large. In the following section, the various approaches to analyzing the process of democratization will be reviewed, after which the different meanings attributed to the process and the rhetoric used to describe its "failure" will be examined. It will become apparent that this rhetoric hides, although not too effectively, an ideological perspective according to which the project itself can never succeed.

2.1 Variations in Analytical Approaches to Democratization

Jean-Claude Passeron distinguishes four different approaches to the democratization of culture (Passeron, 2003). Initially, the concept was understood in terms of the number, or "growth in volume," of people at the ticket desks of various cultural institutions. The problem with this definition is that it does not take into account the cultural composition of that population. It was, therefore, impossible to know at the time (1950–1960) who (what kind of person) benefitted from strategies of democratization. The definition became "a sociologically misleading indicator of the democratization of culture which functioned as a kind of decoy." The second meaning assigned to the notion was that of the "democratization of a practice in terms of decreasing the practical discrepancies between different categories of practitioners." In the 1960s, an increasing number of surveys focused on cultural inequalities, a subject that attracted the interest of a growing number of sociologists. This second, more precise definition evolved from an approach consisting of categorizing people who practiced a certain activity into sub-groups and analyzing those sub-groups with a view to establishing a statistical comparison. The third approach consisted of applying social categories.

> Since the 1970s, sociologists have acquired the habit of thinking and calculating in terms of weighted probabilities (*a priori* and *a posteriori* according to the data used and the questions posed) when dealing with inequalities of all kinds, or, in other words, with the chances of being either the user or owner of a commodity. Publics are thus not analyzed merely in terms of their social composition but also in terms of the chances of each member of a specific category being involved in one practice rather than another, or being involved to a greater or lesser degree in such a practice. (Passeron, 2003)

The advantage of this approach is that it seems to more accurately reflect reality; it is closer to what people perceive of that reality. Lastly, Jean-Claude Passeron alludes to democratization in terms of the "democratization of a social rapport."

2.2 Three Definitions of the Democratization of Culture

A body of doctrine of the Ministry of Cultural Affairs since 1959, dismissed as a mere belief in 1968, taken up once more as a utopia in the Beaubourg Center project, the very notion of the democratization of culture raises a series of problems, primary among which is the phrase's many-faceted meaning.

Political project, historical process, technical procedure, the phrase lends itself to these three possible definitions. For Jean-Claude Passeron (1991: 293–299), the democratization of culture is first and foremost a *political project*, or, indeed, a series of political projects since, in reality, cultural democratization implies three possible approaches. First, it can be seen as a project to *convert* the public to prestigious symbolic forms, which presupposes a strategy of proselytism focusing on the masses and promoting learned and literary works with the objective of encouraging as many people as possible to accept the superiority of a particular corpus of works adjudged to be legitimate. If the "noble" definition of culture is accepted, such a project will aim to convert all of society, ensuring a universal admiration of these consecrated works. But if culture is understood in a second, broader sense, then democratization is a project of *rehabilitation* focusing on popular forms of culture, a project which is part of the paradigm of "cultural democracy." According to a third hypothesis, the frontier between "shared culture" and "elite culture" should be abolished. In this instance, democratization is a project of *revolutionary renewal* aimed at encouraging and legitimizing popular culture. But this meaning has become obsolete since the Popular Front gave up on the approach in the 1930s, preferring instead a top-down conception of cultural policies.

Democratization can also be understood as a *historical process*, or, in other words, as a gradual equalization of the conditions of access to culture, an idea reminiscent of the "providential fact" evoked by Tocqueville to describe what he saw as the inexorable movement toward democracy. The secular history of the popular theater—marked by Victor Hugo's declaration in favor of a theater for the people (1848), the setting up of the Théâtre du Peuple by Maurice Pottecher (1895), and the creation of the National Popular Theater by Firmin Gémier in 1920, the reins of which were taken up by Jean Vilar in 1951—is characterized by continuities and discontinuities. The democratization of culture can be defined as the product of this long historical process. But the evolutionism implied by this second meaning constitutes the limits of such a perspective.

Last, democratization can be read as a *technical procedure*. From this perspective, it consists of a series of mechanisms of social change. The decentralization of the theater falls into this category in that it was a strategy designed to "cover the territory," to conquer and make loyal a provincial public in a country in which the provinces were, after the Second World War, viewed as a "cultural desert." The National Popular Theater's revolutionary approach was based on the introduction of three innovations: the assertion of the principle of the theater as a public service imagined in terms of a non-exclusive theater (Fleury, 2005a: 29–34); the constitution of a popular public; and the introduction of a series of approaches breaking with the intimidating rituals of the bourgeois theater of the 1930s, including earlier performance times, reservations and rented facilities, no tips, free cloakrooms, and popular subscriptions for rehearsals, all aimed at softening the cold geometry of the Palais de Chaillot and doing away with the rituals of distinction that bourgeois theater-goers habitually took part in (Fleury, 2003a). These procedures, introduced in the 1950s in a Republican perspective, were deployed in the 1970s by the Pompidou Center in the form of free circulation, an approach which enabled people to access works of art as they pleased. Later, in the 1990s, innovations such as a free Sunday every month at the Louvre proved highly successful (1996). Over ten years later, an experiment was carried out in fourteen national institutions, ten museums and four monuments by the Ministry of Culture and Communication, the Ministry of Defense, and the Ministry of Higher Education and Research to gauge the effects of free entry on visitor rates. As well as measuring an increase in those rates, the objective of the survey, carried out in the first quarter of 2008, was to evaluate the effect of free entrance on the diversification of publics. Results demonstrated that visitor rates increased significantly among all segments of the population, especially students and people under thirty years of age. The positive effect of the introduction of free entry on the democratization of access to museums on both those already familiar with museums and people who had never visited them before was clear (Eidelman and Céroux, 2009).

Another approach is to apply a positive discrimination strategy to certain targeted populations, often, but not always from the culturally and economically less favored classes, the members of which do not, as a rule, frequent cultural institutions. Targeting certain populations rather than others is tantamount to favoring certain potential publics over others. This new approach to the democratization of culture is not entirely consonant with the French Republican ideal according to which everyone should receive equal treatment. Taking into account the fact that, in terms of access to culture and the arts, certain individuals are advantaged while others are disadvantaged, this approach to democratization deploys a series of procedures designed to reduce the gap between individuals in terms of their relationship with art. If we are to agree that these different aspects of the democratization of culture do not mutually cancel each other out, but that, on the contrary, cultural institutions help to articulate them, then a sociological approach becomes relevant.

2.3 The Democratization of Culture on Trial

The French Ministry of Culture was founded on the idea that culture could be democratized by providing a supporting framework for a high-quality artistic offer. The brutal delegitimization of the mission to democratize culture is a key moment in the history of French cultural policy. In effect, from May 1968, "cultural democratization became a belief" (Urfalino, 1996: 216). The discourse on the failure of democratization imposed itself in the mid-1960s as a category of thought, not only among sociologists of culture, but also among numerous men and women working in the field of cultural policy. The discourse has a self-evident character which sometimes acquires a kind of force of law in the literal sense of the "rules of cultural diffusion" (Bourdieu and Darbel, 1997: 71–107): "Statistics show that access to cultural works is the privilege of the cultivated class" (Bourdieu and Darbel, 1997: 37). And, since "'cultural need' increases the more it is satisfied, the absence of practice being accompanied by an awareness of this absence [. . .] the wish to take advantage of museums can be fulfilled as soon as it exists, it must be concluded that such a wish only exists if it is being fulfilled" (Bourdieu and Darbel, 1997: 37).

Three charges have been leveled at the democratization of culture: illegitimacy, inequity, and inefficiency. The charge of *illegitimacy* focuses on the project itself and is based on a debate on values which provides, at best, shaky grounds for informed argument. The critique focuses on the questionable nature of public intervention, which, advocates claim, transforms the status of culture and provokes its decline: the denunciation of cultural relativism deriving from an "ethnologization" of culture, itself provoked by forms of political demagogy, provides a framework of ideological opposition favoring a hierarchy of aesthetic values. The charge of inequity underlines the anti-redistributive effects of policies on the democratization of culture; those who support the idea of funding culture from the public purse are taken to task on the grounds that taxes collected from the population as a whole would be used to subsidize artistic productions of benefit only to the minority of people who go to the opera or the ballet. The liberal argument underlying this position has a number of dangerous consequences, since the absence of support for artistic productions would only accentuate the inequality at issue. The third discursive figure in the rhetoric of "failure" is the *inefficiency* of policies implemented by cultural institutions. Those defending this argument claim that, in spite of forty years of public intervention, inequalities in terms of access to culture have hardly diminished and that, with the conceptual arsenal of the sociology of culture advancing socialization, *habitus* and distinction as explanatory factors of the social distribution of cultural practices, any attempt to democratize culture would be doomed to failure. However, the idea that the policies employed by cultural institutions are inefficient was not shared by Pierre Bourdieu, for whom it "is established that an intensification of the action of the school is the most efficient means of increasing cultural practice [. . .] at the same time as being the necessary condition for the effectiveness of all other approaches" (Bourdieu and Darbel, 1997). The accusation that public intervention is futile is contradicted by studies carried out on the quantitative and qualitative impact of policies concerning the public. From a political point of view, accusing a policy of being inefficient can lead to institutional innovations being withdrawn, which, in turn, may lead to a fall in visitor numbers, thus ensuring that the prophecy comes true.

If we accept that the democratization of culture can be seen as a political project, a historical process, and a technical procedure, then it has to be admitted that the three charges, established by means of a categorization of discourses, are aimed at three meanings of the term "democratization." Thus, the charge of illegitimacy brings into question the political project that is democratization; the charge of inequity implies a criticism of the meaning of a historical process which, renouncing an optimistic, Tocquevillian view, takes the form of a more Marxian prophecy of an ever-widening gap between the working classes and the upper classes. Last, the charge of inefficiency concerns *a priori* institutional approaches to resolving the question of the inequality of access to culture. These rhetorical figures are typical of "reactionary rhetoric," in which Albert O. Hirschman identifies three topics: jeopardy, perversity, and futility (Hirschman, 1991). A transition occurs between the unarguable *sociological* observation that there are different rates in visitor numbers to cultural institutions, and the more ideological discourse of the invalidation of the very project of the democratization of culture itself, as is witnessed by certain positions taken by researchers in unequivocally pessimistic articles and essays on its so-called failure (Donnat, 1991; 1994). This could be linked to involuntary effects or to an absence of thought about the effects of the diffusion of knowledge from the social sciences. Indeed, Karl Mannheim has demonstrated that the act of criticizing an ideology itself invariably takes on an ideological turn (Mannheim, 1985). The charge of the failure of democratization is thus replaced by a more ideological discourse invalidating the project itself and, along with it, a whole series of institutional innovations by which it accompanied.

3. CULTURAL INSTITUTIONS AND THE REALIZATION OF DEMOCRATIZATION

Against the ideological discourse denouncing the democratization of culture as a utopia or an ideology, the following, extremely important question should, if we don't want the fashionable discourse on the "failure of democratization" to become entrenched, be asked again, namely, what responses does sociology bring to the question of whether a process of democratization has been triggered or not? A sociological understanding of cultural practices which provides access to the meaning given to those practices by individuals presupposes using cultural institutions as a relevant point of observation from which to start to describe people's aesthetic experiences. Cultural institutions are places which can potentially structure behaviors and the representations that accompany them. Furthermore, they can be seen as a potential vector of the realization of the ideal of democratization (Fleury, 2009).

3.1 Forgetting Institutions and Secondary Socialization

The fashionable discourse on the "failure of democratization" is based on the idea that institutions are incapable of countering the determinants of the social distribution of cultural practices. According to this idea, cultural institutions lack the capacity to counter the influence of the education system and the family, considered determining instances of future cultural practices and of the development of taste. Moreover, cultural institutions provide an ideal space for manifesting distinction. The conclusion we are invited to draw is that such institutions are powerless in the face of the social determinants of cultural practices. That is how sociological explanations of inequalities in visitor numbers confirmed by the longitudinal survey of the cultural practices of the French lend credence, on a secular level, to the myth of predestination. The results of such surveys, which have become classic, are viewed by numerous directors of institutions as unquestionable and serve as the foundation of the discourse of impotence of which, paradoxically, they have become the vehicles. The project for the democratization of culture is rendered invalid due to the "translation-betrayal" (*traduction-trahison*) of those results in the form of a deterministic presupposition casting any attempt to attain the ideal as hopelessly vain. The resurgence of the now secularized myth of predestination serves as a justification for the absence of political thought about the most effective ways of mitigating (if not actually abolishing) the effect of symbolic obstacles limiting the access of most people to culture.

The failure of the democratization of culture has become the dominant discourse. However, there are exceptions to the rule. Voluntaristic policies have enjoyed a number of unquestionable successes. Those successes can be used as counter-examples to argue against a theory which is not bereft of ideological effects, for, and this bears repeating, the observation that there is a distribution of cultural practices is sometimes presented as sufficient reason to reject the project of the democratization of culture. The problematic of the *social reproduction of heirs* even seems to have prompted some commentators to dispense with the need to investigate the potential existence of conditions of counter-socialization.

A change in scale of observation enables us to glimpse aspects of reality which have, up until now, been invisible, and to suggest that the question of the democratization of culture demands an analysis of its potential conditions of realization (Lahire, 1996; Revel, 1996). An examination of the role of cultural institutions reveals that they can be used to diminish, rather than exacerbate social differences (Fleury, 2004). How can cultural institutions further the cause of cultural democratization? The conditions of possibility of the *realization* of the ideal have been observed, or at least glimpsed, in empirical surveys. The ideal implies that cultural socialization is not over by the age of fifteen or twenty-five and that secondary socialization has an influence in encounters with art and culture.

3.2 The Power to Provide a Structure for Cultural Practices

Against the widespread idea of a "failure" of the democratization of culture, it is important to consider the conditions which render possible a realization of this ideal. Cultural institutions like the National Popular

Theater, directed by Jean Vilar from 1951 to 1963, and the Pompidou Center, which was opened in 1977, provide two counter-examples to the discourse of the failure of democratization. However, an analysis of the multi-dimensionality of the public and a study of the ways in which relations between institutions and individuals are structured reveal that democratization is intimately linked to the process by which those relations are institutionalized. Exercising genuine power in terms of structuring cultural practices, the National Popular Theater and the Pompidou Center represent two examples of how this ideal could be achieved. Indeed, the two institutions can be viewed as authentic actors in terms of defining cultural policy in France in the post–War period.

If we are to agree that the National Popular Theater was a model, what can we say about its public? Did its spectators belong to the working class? An analysis of the questionnaires filled in by the spectators of the National Popular Theater (Fleury, 2006b) reveals that the task of conquering a working class public and ensuring that it stays loyal is dependent on the institutionalization of the category of the "working class." Because identity can be defined as the fruit of an incessant negotiation between *acts of attribution*, with principles of identification coming from other people, and *acts of belonging* designed to express the categories in which individuals would like to be perceived, the discourse on the public provides a range of potential individual and collective identifications, just as the National Popular Theater's policy towards its spectators could be seen as a series of acts of attribution, themselves at the origin of acts of belonging expressed by those spectators. The category of the "working class public," referring to the ontological model of the political body, was thus largely achieved by introducing the category of the spectator which, in turn, referred to the model of the critical public space.

Far from being impotent in regard to the effects of the cultivated *habitus*, cultural institutions have the power to model people's relationship with the arts and the capacity to produce social effects either supporting or militating against the *habitus*. Because implementing public policies can be seen as enabling institutions to act on the actions of individuals, institutions exercise a structure-giving power on practices representing the foundations on which the ideal of the democratization of culture can be built. The power of cultural institutions can also be demonstrated negatively by means of the fragility inherent in the actions of institutions: more often than not, the disappearance of institutional innovations leads to the public staying away in droves (Fleury, 2002a).

Paul DiMaggio examined the influence of museums on the democratization of culture (DiMaggio, 1996). In tandem with Michael Useem, he explored the question of "cultural democracy," analyzing arts audiences in the United States and highlighting the power of the theater by focusing on the influence exerted by various companies and the extent to which they chose to exert it (DiMaggio and Useem, 1983; 1985). This influence can be described in three ways. First, cultural institutions can be seen as a banal form of political intervention. Second, they make a substantial contribution to defining public policies. And last, they provide spaces in which collective identities, ways of experiencing relations to art, and cultural experiences and social practices are expressed and crystallized. An analysis of their cognitive and normative impact on individuals reveals that the logic underlying cultural practices cannot be reduced to a mere logic of distinction; indeed, other logics are at work, revealed in the transformation of perceptions of how works of art should be received and in the transformation of forms of sociability (Fleury, 2002). The cultural institution thus fully constitutes an instance of socialization.

3.3 Institutions: The Invisible Aspect of Cultural Policy

Toby Miller and George Yudice demonstrate the importance of cultural policy and the approaches taken by cultural institutions in structuring practices (Miller and Yudice, 2002). Far from being neutral, the organization of the relationship between individuals and works of art produces effects which suggest the power of cultural institutions. This is at least what is highlighted by the study of the normative and cognitive impact of public-focused policies implemented by institutions, which reveals that variables other than the artistic offer influence the development of cultural practices. In regard to the effects of policies on the public, it is legitimate to conclude that cultural institutions are central actors in cultural policy.

This recognition of the power of cultural institutions opens the door to a neo-institutionalist program articulating two questions. First, what are the roots of cultural institutions and what bodies institute them and are, in turn, instituted by them? And, second, what relationship do they have with individuals and how do they develop that relationship? These two questions inform the potential realization of the ideal of democratization. Modeled by the state and society, cultural institutions have revealed themselves to be capable of modifying the practices of individuals, thereby helping to transform the presuppositions underlying public policies by helping to elaborate the norms of public action that they produce.

The fact that the power possessed by cultural institutions is hidden renders the institutions themselves invisible. Or, at least, their social and political clout, their capacity to produce social and political effects, is invisible. This may seem paradoxical in regard to the high profile of many cultural institutions. What becomes invisible, and what is forgotten in traditional analysis—thus reinforcing that invisibility—is the capacity of institutions to inform activities, govern practices, and make individuals aware of culture and its multifarious aspects. Thus, cultural institutions like the National Popular Theater and the Pompidou Center have not only produced norms and rules, but also instituted apparently insignificant routines. The fact that the power of cultural institutions is generally forgotten explains why they represent the invisible aspect of cultural policy. In this sense, they not only contribute to implementing cultural policies but also to elaborating the way in which those policies are defined.

Another blind spot in the sociological approach to the democratization of culture is the temporal variable or, in other words, the lack of analysis of temporality in terms of culture. There is a disproportionate contrast, with which sociologists of culture, often close to sociologists of education, are familiar, between educational democratization—deployed for over a century—and the democratization of culture, for which the first public policies were only introduced in the 1960s. While it is difficult to say at what point in the course of the last five decades the sociology of culture started to observe, meticulously and methodically, even the most modest leveling out of the opportunities of various publics and social groups to accede to elite culture, it should be borne in mind that the period of time so far "assessed" is a relatively short one in regard to the period of time required for processes of socialization to make a lasting impact. We should thus avoid concluding that the democratization of culture, announced in 1959 as the guiding principle of public policy in France, is an impossible ideal merely because it has not been attained. Because such a process is, by definition, unattained and, ultimately, unattainable, does not mean that it should not be pursued. The democratization of culture, too often analyzed in terms of a *political project* with the associated question of its success or lack of it, would therefore be worth studying as a *technical procedure* (with the accompanying sociological question of the appropriation of public apparatuses by social actors) or, more to the point, as a *historical process*, incorporating the comparatist aspect of a historical sociological perspective.

In conclusion, the democratization of culture can be seen as an approach to instituting culture politically. Criticized by many sociologists for being an unrealizable ideology and an "exhausted utopia" and abandoned as a project by numerous elites, the democratization of culture found itself sidelined even as it was being partially implemented by certain cultural institutions. But a sociological analysis highlights the impact of the actions of cultural institutions both quantitatively, in terms of increasing arts audiences, and qualitatively, in terms of individual and collective identifications, sociability, and socialization, and relationships with the question of meaning and values. The program of a sociology of reception casting members of the public, not as crucial consumers of cultural products, but as indispensable actors in the construction of the meaning of works of art, provides an alternative perspective for those who prefer not to reduce cultural goods to the status of economic commodities, but who are instead interested in cultural socialization and aesthetic experience.

FIVE
Contemporary Reorientations

Criticism of the early sociology of culture prompted researchers to explore new themes, triggering an increase in the number of empirical studies on cultural practices, and contributed to the emergence of a sociology of reception focusing on the question of the constituent elements of aesthetic experience.

1. THE CRITIQUE OF THE THEORY OF CULTURAL LEGITIMACY

The theory of "cultural capital" has been put to the test in a number of empirical studies, most of them published in the journal *Poetics* starting in the 1990s. The primacy of the "legitimist" analysis of cultural objects and practices was brought to an end by a tripartite empirical, epistemological, and methodological critique.

1.1 Empirical Critiques

The models suggested by Pierre Bourdieu were discussed without the theoretical framework supporting his concept of "distinction" being radically called into question. Although empirical studies acknowledged the importance of culture in promoting class cohesion, the introduction of analytical categories such as gender and ethnicity helped to better describe not only the relationship with "distinction" constructed by various social groups but also the variables and parameters used in the definition of cultural choices and practices (Ostrower, 1998). Michèle Lamont has studied the potential impact of symbolic boundaries on relationships of inequality; her comparison of the cultural repertoires of the French and American elites demonstrates that cultural boundaries associated with levels of education, intelligence, refined taste, and cosmopolitanism are less strictly defined in France than they are in the United States (Lamont, 1992). Symbolic boundaries should thus be considered as a necessary, although insufficient precondition of the production of inequality and exclusion. This comparatist approach makes it possible to nuance the contribution of national cultural differences in the (re)production of symbolic boundaries.

Mirroring such studies, in a survey on the "cultural repertoires of the elites," Guy Bellavance compares the cultural and professional worlds of a population generally seen—notably in polls on cultural practices—as the leading consumer of art and culture. This potential public is that of the new upper middle classes, well-educated and highly qualified, disposing of a double capital, cultural and economic, that, theoretically, facilitates access to a repertoire of legitimate objects and activities and that, above all, predisposes it to a "correct" usage of that repertoire, a classic example of the *habitus*. After having revealed in this ideal (or idealized) public an ensemble of attitudes of non-participation or indifference characteristic of "non-publics," Bellavance analyzes the composition and use of those repertoires, demonstrating that repertoires of taste, like the forms of legitimacy and modes of legitimization that underpin them, have substantially evolved over the course of recent decades (Bellavance, 2004).

However, livelier critiques, both empirical and theoretical, of the theory of distinction have also emerged (Gartman, 1991; Lamont and Lareau, 1988),[1] highlighting, among other things, the existence of disjunctions between cultural repertoires, levels of cultural participation, and symbolic boundaries (Kane, 2003). Paul Kingston (2001) poses the question of the decline of the role of the arts considered as "cultural capital" and observes an unprecedented depreciation of their value in this regard: rates of participation in arts associated with high culture have declined spectacularly, especially insofar as younger people are concerned. Empirical surveys show that a status hierarchy involving the notions of "omnivore" and "univore" has replaced the older idea opposing the elite to the masses (Peterson, 1992; Peterson and Kern, 1996). Paul DiMaggio and Toqir Mukhtar also point to a gradual decline in the number of people attending cultural events (all ages, genders, and levels of education included), a phenomenon that can be explained by competition from home entertainment technology and changes in the composition of the population and the structure of the family. The trends revealed (DiMaggio and Mukhtar, 2004) confirm a transition from the figure of the "snob" to that of the omnivore, first observed by Richard Peterson in 1996. Although he underlines notable changes in the field of cultural consumption, which is a good deal more complex than it once was, Peterson also highlights the fact that the middle and upper classes continue to distinguish themselves from the working classes, with the displacement of meanings in terms of boundaries constituting a major difference between the two groups.

Thus, even if cultural choices are neither diversified nor complex within a specific group, they are never the product of chance. Alongside a pre-existing hierarchical space in which cultures are defined around a dynamic of familiarity with and rejection of popular culture, processes of social reproduction are still at work.

1.2 Epistemological Critiques

Claude Grignon and Jean-Claude Passeron's epistemological critique is based on an analysis of the various positions taken by sociologists in regard to popular culture (Grignon and Passeron, 1989; Passeron, 2006: 445–508). Two major postures are identified, namely *relativism* and *legitimism*, both of which run the risk of falling into specific traps, respectively *populism* and *miserabilism*. Because the sociology of popular culture is a prisoner of the contradictions inherent in its own methods, or, in other words, a prisoner of the paradox that encompasses the study of popular culture within a framework of learned culture, the value judgments made by sociologists must be taken into account. The first approach—*cultural relativism*—focuses on the norms and values of popular culture without locating that culture in a power relationship or a relationship of submission or subjugation vis-à-vis legitimate culture. The descriptive method applied in this theory is based on *cultural autonomization*, a notion summed up as follows: "even if it is dominated, a culture still functions as a culture" (Grignon and Passeron, 1989: 21). The use of a descriptive method induces a *populist* error which consists of maintaining that "real values" belong to the people. On the other hand, the second attitude—the theory of *cultural legitimacy*—describes the working classes and their culture in reference to the symbolic domination to which they are subject. Popular culture is not viewed as *autonomous* but, on the contrary, as *heteronymous*, and dependent on a dominant culture. This analysis uses a descriptive method based on negative differentiation, which effectively betrays a form of *class ethnocentrism*. The observer considers his or her system of norms and values as primary, as better than anyone else's, thus inducing a kind of *miserabilism* focusing on the shortcomings of popular culture compared to dominant culture.

Grignon and Passeron's vigorous critique focuses on the question, close to the heart of Max Weber, of the "relation to values" of the sociologist or, more precisely, of the clarification of her relation to values or the lack thereof. Other critiques, focusing specifically on Pierre Bourdieu's theory, underline the effects of the imposition of learned culture, for example Louis Gruel's vitriolic portrait of Bourdieu as an "impostor" in his critique of *The Inheritors* and *Distinction* (Gruel, 2005).

1.3 Methodological Critiques

The first *methodological* critique contrasts a sociological approach with Bourdieu's positivist arsenal of analytical weapons. While some observers criticized the author's use of factorial analysis, others went further, lambasting his habit of transforming statistical probability into a social "law" based on statistics—an approach he used in both in *The Love of Art* and in *Distinction*—thereby raising the more general question of how statistics should be generated and applied. Norbert Elias had already demonstrated the weakness of statistical "proof" of this kind, stating that the "impoverishment of sociology as a science which has resulted from the prevalent evaluation of sociological methods—from the assumption that it is enough to use statistical methods if one wants reliable answers to sociological problems, is obvious enough" (Elias, 1994: 9) and adding that "social data can be sociologically significant without having statistical significance and that such data can be statistically significant without having sociological significance" ([1965] 1994: 11).

A number of sociologists have rejected the traditional, caricatured, tripartite hierarchical typology of culture, which features, at the top, "legitimate culture" (classical music, *auteur* theater, opera, etc.) consumed by the "dominant classes"; in the middle, "middlebrow culture" (jazz, film, etc.) consumed by the middle classes; and, at the bottom, a popular culture marked by exclusion. They demonstrate that, on the contrary, boundaries between the learned arts and the popular arts, between "highbrow" and "lowbrow culture" (Gans, 1974; 1985), are extremely unstable and evanescent and are subject to endless realignment. Referring to what he terms "imperfect transfers" (2004: 166–174), Bernard Lahire recalls that a "concept has no scientific use unless it enables us to observe elements of reality and to order those observations in a specific manner." This approach, which takes into account new elements and the way in which they are inserted into a coherent system of analysis based on previously existing phenomena, is the one that should be retained. At issue here are the *modes of analysis* which should be applied to cultural practices. By observing their relations with cultural institutions, by changing the scale of our analysis, and by applying a sociological approach, we can obtain a precise idea of the meanings accorded by individuals to their practices, meanings which remain invisible to statistical techniques.

2. THE REORIENTATION OF PROBLEMATICS AND OBJECTS

2.1 Changes in Society and Culture

The transformation of the status of culture accompanied by the emergence of new technical, scientific, and managerial cultures among the traditionally cultured elites and the professionalization of the artistic field provides a valid area of research. As is witnessed by sociological analyses of cultural crises in the field of education (Dubet, 2002), academic performance at school and university is no longer as accurate in terms of predicting cultural behaviors as it once was. Schools, whose traditional purpose was to transmit culture, now have to accommodate the pragmatic objectives of young graduates concerned with preparing for the labor market and professional specialization. The increase in the number of young people from social milieus unfamiliar with the consecrated culture serves to undermine the idea according to which having a degree indicates a certain level of "cultural capital." The number of "non-cultivated" degree courses is increasing. Last, schools no longer have the exclusive right to define legitimate repertoires and uses of culture. The number of sources of access to culture has increased substantially, notably thanks to public cultural action, and, above all, to the media and the market (Moulin, 1992).

The decline of belief in the superiority of high culture is becoming increasingly generalized. Indeed, attitudes, even amongst the best educated, are changing. The culture industry is developing and gradually being rehabilitated by a large proportion of the cultural elite, as well as by government agencies. In a different light, multiculturalism, and the rehabilitation of the "sub-cultures" and minority cultures by which it is underpinned, suggests an equally important change in forms of legitimization by distancing itself from traditional ideologies of the democratization of culture focused exclusively on the most legitimate repertoires. Multiculturalism lays claim to the status of singularity in a homogenized world. According to the anthropologist Jean-Loup Amselle, "the implementation of the policies of liberalization on a global scale does not translate, as might be expected, into a triumph of individualism but, on the contrary, generates a proliferation of collective identities" (Amselle, 2001: 45).

These phenomena are all the more evident in North America, where, faced by the culture industry and popular culture, traditional cultural institutions, notably those focusing on the arts, are unable to command the kind of tradition-based prestige enjoyed by their counterparts in Europe. In this context, critiques of the behaviors of the elite, like those developed by Pierre Bourdieu in *Distinction*, are all the more likely to be inaccurate, especially since the surveys on which those analyses were based date from the early 1960s. Following the surveys conducted by Peterson showing that the dominant actor in the cultural game is no longer the purist, the snob, or the pedant—the "univore" consumer of an exclusive repertoire—but an eclectic and inclusive "omnivore," the number of surveys in the field has increased (Bellavance and Fournier, 1996).

The work of Terry Clark is among the most suggestive in the field. Using quantitative data in a perspective of international comparison,

Clark demonstrates that culture appears as a *primary factor* in the constitution of American and French cities. His monographic study on Chicago charts the city's transition from an industrial center to a cultural megalopolis (Clark, 2011). While the attractiveness of a metropolis can be measured in terms of its major assets (tourism, global competition), and its more modest social mechanisms (social cohesion, the insertion of problematic neighborhoods), it is primarily associated with the conjunction of various modes of cultural consumption (Clark, 2007). It is not a question of choosing between "major projects" and policies designed to provide support for popular culture; what this new approach aims for above all is to work with existing *ambiances* and to eschew received ideas about what culture is, in favor of a real understanding of day-to-day practices and their relations to cultural facilities. Terry Clark, professor at the University of Chicago, combines urban sociology with the sociology of culture in an attempt to describe *ambiances* characteristic of *scenes*.[2] Composed of specialists in urbanism, sociology, and psychology, the team directed by Clark has developed an original method for measuring *ambiances* by correlating them with more traditional indicators such as employment, demography, environmental costs, civil commitment, and political participation.[3]

Focusing on a cartography of *ambiances* and modes of cultural consumption rather than on a cartography of cultural facilities substantially transforms the perspective and provides greater insight into the effects on culture of the concrete choices of individuals. It transpires that people are more involved in artistic activities than political ones (Putnam, 2000; 2004) and that the influence of artistic activities is greater than that of political activities, not only in terms of changing individual and collective identities, but also of reinforcing the trust in society and its *leaders* and their legitimacy (Clark and da Silva, forthcoming), both of which can be considered as social and political effects properly so-called. This approach shows that several *arrondissements* in Paris (Sawyer, 2011) and communes in northern France are losing talented young people, who are moving to the south and west of the country (Silver, Clark, Navarro, 2010). An analysis of the factors associated with these changes indicates that more traditional and hierarchical cultural activities are characteristic of regions which are losing inhabitants (large museums, traditional spectacles), while other regions are characterized by cultural innovations (small music groups, eclectic performances), for example in cities such as Montpellier, Aix-en-Provence, and Grenoble (Clark and Sawyer, 2009–2010), whose local governments often support diverse cultural activities that frequently attract visitors from Paris (Clark and Hoffman-Martinot, 1998). This research underlines the weakness of traditional approaches advancing factors such as class, race, gender, and ethnic origins, which individuals cannot change, as determining cultural activities. In effect, only 15 percent of cultural practices can be explained by these types of factors. Rather than refuting other approaches, analyses of ambiances help us to understand the countless ways in which various publics appreciate culture in their many different relations to various cultural activities.

2.2 Transforming Scales of Observation

Networks of Sociability

Sociability networks have long been neglected in the analysis of cultural practices. Sociability, the importance of which was underlined by Simmel in his analysis of the life of social forms (Simmel, 1997), is central to an understanding of the number of exceptions to the rule of cultural socialization theorized by Pierre Bourdieu. The effects of social contiguity employed to explain singular trajectories constitute, in and of themselves, a crucial object for the understanding of cultural practices and aesthetic experiences. The influence of *sociability* in the formation of aesthetic judgments explains both their dynamic and the plurality of identifications characterizing the field. The cultural sociabilities approach developed by Katz and Lazarsfeld in their influential book, *Personal Influence: The Part Played by People in Mass Communication* (Katz and Lazarsfeld, 1955) can be applied in this perspective to gain a deeper insight into aesthetic judgments, which can be understood here within the context of an "economy of singularities" (Karpik, 2007).[4] Comparing the range of cultural practices of individuals, Bernard Lahire insists on the many different contexts which frame them and on the idea of the numerous cultural identities of the "plural" individual. François de Singly addresses the theme of sociability by presenting "the library as a space of public discussion" (de Singly, 1997: 100–130) and develops the problematic of individualism (de Singly, 2003a: 43–60) and the institution of social bonds (2003 and 2005). Practices of sociability focusing on books and reading demonstrate that readers are not the solitary, introspective characters that they are too often imagined to be, but, on the contrary, that they develop a real or imaginary sociability with other readers or authors (Burgos, Evans, and Buch, 1996). Museums (Poulot, 1986) and music fandom (Le Bart, 2000) are characterized by a similar dynamic. Sociability is a key concept in studies on the reading habits of young adolescents between eleven and fifteen years old (de Singly, 1989; Baudelot, Cartier, Detrex, 1999), and, more generally, on the cultural leisure pursuits of six- to fourteen-year-olds (Octobre, 2004), and on high school cultures (Dominique Pasquier, 2005).

Frameworks for New Meanings and Values

For some sociologists, objects are central to any analysis of mediation. Like Antoine Hennion, much of whose research focuses on the emergence of aesthetic taste (Hennion, 2003), these authors focus on the relationship between cultural objects and their publics. Following in the footsteps of Callon and Latour (1981), Hennion develops, in his book *La passion musicale* (1993), an anthropology of cultural objects in which objects fashion the representations that people have of them. Applying an approach reminiscent of Latour's perspective on scientific objects described in *Laboratory Life* (1986)—in which the author takes issue with the sociology of science—Hennion underlines the *irreducible specificity* of works of art as cultural objects and the importance, for all those interested in understanding the dynamics of taste, of how such works are mediated.

In a different perspective, a number of surveys have focused on festivals (Ethis, 2001 and 2002) and other cultural institutions, taking into account their various effects and their role in structuring the cultural practices of spectators, listeners, and readers (DiMaggio, 1996). Foregrounding the notion of aesthetic reception, these surveys are informed by Nietzsche's critique of the romantic vision of artistic genius (Uzel, 2001) outlined in the third dissertation of the *Genealogy of Morals*. In opposition to the disinterested pleasure described by Kant, Nietzsche rehabilitates the role of the spectator in the creative process, an idea that was later to be developed by Walter Benjamin in his influential essay, *The Work of Art in the Age of Mechanical Reproduction*(1935–1938). All these approaches convincingly suggest that the articulation between politics and art, one of the fundamental issues in the sociological analysis of aesthetic experience, should not to be sought in objects (form, content, material), but, rather, in the relationship, mediated by the work of art, between the spectator and the creator (Halley, 2004). Indeed, the idea that a work can possess a value in itself has been called into question by a number of sociologists. For Pierre Bourdieu, the value of the work is that which social groups accord to it. Although at the opposite end of the spectrum insofar as this notion is concerned, the sociology of reception is also based on the idea that the value of objects is bestowed on them by people, which means that a work cannot exist in and of itself, but that it is, rather, an object subject to multiple interpretations. This definition of the work of art as an infinite process of interpretation has methodological consequences. Insisting on the breadth of attitudes displayed by individuals, on the multiple functions of culture, and, on the diversity of styles of belief, Paul Veyne has shown how the generally received meaning of works of art is not the one implied by their content or desired by their creators (Veyne, 1988). Thus, sociologists of culture cannot claim to be able to interpret all the possible meanings of a given relationship with culture. To understand the meaning of a work of art is not, therefore, exclusively dependent on a thoroughgoing knowledge of the context in which it was produced, but, rather, on an analysis of the meanings it has for interpretative communities (Heinich, 1991). Processes of interpretation escape the control of artistic creators who address a public that they only imagine. And the act of interpretation, since it involves the selection of a series of structuring traits, generates meaning. In fact, all works are reconstructed by individual interpretations. They are taken on a transformative journey. In other words, the object of a sociology of reception is to understand how meanings are attributed to works of art via the historical articulation of processes of production, mediation, and reception. In a sense, the sociology of reception, or, more broadly, the sociology of culture, is defined by an understanding of the "cultural meaning" of artistic and cultural phenomena.

2.3 Exploring New Inter-Disciplinary Approaches

The various and complementary perspectives characterizing inter-disciplinary approaches to cultural analysis can be viewed as a welcome reaction to the kind of "sociologism" that marked the early years of the sociology of culture. In a more positive light, they can be seen as reflecting a desire to exploit the kind of contiguity of ideas potentially contained in such approaches.

Maurice Halbwachs's work on the fruitful relations between sociology and psychology (Fleury, 2006d) was developed by Bernard Lahire with a view to providing sociologists with the kind of conceptual and methodological tools required to analyze the more arcane and eccentric aspects of the social world (Lahire, 1999). A number of sociologists of culture refer to recent research in cognitive psychology, which describes a fragmented vision of culture informing individual experience, in order to highlight the importance of institutions and networks in any understanding of cultural practices. Paul DiMaggio underlines the heuristic value of these approaches in terms of appraising processes of identification, collective memory, and the logics of action (DiMaggio, 1997).

The familial link between sociology and anthropology is evident in the quantitative ethnography of Jean-Claude Passeron (Passeron and Pedler, 1991; 1999). The work of Marie-Madeleine Mervant-Roux on the role of the spectator in theatrical representations is articulated around a series of field studies in which a number of disciplines were applied, including ethnography, sociology, historical, and cultural anthropology, aesthetics of the theater, and the stage arts (Mervant-Roux, 1998). And dialogue between sociologists and economists of culture has highlighted the material (tickets, transport, time) and immaterial (information, training, communication) costs associated with visits to the theater, the concert hall, or the opera (François Rouet), as well as the importance of "price-elasticity" in assessing the effects of introducing a free Sunday a month at the Louvre (1996). Such an approach foregrounds both the issue of the relationship between cultural practices and economics and the anthropological perspective of the theory of the gift (Fourteau and Godelier, 2002).

Similarly, sociologists of culture and cultural historians have worked together on the material forms in which texts are transmitted and received, examining, among other things, the role of publishers and printers in relations between authors and their readers. A combination of methodologies deriving from sociology and political science has been applied to highlighting the fact that cultural institutions are not only the product of public policies on culture but are also central to the very existence of such policies (Fleury, 2006). *Instituted* by cultural policy, cultural institutions also act as agents *instituting* not only new cultural practices but also new public policies. The development of a sociology of institutional frameworks of aesthetic reception (Fleury, 2006c; 2007) has thus helped to introduce a political aspect to the sociology of culture.

3. TOWARD A SOCIOLOGY OF RECEPTION

The transition from an *aesthetics* of reception to a *sociology* of reception led to the emergence of a new program of research.

3.1 The Precursors: From Kant to the Constance School

In publishing his *Critique of Pure Reason* in 1790, Kant became a precursor, or even a revolutionary. Thanks to the German philosopher, aesthetic experience acceded to the rank of a philosophical question. The classic problematic of philosophy had until then often focused on artistic creation. However, Kant took into account the universality of the judgment of taste. Pierre Bourdieu contested this position: the subtitle he chose for *Distinction* (1979) — "*A Social Critique of the Judgment of Taste*" — is not only a clear expression of his opposition to Kant, but also serves as an effective diversionary tactic obscuring his project to differentiate sociological discourse from its philosophical counterpart (Péquignot, 1993: 169–183). On another front, Hans-Robert Jauss is opposed to Theodor Adorno. In his *Aesthetic Theory* (1970), Adorno rejected all experience linked to *jouissance* and instead promoted asceticism, thereby founding the aesthetics of negativity. As well as rejecting the enjoyment procured by art, Adorno fustigated any form of identification between spectators and readers and the objects of their attention, an attitude which he regarded as philistine. Taking a contrary stance, Jauss rehabilitated both enjoyment and the processes of identification at the heart of which Wolfgang Iser described an "aesthetic effect," the *event* represented by the text which so moved the reader (1978). Jauss presents this enjoyment as the foundation stone of aesthetic experience. In his "Apology for the Aesthetic Experience," a paper delivered at a conference held in Constance, he drew up a program whose themes were later appropriated by sociologists. The Constance School insists on the importance, in the production of a text, of its potential reception: the text is written and felt in function of what Jauss calls the readers' "horizon of expectation." According to the author, the strength of aesthetic experience depends on three key concepts of the aesthetic tradition: *poesis, aisthesis,* and *catharsis* (p. 131). *Poesis* is the experience of belonging to the world. Through *aisthesis*, the work of art reinvigorates perceptions dulled by habit. Individuals are thus *uncoupled* from the chains linking them to the interests of daily life, thereby recovering their freedom of aesthetic judgment. Last, *catharsis*, described in Aristotelian theory, offers *deliverance*.[5] This liberation through aesthetic experience functions on three levels: consciousness as a *productive activity* creates a world which is its own work; consciousness as a *receptive activity* grasps the possibility of renewing its perception of the world; *subjective experience* introduces the Kantian problematic, later developed by Simmel, of inter-subjective experience, whence the problematic of the "horizon of expectation," a useful concept in terms of understanding the paradox of an expected unexpected event, combining the notion of "change of horizon" (*Horizontwandel*) with that of "horizon of expectation" (Fleury and Vazereau, 2005).

Although they have not been tested by a defined methodology, the hypotheses presented by Jauss in *Toward an Aesthetic of Reception* (1978) and *Aesthetic Experience and Literary Hermeneutics* (1988)[6] still have a programmatic value. A number of critiques of the concept of the "horizon of expectation" developed by the German school of *reception aesthetics* provide us with a glimpse of the value of a sociology of reception. Recent approaches undermine the traditional idea of a homogeneous public, which receives written works solely in function of its *horizon of expectation*. The problematic implied by this perspective represents a break with the traditional conception of transparent communication and that of the imagined expectations of a public whose wishes are satisfied by a cohort of busy writers. In his 1985 book, *La Naissance de l'écrivain* ("The Birth of the Writer"), Alain Viala discusses the links between the development of a literary field and that of a public (Viala, 1985). In this same literary field, Roger Chartier, rejecting the idea of a preexisting homogeneous public, reveals the importance of the role of publishers and printers: the material forms in which texts are transmitted (for example, the kind of typographical elements used) and the way in which they are received (plays, public readings, intimate readings) provoke variations in the ways in which texts are interpreted (Chartier, 1996). Jacques Leenhardt has also worked on the sociology of reception by comparing the ways in which texts are appropriated in terms of the constitution of their meaning and the development of communities of readers (Leenhardt and Jozsa, 1999).

3.2 The Program of a Sociology of Reception

"In order to increase the presumption of truth, *description* must be dense and compact; the more closely the field is inspected, the more taught the description will be." Jean-Claude Passeron certainly followed his own advice on how to approach research conducted by means of studies on the ground. His broad-ranging survey on the introduction of audiovisual services in libraries provides an accurate description of the actions and interactions of the various players involved. The results of the survey run counter to received ideas; the people who took most interest in the new media were those who read the most books (Passeron, 2006a: 289–299; Passeron, Grumbach, de Singly, et al., 1984: 5–24). Another major research project focused on the reception of works of art at the Granet Museum in Aix-en-Provence (Passeron and Pedler, 1991; 1995) in which the time visitors spent looking at various pictures was measured. Highly variable from one individual to another, *the time spent looking at pictures* is considered the most easily observable aspect of what the authors call "non-verbal semic acts" characteristic of looking at images and listening to music.

This quantitative ethnographic approach to the way in which paintings are perceived (Passeron, 2006b) undermines received ideas about academic qualifications. The time spent looking at works of art, studied by Jean-Claude Passeron and Emmanuel Pedler (1991), raises the question of the causal monism of *The Love of Art* (1969) which defines the level of education as the principal, if not the only, variable of changes in cultural behavior. The authors reveal a paradoxical effect of levels of education on behavior in museum visits. Categorized in reference to their level of qualifications and the length of time they spent in the education system, "subjects with an average level of qualifications are those who spend most time in museums" (Passeron and Pedler, 1991: 37). Academic qualifications cannot be considered automatically to reflect levels of interest in culture. In regard to current cultural practices, the theory of legitimacy, in spite of its undoubted value, must be revised. And another lesson to be learned from the approach is that the sociology of publics, understood in this manner, is an exercise in patience whose reward is to provide us with a new way of analyzing cultural consumption. The report on the survey undertaken at the Musée Granet thus marks an important stage in the exploration of the sociology of reception suggested by Jean-Claude Passeron.

The ethnographic approach (the observation of how much time the subject spends in front of a painting) provides researchers with access to certain components of the aesthetic experience, including "sensorial originality"[7] (the direct effect of sensation produced by the materiality of the iconic message) and "formal originality" (the recognition of forms nonrandomly arranged in space). Indeed, it also demonstrates the need, in Passeron's own words, for "a cognitive or technical skill," for "ideological connivance"; for the "representation of a cultural legitimacy" of the artist, her oeuvre, her style, and the genre of painting in which she works; "the feeling of uniqueness" of the work; "the feeling of escaping from time"; the "aesthetic gratification" of possessing or having personally gathered a capital of information on the work, its creator, its past, and its context; and the "affective impact" of an encounter with a work of art or one of its motifs to the degree that the subject matter, structure, and ideas associated with any of its preceding components arouses an emotion in the person looking at it.

Passeron thus suggests applying a phenomenology of pleasure in which "the taste for works of art is an irrevocably *mixed* taste, recognizable, in all eras, by its very *mixity*, made more vigorous by its diversity, exalted by the porosity of the borders between multiple reactions, from the most intellectual to the most emotional to the most sensual" (Moulin and Veyne, 1996: 351). This phenomenology of the "impure pleasure of art" is one of the most consistent factors in the sociology of reception, whose unity contrasts with the dramatic dualisms which characterized the sociology of culture in its early stages of development. Distinct from the standardized sociology of cultural consumption, which contents itself with comparing the frequency of cultural practices with socio-demographic characteristics, the meticulous description of the interpretative activity of individuals is vital to the progress of the sociology of culture. Revealing the components of the aesthetic experience highlights the degree to which cultural socialization is potentially infinite and always incomplete and how the sociology of reception remains, for the time being, programmatic. Much work is yet to be done if another form of objectivization is to be successfully combined with quantitative ethnography, namely the form revealed by a sociological understanding of the emotions felt during an aesthetic experience.

3.3 A Sociology of Emotions and of Aesthetic Experience

Taking an interest in works of art and their effects presupposes taking into account the question already asked by Wolfgang Iser in his *The Act of Reading: A Theory of Aesthetic Response* (1976) and carrying out research into some of the most recurrent of those effects, namely the *distancing effect* from day-to-day life in which cultural practices constitute counterpoints to quotidian activities; the *conversion effect* revealed in the observation that the reader's encounter with a particular work at a particular time "changed their lives"; and the *vocational effect* in which relations with culture provide the possibility of discovering other ways of living, a phenomenon linked to the Foucauldian problematic of the technologies of the self (Nègre, 1996) and to the ensemble of aesthetic techniques of existence which become an ethics.[8]

"It changed my life." This phrase, which crops up again and again in the surveys, expressed by numerous individuals to describe their relation to particular authors or works of art, signals a change in the course of a life and a transformation in the subject's relationship with that life. It is as if art, like religion, work, and politics, provided a structure for existence. Ontological upheavals of this kind are linked to the passage of time, suggesting a temporality of cultural practices worthy of examination. For this declaration is more than just a simple evocation of an escape from the cares of daily life. Because the temporality associated with cultural practices is part of a chronological *mise en scène* that provides a kind of rhythm for our experiences, we should study the ways in which emotions are expressed and represented. Grasping the significance of a life-changing event of this kind in the existence of an individual, a life-changing event that can, due to the upheaval it causes, be considered as a metaphorical "deviation" or "re-routing," presupposes a thoroughgoing study of the influence of institutional apparatuses on aesthetic reception and on the rhythms of the dynamic of judgment. Such a conclusion implies the idea that the institution may (or may not) exert a structuring power on cultural practices. Thus, the ritual form offers individuals encountering culture not only a framework in which meanings are attributed, but also the potential to express and represent emotions. Consequently, the way in which rites and rhythms are articulated cannot be simple, since it involves the emotions, a fact which obliges us to think in terms of the development of a sociology of emotions (Fleury, 2005).

However, such a sociology will inevitably be confronted by a *methodological and epistemological difficulty* in that emotion is not an ordinary subject of research but one which defies the exclusive logic of definitions and seems to escape all rational explanation. Anyone undertaking research in the field will immediately be confronted by an initial methodological difficulty. How can emotion be grasped? How can we take into account the instantaneous nature of the shock and duration of astonishment? The problem becomes epistemological when the question of whether or not this *ravishment*, which simultaneously mobilizes and immobilizes the subject, can be defined rationally. To be moved is to be "re-routed." The individual, suddenly bereft of his powers, apparently reduced to a bewildered silence, feels the full force of the experience. The question then becomes what method or methods should be applied to the task of describing emotion rationally. How can we develop a reflexive approach that rigorously holds to the middle ground between cold analysis intended to be strictly objective and subjective empathy, and that strenuously avoids the use of inflexible definitions which fail to grasp the protean nature of emotion and the facile vagueness of purple prose descriptions?

The inversion of a *theoretical perspective* provides an opportunity to move beyond this dualism (Fleury, 2006a). The singular and universal trust implicit in admitting that one's life has been changed stands as an invitation to transform the very status of aesthetic emotion by casting it not as an *object to be explained* in reference to previous forms of socialization but as an *explicative variable* of cultural socialization. The relationship between emotion and knowledge can be interpreted in two ways: emotion can either be seen as a mode of knowledge, or as an access point to what affects us or what we affect. A wealth of social connotations are revealed in the etymology of the word (*motion*), which suggests movement away from a specific point, a transformation of identity, a process of re-socialization, and the introduction of a new relationship with the self, the world, and one's own life. Since emotion suggests a loss of control, how can the fundamental experience of aesthetic emotion be synonymous with a paradoxically "desocializing" socialization? Emotions can change an individual's aesthetic values. The judgment of taste and, consequently, the values which constitute it, are destabilized by emotions. The sociological approach sheds light on the behaviors and representations underpinning individuals' relationships with works of art, as well as on the social and cultural practices which contribute to defining their artistic value. Thus, the sociology of reception represents a kind of third way that leaves the question of meaning open to interpretation and that it makes possible to grasp the many facets of aesthetic experience.

CONCLUSION

The sociology of culture presented here is a sociology of reception in the strong sense of the term. Other perspectives focusing on cultural production are worthy of exploration, for example the critical approach to cultural content offered to the public. But that approach is not included in the scope of this work. In the preceding chapters, I have attempted to understand and explain three metamorphoses: the upheavals in relations between individuals and culture, the changes made by the state in its relation to the democratization of culture, and, last, the modifications in approaches applied by sociologists to the question of cultural practices and aesthetic experience. All of these changes affect the very definition of culture and the way in which relations to it are perceived. Three final remarks will enable me to clarify my conclusions.

The first touches on the *notion of cultural socialization*. This observation, which is slightly perturbing in view of the chronological, thematic approach taken in this chapter, is the idea that, for individuals, there are no simple, univocal links between childhood attitudes and adult behaviors in terms of culture. This conclusion obliges us to think of cultural socialization in complex terms, taking into account both transformations in instances of primary socialization (family, school, peer groups), and variations in processes of secondary socialization (processes of individuation, phenomena of contiguity, cultural institutions). Even when primary socialization provides a non-decisive degree of structure for future practices, it is never a necessary or sufficient condition of those practices. An examination of secondary socialization reveals that socialization is radically *incomplete,* an ongoing process which defines itself to the extent that it is indeed a process. Nevertheless, sociologists must rise to the challenge of understanding and explaining what it is to experience a cultural act.

A second remark should be made, namely that modesty in research in the field of the sociology of culture is always a good thing. The fact that globalizing explanations have been increasingly undermined by the results of empirical surveys imposes, as Max Weber suggested, a number of duties on researchers in the social sciences, including a *refusal of causal monism* (for example, overestimating the influence of education) which consists of rejecting all forms of simplification in the description of cultural practices, and elucidating one's own *relationship to values* by developing an axiological neutrality in order to avoid falling into the traps of miserabilism and populism and to overcome the confusion between the *learned* and the *political*. Even more importantly, a *sociological understanding,* indispensible for researchers focusing on the meaning and signification to individuals of their outings to the theater or the museum and of the books and articles they read, reveals that such activities introduce a relation to values, sometimes ultimate values, which goes some way in explaining the oft-repeated idea of "upheaval" and "transformation" expressed in the phrase "it changed my life," reported by individuals talking of their relation to a work of culture.

Last, a third remark should be made concerning a point shared by anthropological and sociological approaches to culture which are too often opposed to one another: *the function of the symbolization of culture*. This approach enables us to take into account both cultural *reproduction,* a phenomenon which has been extensively studied, and *emancipation,* on which less emphasis has been placed. Rather than focusing on the purely reproductive aspects of culture, it would be more useful to shift our sociological attention to the normative and cognitive aspects of the ways in which it is appropriated. It is in this regard that culture in its restricted sense, that of the "culture of the arts," can serve as a key to the reflexive dimension of all forms of symbolism, since everything, even the most apparently simple forms of artistic expression, implies the problematic of the distance from the self that conditions the relative efficiency of symbols. The reorientation of problematics and the program of a sociology of reception suggest that the crux of the sociology of culture is located in a sociological understanding of the processes of symbolization that constitute life in society. It is in this area that the most sophisticated developments in contemporary research can be applied to an exploration of as yet unknown aspects, while at the same time incorporating the founding questions of the sociological tradition.

NOTES

1. I would like to thank Mary Leontsini, professor of sociology at the National and Kapodistrian University of Athens, for having informed me of a number of important articles quoted in this section.
2. A combination of a place and an atmosphere, an *ambiance* is much more than just a concert hall, a museum, or an open-air festival; it takes into account the people in the street, the mixture of commercial and residential activities, the diversity of cafes and restaurants, all the "little things" that make a neighbourhood attractive and encourage people to stay there.
3. The "ambiance" approach has been developed by Terry Clark and other researchers in the United States, Canada, France, Spain, Korea, China, and other countries. A combination of a place and an atmosphere, an ambiance is much more than just a concert hall, a museum or an open-air festival; it takes into account the people in the street, the mixture of commercial and residential activities, the diversity of cafes and restaurants, all the "little things" that make a neighborhood attractive and encourage people to stay there. Note: ambiance is the normal French translation of the English term scene.
4. I would like to thank Federico Tarragoni for having drawn my attention to this concept.
5. Max Weber also suggested this "function of deliverance" (*Erlösung*) characteristic of art: see chapter 1.
6. The German title, *Ästhetische Erfahrung und literarische Hermeneutik* (Suhrkamp, 1982), emphasizes the importance of "aesthetic experience."
7. All quotes in this paragraph can be found in Moulin, Raymonde, and Veyne, Paul, « Entretien avec Jean-Claude Passeron. Un itinéraire de sociologue » in *Revue européenne des sciences sociales* XXXIV, 103 (1996): 351.
8. On the influence of Nietzsche's concern with the aesthetics of existence, see Colin Gordon, "The Soul of the Citizen: Max Weber and Michel Foucault on Rationality and Government," in *Max Weber, Rationality and Modernity*, edited by Scott Lash and Sam Whimster (London: Allen & Unwin, 1987), 293–316.

II

The Transformative Power of Institutions

SIX

The Work of the Institution

The Democratization of Culture in the Light of the Legacy of the TNP

Imagining the TNP as a cultural institution that *instituted* practices and norms provides a new perspective on the *institution* no longer thought of exclusively in terms of an organization, but, rather, as a *process*. The institution is no longer considered as an already constructed given, but as a dynamic, dialectical process resulting from a permanent tension between that which is instituted and that which institutes, in which instituted forms are ceaselessly corroded, subverted, and de-structured by the pressure of *instituting* forces. If institutions protect values and produce norms, they create the *institution*, in the strong sense of the term. The institution cannot, therefore, be reduced to a finalized, coherent, and stable "totality," but defines a permanently ongoing *process*. And if the institution only exists in this continuous, twisting movement of deconstruction and reconstruction of social forms, the case of Vilar's TNP not only makes it possible to understand the "instituting processes" characterized by the innovations that he succeeded in deploying in time and space, but also to imagine the institution itself, historically, in acts, of the democratization of culture. This is, at least, what I propose to outline in this chapter.

Jean Vilar crystallizes a paradox: he represents a figure that, one might imagine, belongs to the past, incarnating both the expression of a truth that belongs to the present and that manifests itself on a daily basis in the shape of the questions that he has bequeathed to us. Beyond the fact that we are all, as spectators at least, the heirs of Jean Vilar due to the revolutions for which he was responsible and of which we are still the beneficiaries, the question of his legacy should be posed. A possible reply to the question is to be sought in the idea that we can do more than just proclaim the ideal of democratization of culture; we can also think in practical ways about how to ensure that it happens. The actions of the TNP provide at the very least an empirical illustration that forces us to examine what the organization succeeded in instituting.

The National Popular Theater (TNP) directed by Jean Vilar from 1951 to 1963 was an institution unique of its kind in France. The TNP's value as a model for future action can be explained primarily in reference to the three innovations introduced by Vilar, by the success subsequently encountered by his approach, and, lastly, by the support and criticism that the approach engendered. In attempting to understand how the TNP effected a transformation in terms of practices and representations, this chapter aims to explain how it became a model of cultural action which was later used as a point of reference by numerous institutions which drew inspiration from the various ideas promulgated by it.

Conquering a public and encouraging it to remain loyal: Vilar's TNP approached these goals in two ways, firstly by "reaching out to the public" and, secondly, by establishing a relationship of mutual loyalty between theater-goers and the theatrical institution. In what respects does Vilar's TNP constitute a model for the development of policies targeting the public? The question raises a series of problems: the *practical* issue of how "audience policy" should be defined; the *methodological* issue of quantifying the effects of such policies; and the degree to which the TNP's public can be classified as "popular." Lastly, there is the *theoretical* question of how to characterize the impact of audience policies.

In regard to these points, remarks should be made about the following three issues, first, the development of audience policies within Vilar's TNP; second, the evaluation of those policies in terms of encouraging the loyalty of a working class audience; and, third, the explanation of the popular success of the institution. Only then will it be possible to reach a conclusion concerning the validity of the term "model" as applied to the TNPs institutional innovations.

1. A MODEL FOR DEFINING POPULAR THEATER

The audience policies elaborated by Jean Vilar during his twelve years at the helm of the TNP (1951–1963) gave authentic meaning to the term "popular theater." Those policies were based on a tripartite process: the affirmation of the idea of theater as a public service; the invention of the term "public" as a category of action; and the elaboration of a series of approaches to building a relationship between spectators and the theater.

The proclamation of the theater as a public service "like water, gas and electricity," according to the now consecrated phrase used during the attack led by Jean Vilar on the public authorities which, after the departure of Jeanne Laurent—who had appointed him director in 1951—seemed intent on denying Vilar the opportunity of running Chaillot, is based, on the one hand, on a critique of the bourgeois theater, and, on the other, on the affirmation of its working class counterpart. Vilar's critique of the bourgeois theater, which was seen as *dividing* people rather than bringing them together, is informed by the memory of the social codes of the bourgeois theatrical outing described in his book *Chronique romanesque* (1971).[1] Defined by a high degree of class consciousness, the bourgeois theater—a distinctive environment—is opposed to the working class, or popular theater which, according to Vilar, must, unlike the former, assign itself the task of "*uniting* in the dramatic communion of the audience, the modest Suresnes shopkeeper and the senior magistrate, the workman from Puteaux and the stockbroker, the postman working in a poor area, and the tenured professor" (*Petit Manifeste de Suresnes*, 1951). As a *national* and *popular* theater, the TNP's objective was to embody the founding principle of equality underlying individualist society. Recalling this normative dimension makes it possible to understand the TNP's status as a "model." Appearing in the wake of the Republican model to which Jeanne Laurent, like Vilar, was so attached, public service, discussed in reference to the theater from the 1920s, became the point of reference for cultural policy after 1945. The roots of the idea of the theater as a public service are to be sought both in the historical context, with the success of the Popular Front and what Simone de Beauvoir described as the "outpouring of fraternity" which accompanied the Liberation, and the readings of Jean Vilar, who was as attached to the idea of the Rousseauist civic festival as he was to the resurgence of the model of the ancient theater.

The invention of "the public" as a category of action. The public did not wait for the arrival of Jean Vilar in order to exist. However, thanks to Vilar, it became, for the first time, a category of public action. For Vilar was the first person to ask himself just who was in the auditorium. By analyzing not only the social and spatial origins of the audience but also various ways of getting around the material and symbolic obstacles which prevented people from going to the theater, Vilar's TNP constituted its public as a category of action requiring a whole series of measures and approaches to accommodate it. At the same time, Vilar developed an approach to the public based on ideal representations. For Vilar, the public was a synecdoche of the people, which he defined in terms of the *populus*, or, in other words, of the people of the unified, non-exclusive city, rather than the *plebs*, or plebeians, a term implying principles of differentiation and hierarchy. For Vilar, the idea of the people was dependent on the type of theater in question: the bourgeois theater belittles the people, casting them as *plebs*, while the popular theater dignifies them, treating them as *populus*. A double metaphor, recurrent in his writings, defines the ideal type of the public-*populus* for the TNP: the ontological metaphor of the political body and the metaphor of the public literary sphere. To judge by the reactions it provoked in terms of identification, a subject which will be broached later in this chapter, the image of the public thus created generated a number of very real effects. The perception, even if it was imaginary, of the unity of the public, presupposes the formation of a communitarian space characterized by the sentiment of an equality encouraged by approaches taken to making spectators feel important to the TNP and promoting their loyalty to it.

The elaboration of ways of creating bonds between the TNP and theater-goers accounts for the third process. The foundation stone of the public policy was, in Laurent Thévenot's words, the panoply of "investment of forms" or "institutional frameworks" which modeled and informed relationships between individuals and institutions with a view to creating "regimes of familiarity." One of the first series of innovations was based on the transformation of traditional ritual. Jean Vilar, who possessed a finely honed awareness of the bourgeois theater's codes of social distinction (Vilar, 1971: 110), modified the traditional approaches to an evening out at the theater. By changing the time at which plays started to 8.15 pm, he enabled theater-goers, especially those who lived in the suburbs, to get home earlier. TNP theaters opened at 6.30 pm, giving spectators the opportunity to eat before watching a play. The fact that cloakroom facilities were free and tipping banned removed any notions of a captive audience falling prey to the exploitative mores of the theater and of the kind of humiliation associated with not having the wherewithal to provide a tip. Theater-goers were made to feel at home by the presence of an orchestra and the opportunity of dining to the sound of music. By such means, Vilar was able to remove the kind of sacred aura associated with an evening out at the theater, which had previously been considered a kind of temple, access to which was denied to a large part of the population. The kind of welcome afforded to spectators made a powerful contribution to the institutionalization of their status of theater-goers. A second series of innovations consisted in inverting the protocol regarding dress rehearsals. By inviting the public to attend TNP shows before the members of the press and the Parisian upper classes, who were habitually present at dress rehearsals in other theaters, Vilar continued his transformation of bourgeois ritual. If we accept that protocol designates an ensemble of conventions which inscribe power relations and influence behaviors, the inversion of the ritualized order between public and critics constitutes a revolution (Fleury, 2003a). The apotheosis of the TNP's audience policy, the creation of the "popular season tickets" system, the size of the public already conquered, and the climate of trust established with the leaders of collective bodies enabled the institution, in 1957, to offer an entry ticket which was valid for five plays in the season. Theories regarding such practices, which had been developed at the start of the twentieth century, were systematically implemented by the TNP. Such institutional innovations were the practical expression of an emphasis on the working class audience which Vilar ceaselessly conquered and rendered loyal, and the affirmation of a public theater which accommodated all sectors of society.

2. A MODEL FOR ENCOURAGING THE LOYALTY OF A WORKING CLASS AUDIENCE

Due to the dearth of studies on the TNP's socio-demographic characteristics, it is difficult to define exactly who made up the institution's audience. We can nevertheless present three elements which give some idea of the TNP's public and of its public policies. In order to highlight the quantitative impact of the approaches taken by the TNP, we will provide a positive demonstration of the effectiveness of public policies implemented between 1951 and 1968, followed by a negative demonstration of those policies, based on a statistical analysis, between 1968 and 1972.

Between 1957 and 1963, the number of season tickets purchased nearly doubled, rising from 99,000 in 1957-1958 to 165,000 in 1963–1964, as marketing became increasingly effective. In one season, the TNP attracted 498,000 theater-goers to Chaillot. At the same time that the season ticket system was introduced, the TNP started to prospect theater-goers in order, for the first time ever, to invite members of the public to its dress rehearsals. Potential spectators were contacted, generally by telephone, after which "TNP delegates" (actors and technicians) visited companies (banks, head offices of large companies). Statistics demonstrate that the season ticket system, combined with prospecting operations, had the effect of substantially increasing the number of spectators. During the 1956–1957 season (when there was no season ticket system in place), 62,635 spectators attended the thirty-one previews, giving an average of 2,020 spectators per dress rehearsal. During the 1957-58 season (when season tickets were available), the thirty-nine dress rehearsals attracted a total of 17,320 season ticket holders, or 96,188 spectators, giving an average of nearly 2,500 spectators per performance. The involvement of popular cinema stars like Gérard Philipe made initial contacts with this new public easier.

By casting aside what had become the kingpin of the TNP's audience policy, Georges Wilson—Jean Vilar's successor at the head of the institution—ushered in the end of an era. The decision provided another demonstration of the effectiveness of Vilar's audience policy. Putting an end to season tickets immediately generated negative effects: the public became disaffected, government subsidies declined, and the very idea of a public theater received a crushing blow. The public's disaffection manifested itself in two ways: not only were they disappointed; they also stayed away in droves. The suppression of season tickets had a devastating effect as attendance at Chaillot dropped to 25 percent of what it had been in the glory days; a dramatic contrast with the packed theaters of the Vilar era. Furthermore, in brutally discrediting the system of relations patiently forged by his predecessor, Wilson implicitly disqualified the spectators who were such an integral part of it, sacrificing them to the dominant ideas of the time. In May 1968, Wilson, along with a number of other theater directors and heads of drama centers, arts centers, and popular theaters, signed the "Declaration of Villeurbanne" at the *Théâtre de la Cité* directed by Roger Planchon. Promoting the slogan "Power to the Creators," the Declaration relegated the ideal of democratization, adjudged to be unattainable, to the status of ideology, with, as a corollary, the invention of the notion of the "non-public" (Fleury, 2003). The inversion of values underlying this reduction of the audience to an excluded third party effectively destroyed the pact established between the public and the institution. The change of policy generated a vertiginous fall in attendance figures which, in turn, led to a harsh reaction from the government. Appointed as Minister for Cultural Affairs in January 1971, Jacques Duhamel asked Wilson to restore the image of the TNP. Faced with the institution's inability to react, an inability which derived from the paucity of its relations with the public, Duhamel announced that the TNP would be restructured. The institution was transferred to Villeurbanne, near Lyon in eastern France, and the triumvirate of Planchon, Chéreau, and Gilbert were invited in as directors. The dismantling of the TNP, now deprived of its historical roots, marked the end of an era.

Last, a word about the working class nature of the TNP's spectators. Challenged in 1955 by Jean-Paul Sartre in the journal *Théâtre Populaire* (Sartre, 1955) and in 1957 by Jean-Louis Barrault (1957), the working class character of Vilar's theater was confirmed by writers including Louis Aragon and Elsa Triolet, as well as by museum curators like Bernard Dorival. Even more so, founders and promoters of the popular theater including Maurice Pottecher[2] and Joseph Paul-Boncour,[3] recognized Vilar as their worthy heir. And the popular character of the TNP's audience was based on the audience's perception of itself. Letters from spectators reveal a sentiment of belonging to the TNP as an institution. In order to get an idea of this sense of belonging, it is necessary to see how members of the audience themselves defined it in their writings.[4] Three types of "belonging" are expressed: to the people, to a national tradition, and to the popular theater. In order to better understand such attitudes, we will examine a number of those letters. One spectator, expressing a kind of primitive sociology by listing the kind of people in the audience and emphasizing the presence of working class spectators, wrote that, "while there were a good many well-dressed gentlemen and perfumed ladies in the audience to applaud you, they were not the ones who provided the triumphal reaction that saluted your performance at the end of the play.

That is what makes your success so much sweeter and so much more complete."⁵ An inhabitant of Paris's eighteenth arrondissement also attempted to express in words her feelings about her experience: "[A]fter watching the production of *El Cid* on the evening of Monday 11 in Clichy, I am entirely reassured. I feared that your efforts would not arouse the kind of appreciative reaction they deserved. But my anxieties proved groundless; the *working class* or *popular* audience (as you wish) is capable of appreciating and loving the theater when the theater comes to them. I am all the more happy in that I am myself *the granddaughter of workers and artisans*."⁶

A sense of national belonging was most frequently expressed by laying claim to a cultural tradition. The TNP's classical repertory seemed to offer its spectators the opportunity of participating in processes of identification with a body of literature constituting the national identity. How can the triumph of the classics at the TNP best be interpreted? The explanation is doubtless of a general order, as Patrice Pavis suggests in advancing the idea of a "classical effect" (Pavis, 1990: 54). In fact, many spectators saw themselves as belonging to a theatrical tradition based on a belief in the existence of a national tradition. And many also saw themselves as belonging to the popular theater: "*Populo*, populace, popular . . . ; why 'popular'? We know full well that we belong to the people!"⁷ The popular theater is defined by a climate, the main criterion of which is the absence of hierarchy both in the auditorium and on the stage. "I enjoyed an absolutely delightful evening and the 2,500 spectators left with a relaxed, happy smile on their face . . . at the TNP where the public is marvelous and experiences the play intensely with the actors. . . . Let me thank you once again for the generous idea of a popular theater which mixes all the social classes together. So few people put their ideas into practice."⁸ We have yet to explain the enigma of this popular success.

3. A MODEL FOR INSTITUTIONALIZING THE CATEGORY OF THE POPULAR AUDIENCE

Rather than, at this juncture, recalling the well-known socio-historical context of the *Libération*, characterized by the setting up of works committees, the burgeoning of major movements promoting popular education, and an aspiration to upward social mobility through education, it would be more useful to outline the work carried out by the TNP and by Vilar himself with a view to institutionalizing the category of the popular audience.

This process of institutionalization was primarily based on the creation of an identity. The TNP provided a number of symbols of identification, including the three-letter logo designed by Marcel Jacno, the creator of the

Gauloises cigarettes symbol, who employed the Didot font, used during the French Revolution, to underline the values of the Republican trinity stated in 1789. Like the totem or flag, whose functions of integration were outlined by Durkheim (1990 [1912]) the TNP's banners represented the common good around which the spectators were gathered. Similarly, on the programs containing the text of the play and a number of photos of the actors performing on stage, the title of the play positioned under the name of the author in red on a white background appeared in the same font as the TNP logo and the posters announcing the institution's productions. The name of the collection published by L'Arche éditeur—the *Collection du repertoire*, or "Repertory Collection"—evoked at once the constitution of a memory and the possibility for the public to identify with *its own* theater: from a repertory to a collection. Thus, the TNP's programs represented an innovation in regard to those of other Parisian theaters of the time, making the spectators into potential readers and offering the possibility of constituting a memory. If we are to accept Maurice Halbwachs's contention that all memories are social and that memory is neither a function of the thought of the subject nor a psychic faculty of human beings but, rather, an "institution" (Halbwachs, 1925; 1950), then the approaches described above are integral to the constitution of a collective memory that underlies the feelings of belonging expressed by the spectators. The TNP also provided a specific status—season ticket holder—to thousands of theater-goers. This act of attribution provoked a process of identification that was especially strong in that individuals discovered a plural identity, whereas before they had possessed a social status with which they tended to identify exclusively (Lahire, 2005). Last, Vilar's TNP inverted the established order by inviting season ticket holders to watch dress rehearsals, thereby giving them the opportunity to see shows before professional theater critics, who had to wait their turn to cast an eye over new productions. These changes in protocol made a major contribution to instituting the status of a critically involved public.

This process of institutionalization later took an approach involving the production of a fictive equality. By inviting spectators to fill in a questionnaire after every play, the TNP encouraged theater-goers to express a judgment about the aesthetic value of its productions and, in so doing, to make public use of their critical faculties. The TNP thereby encouraged the creation of an isonomic space by rendering theater-goers equal to one another and instituting the quality of "spectator." For the quality of spectator, like that of citizen, is characterized by the universality of the possibility of judgment. Spectators gained in terms of universality what their social origin or the socio-professional category to which they were assigned often denied them. Like the socialization of the citizen through the electoral process, the techniques introduced by the TNP—the questionnaire, debating facilities—provided members of the public with a kind of education, transforming them into critical spectators. The TNP thus satisfied the desire for recognition shared by many members of its audience by providing it with a status traditionally denied to the working classes (Fleury, 2002). The creation of a public critical space was also rendered possible by the nature of the program, the monthly journal *Bref*, and the debating facilities. The "debating spaces" and discussions with the public launched at the festival held in Suresnes in 1951 became definitively ingrained. Among the many comments concerning the creation of a public critical sphere, in the sense that Kosseleck gives to the term (Kosseleck, [1959], 1979), the following extract from a letter written by a TNP spectator in 1952, is worth examining:

> *It's true that working class people have a terrible inferiority complex.* They find it hard to express themselves properly, which leaves you with another difficult task, but one well worth accomplishing. . . . That is why I am entirely in favor of your discussions. . . . That is your task: to force those words out from the heart where they have been trapped, where you cannot hear them. You see, the microphone should be present everywhere to capture, randomly, the emotion and joy of the audience. It should be like a game in which those asked a question have to reply. Clearly, the audience will have been told not to prepare any grandiloquent responses beforehand but simply to say what they think. . . . Perhaps, in the beginning, people will be a little uncertain, but I'm sure that everything will get better with time.[9]

In addition to meetings and discussion spaces, spectators were provided with information in the form of the didactic journal *Bref*, and a program was produced for each play. *Bref, Journal mensuel du Théâtre National Populaire* contained background information about the productions in the repertory. The programs accompanying the plays contributed to establishing the possibility of a public space. Composed exclusively of the integral text of the stage version of the play and of photographs of the production, all forms of advertising were absent. To judge by reactions to the questionnaires, spectators appreciated the access to the work afforded them by the programs and were happy to prolong the emotion of the production and add to their pleasure at seeing the play by being able to read it later. These factors encouraged the creation of a public critical sphere. For Habermas, the bourgeois public sphere was born of the decline of courtly society, and the rise of egalitarian practices of conversation, and literary criticism. Jean Vilar's theater has more to do with what Habermas calls a "culture-debating public" than with what he terms "a culture-consuming public" (Habermas, 1989: 159–175). For the German philosopher, public opinion affirmed itself and continues to affirm itself in literary debates in which, due to aesthetic sentiments being shared, it discovers its first consciousness of itself.

Last, the process of institutionalization also depended on the provision of spaces of sociability. Vilar's TNP could be said to have combined a number of different forms of sociability. For Simmel, "sociability provides Mankind, in his search for depth, a plenitude of life of a symbolic order."[10] It creates a "sociologically ideal world."[11] The TNP seems to have produced sociability by creating what constitutes, according to Simmel, its very condition of possibility: the fiction of equality. Setting up an ideal "society of equals" makes it possible to avoid any contemplation of the contents of socialization, such as the excellence of one's social position (Deroche-Durcel, 1993). The affirmation of a popular form of sociability was expressed in the public spaces provided by Vilar's TNP. The institution initially offered popular forms of sociability in the form of balls,[12] arenas for dancing, a ritualized form of meeting. The TNP then offered popular forms of commensality in the form of banquets and TNP weekends or "nights,"[13] which, to judge by the jokes about the cold veal served at Suresnes,[14] were not only much remarked upon but also highly appreciated. Such events gave spectators the chance to enjoy the surroundings and "feel at home." Last, the TNP offered communitarian forms of sociability by encouraging loyalty among collectives and associations at a time when social ties were particularly class-bound. Jean Vilar's writings on the theater auditorium suggest a quest for a temporary equality of individuals ordinarily separated by their social status. Because the sociology of culture insists on the socio-demographic characteristics of the individual, it sometimes neglects the specificity of the relationship with the theater which resides in the, albeit temporary, loss of such attributes, as has been ably demonstrated by Marie-Madeleine Mervant-Roux.[15] The abstraction of social attributes after the play, when the questionnaire is being filled out, extends the span of time during which those attributes are lost. It is possible to maintain that during the production, spectators forgot about their social identity due to the liminal state thus created.[16] The ritual generates a sense of *communitas*, or, in other words, a moment localized in time, during which equal status prevails. In this state of *communitas*, social attributes are lost and everyone finds themselves, for a short period of time, in a state of strict equality, a state promoting a sentiment that, in addition to a public space, a shared space has also been created.

CONCLUSION

In conclusion, it would be useful to examine two words—"model" and "origin." The term "model" applied to these institutional innovations deserves an explanation. Jean Vilar did not attempt to construct a model as such. It is the judgment of politicians, artists, and professionals of culture, and researchers in the social sciences about the policies implemented by Vilar's TNP which make of it a "model." A model, first and foremost, due to the *political usages* which it generated, with the establishment of the Ministry of Cultural Affairs in 1959 against the background of the institution's success, then at its height; then with the policies implemented by the *Maisons de Culture* after 1961 based on Vilar's model of cultural action; and, last, with the continual references made to Vilar's TNP in the debates prompted by the Charter of Public Service Missions in 1998.[17] A model because of the *historical filiations* to which it later gave birth: a model asserted by the public theater which grew out of decentralization in the 1950s (Denizot, 2005), and, later, a model contested during the events of May 1968 and in the Declaration of Villeurbanne, but finally, against all odds, appropriated in the revolution effected by the Pompidou Center (Fleury, 1999). And, last, a model because of its *heuristic fecundity*: Vilar's TNP also offers researchers the possibility of constructing a Weberian "ideal type" (or "pure type") of the realization of the ideal of democratization. If we agree with Weber's thesis that an ideal type is an abstract construction with a provisional status which expresses only the qualitative aspects of reality, or that, in other words, it is not a vehicle of quantitative data but the accentuation of qualitative features associated with specific patterns of thought, then the TNP provides an example of the institution as ideal type,[18] reducing the gap between reality and the "mental image obtained by means of rationalizations of a utopian nature" which constitutes the ideal type (Weber, 1992 [1904]).

But we should avoid the intellectual lure of a "return to origins." First and foremost, the TNP should not be thought of as a type of "origin"; instead, it should be linked to what gave rise to it, for example, the debates of the first decade of the last century promulgated by the *Revue d'art dramatique*, successive waves of movements promoting popular education, and the cultural policies of the Popular Front. Indeed, rather than being some kind of unique phenomenon, the TNP was at the confluence of multiple traditions. We should also take care not to fall prey to any form of melancholia concerning the issue of origins; after all, the "facts" of the past are not merely inert phenomena that can be sought out, isolated, and then inserted into a narrative. History must be thought of, with Walter Benjamin, as discontinuous rather than homogeneous. We must avoid the temptation of thinking of history as a linear construct running between two points, from grandiose beginnings to an ineluctable final decline, and focus instead on perceiving a present open to the possibility of "resurgences." Uncovering those resurgences involves asking questions about political discontinuities and rejecting old models of historical continuity.

In this sense, we can conclude with the idea of the *institution*, in its multiple meanings, including the meaning given to it by Montaigne, who considered it a synonym of education when, in the vocabulary of his time, he spoke of "the institution of children." For the innovations of the TNP profoundly changed ways of instituting a relationship with the theater. Because the rules and conventions introduced by Vilar in the 1950s had a long-term effect on ways of producing and going to see theater, it is legitimate to conclude that cultural institutions have an *instituting* power. Thanks to the new rules and relations forged in the implementation of those innovations, Vilar's TNP was able to break with previous practices. If we accept that the power of the cultural institution is forged in the process of producing new rules, like those introduced by the TNP, then we can conclude that cultural institutions have the power to create the *institution*. At the very least, when they decide to exercise this *power*, cultural institutions define a place of power, an instituting process.

NOTES

This chapter appeared in an earlier form with the title, "Le travail d'institution: la démocratisation de la culture à la lumière des héritages du TNP," in Olivier Moeschler and Olivier Thévenin (eds.), *Les territoires de la démocratisation culturelle. Équipements, événements, patrimoines : perspectives franco-suisse*. Paris: L'Harmattan, « Logiques sociales,» 2009, pp. 21–34.

1. The twenty-one-year old Jean Vilar, who hailed from the southern French town of Sète, first discovered the Paris theater in 1933, during an era in which it was still very much dominated by the bourgeoisie. On the bourgeoise of the time, see Goblot, Edmond. [1925]. 1967. *La barrière et le niveau. Étude sociologique sur la bourgeoisie française moderne*. Preface by Georges Balandier. Paris: Presses universitaires de France.

2. "Please accept, Monsieur, my brilliant colleague, the joyous compliments of one of the spectators of the play you put on yesterday. These compliments come from an old man whose name is perhaps not entirely unfamiliar to you, an old man who has dedicated his life to creating a theater in his home province in which the elite and the working classes can mix together and finally feel united before a work of art accessible, albeit in different ways, to one and all. You have brilliantly succeeded in setting up this theater of Art for everyone, the kind of theater that I, along with my friends Romain Rolland and Firmin Gémier, to mention but two great men, once dreamt of creating in Paris, but which I found it better to establish on firm foundations in a place in which I felt more at liberty to act and more certain to succeed." Letter from Maurice Pottecher to Jean Vilar, dated December 30, 1951. French National Archives. T.N.P. Visitors' Book. VIP Letters.

3. "How am to express the joy I feel at what you have achieved with this Popular theater, which I so insistently championed in my report for the Beaux-Arts in 1911 and to which later, with Firmin Gémier, I dedicated so much time?" Letter from Joseph Paul-Boncour, undated. French National Archives. T.N.P. Visitors' Book—VIP Letters.

4. This analysis also makes it possible to compare the way in which a given public belongs to an institution with other forms of belonging: professional, partisan, national. Professional belonging is the kind which binds individuals to a trade or corporation, as Emile Durkheim demonstrated. (On professional morale and corporate belonging, see the first three lessons in Durkheim, Émile. 1990. *Leçons de sociologie*. Paris: Presses universitaires de France, "Quadrige," 41–78).

5. Letter from Robert Catu, Saint-Mandé, March 7, 1952. French National Archives: T.N.P. Visitors' Book—Spectators' Letters.

6. Letter from Yvette Aubert, December 15, 1951. French National Archives: T.N.P. Visitors' Book—Spectators' Letters. In a postscript to the letter, she writes: "I also wanted to tell you that you have reconciled me with Corneille's tragedy. The performances of Françoise Spira and Gérard Philipe brought tears to my eyes. I would never have thought it possible."

7. Rose Gage, shopkeeper. French National Archives, T.N.P. holdings, Box 295 AP 215: "Spectator Questionnaires: Chaillot season 1953–54."

The Work of the Institution

8. Mlle Vetois, Saint-Mandé. French National Archives, T.N.P. holdings, Box 295 AP 217: "Spectator Questionnaires: Chaillot seasons, 1955–1958."

9. Letter from Y. Portolcan, Viroflay, February 1952. French National Archives: T.N.P. Visitors' Book—Spectators Letters. My italics.

10. Simmel, Georg. 1981. « La sociabilité. Exemple de sociologie pure ou formelle. » *Sociologie et épistémologie*. Paris: Presses universitaires de France. « Sociologies ». Pp. 121–136 (125).

11. Simmel, Georg. 1981. P. 128. "La sociabilité. Exemple de sociologie pure ou formelle," *Sociologie et épistémologie*, Paris: Presses universitaires de France, « Sociologies ».

12. As Jean Vilar asked rhetorically, "What is this nocturnal gathering [the Opéra auditorium] for, if not to share the same pleasures and experience the same joys? Frankly, in this case, I prefer the *communitarian effusions* of the July 14 dances . . ." Vilar, Jean. 1971. « Deux lettres et un ballet, » *Chronique romanesque*. Paris: Grasset, 110. My italics.

13. "Carrying on with the weekend events, it's a magnificent idea." Mademoiselle Josette Bourbon, SNCF employee. French National Archives, T.N.P. holdings, Box 295 AP 215: "Spectator Questionnaires: Chaillot season 1953–54."

14. On the stage of the totemic meal and the "the act of fellowship between the divinity and worshippers, the communion between the faithful and their god." See Freud, Sigmund. [1912–1913]. 1990. *Totem and Taboo*. New York: W. W. Norton. On communion through the consumption of food, see Emile DurkheimErreur! Signet non défini., *The Elementary Forms of Religious Life*, translated by Carole Gossman. Oxford: Oxford University Press, 2001.

15. On the process by which these attributes are parenthesized during a production, see Marie-Madeleine Mervant-Roux, *L'assise du théâtre. Pour une étude du spectateur*. Paris: CNRS Éditions, 1998.

16. Victor Turner demonstrates how rites can guarantee a regulatory function within a society by permitting, for a circumscribed period of time, an inversion of status. On the inversion of statuses, see the passage on the enthronement of the king who, before taking up his function, must undergo scrutiny and experience the authority and complaints of the group. Victor Turner, « Basses et hautes positions hiérarchiques : la liminarité de l'élévation et de l'inversion de statut. » [1969] 1990. *Le phénomène rituel. Structure et contre-structure*. Paris: Presses universitaires de France, « Ethnologies ». 161–196.

17. When the opponents of the Charter of Public Service Missions for the Living Theater, published in spring 1998, brandished "Vilarisme" as an anathema, they revealed exactly to what extent the notion of public service continues to inform debates and struggles over the definition of the ideal approach to theater policy. Venerated or vilified, it remains a model.

18. The rapprochement between reality and the "ideal type," unusual in the work of Weber, is evoked in his article, « Die Grenznutzlehre und das 'psychophysische Grundgesetz' ," *Archiv für Sozialwissenschaft und Sozialpolitik*, 1908, reprinted in Weber, Max. 1951. *Gesammelte Aufsätze zur Wissenschaftslehre*, Tübingen, Verlag J.C.B. Mohr (Paul Siebeck), 384–399.

SEVEN

The Influence of Mediation Apparatuses on the Structuring of Cultural Practices

The Pompidou Center's "Correspondents"

Is "cultural mediation" no more than a phrase? In other words, what are the differences between the *cultural action* promoted in the 1960s, the *cultural animation* criticized in 1968, the *cultural development* advocated by Jacques Duhamel in the 1970s, and the kind of activity which, since the 1990s, has been known as *cultural mediation*? Should we not rather look for the avatars of a term applied to single ideal, that of the democratization of culture, the substitution of words merely cultivating the illusion of change? Perhaps. But words are not merely labels; they serve to clothe the reality of what one imagined existed before. Their use is political in nature. However, there is another conception of language in which words are a tool, an approach to reality and processes. In this perspective, their use is more scientific. This chapter will focus on an explication of these two aspects of language and the inevitable complementarity between them.

In effect, the meaning attributed to words conceals the fundamental issue of access to works of art. Insisting on the plurality of attitudes displayed by individuals, on the multiple functions of culture, and on the diversity of styles of belief, Paul Veyne has shown how the generally received meaning of works of art diverges from the meaning implied by their content and the intentions of their creators (Veyne, 1988). While aestheticism describes the relationship between the work and the individual in terms of direct contact, Veyne introduces a series of intermediaries. This new vision of our relationship with art implies a social aspect, that of mediation.

The introduction of new degrees and jobs in the field of *mediation* has modified the landscape inhabited by cultural actors. In this context, we need to focus on the kind of mediation services delivered by members of the public rather than by professionals. In order to study both the procedures and processes characteristic of mediation, we need to concentrate on an empirical reference: that of the "correspondents"—or mentors—of the Beaubourg who, from 1970 to 1980, were at the origin of a whole series of effects, including *incentives, regulation,* and the *encouragement of loyalty,* many of which had far-reaching consequences in terms of the transformation of cultural practices. The exemplary character of the mediation processes applied by the Beaubourg correspondents as a historical point of reference for a number of cultural institutions, particularly the media libraries and museums founded in France in the 1980s and 1990s, renders their case all the more interesting.

In addition to this case study, reflections of a general nature will be combined with the results of surveys carried out on the ground. Specific events will be taken into account with a view to defining cultural mediation, a construct in which project, procedure, and process are intertwined. The sheer range of approaches developed by mediators and the multiple effects they produce suggests the existence of an often invisible element of cultural policy, namely the transformative power of the mediators themselves, a power which, since it is rarely studied, is often ignored.

1. DEALING WITH THE DIVORCE BETWEEN ART AND THE INDIVIDUAL: THE FIGURES OF "THE GAP"

Mediation can only be understood in reference to the problematic of the *gap,* or even the *divorce* between art and the individual, of a *separation* which Nietzsche, in *The Birth of Tragedy,* thought of as being concomitant to the deployment of our Socratic civilization. But, perhaps more relevantly, this *divorce* between art and the individual can be viewed from the philosophical perspective that Simmel, as a reader of Nietzsche, expressed in terms of the "tragedy of culture," as a political preoccupation underpinning the development of cultural policies and as a central conclusion of the sociology of culture and of cultural practices since the 1960s.

1.1 The Figure of the "Tragedy of Culture"

The concept of the "tragedy of culture" highlights another point of ambivalence: the tragic opposition between life and form and, beyond that, our own exteriority to cultural forms. For Simmel, life depends on forms in order to express itself, even if those forms stifle its creative élan. Life is thus transcended and alienated in the cultural forms it creates and that it refers to as *objective culture*. According to the author, modern individuals are confronted by an incalculable number of objectivizations of the mind, works of art, social forms, knowledge, and even institutions, so many "kingdoms" governed by their own laws vying to become both the "contents and norms" of our existence. Nevertheless, these "kingdoms" are often perceived as weighing down the existence of the individual.

The tense relationship between the objective and the subjective is also characterized by a problem of quantity embodied by the endless flow of new books, scientific discoveries, and works of art that demand to be "incorporated" by individuals. This oceanic wave of cultural items has the potential to overwhelm individuals in two ways: uncapable of absorbing it all, they are nevertheless unable simply to reject out of hand elements that might belong to their cultural milieu. According to Simmel, this inability either to assimilate or reject characterizes the problematic situation of modern man, who is obliged to confront another danger, that of seeing the task of developing his own, subjective culture rebutted by interests and hopes increasingly centered on the development of objective culture. While objective culture is distinguished by its limitless capacity for expansion, improvement, and speed, subjective culture is restricted and relatively monotonous.

The idea of a *divorce* between *objective* and *subjective culture* thus hoves into view, with the abundance of the first indissociable from the relative poverty of the second. For Simmel, the triumph of objective culture is accompanied by the defeat of its subjective counterpart: individual culture has not been able to keep up with the increase in the sheer numbers of things by which our lives are filled and surrounded; indeed, in many regards, individual culture can be said to have regressed (Simmel, 2004: 486; 1997a). To the degree that objective culture (the ensemble of cultural forms preexisting the individual) becomes autonomous and hypertrophied, it departs from its role as a *mediator* for, faced by this extreme abundance, individuals are overwhelmed by an accumulated wealth which they are entirely unable to assimilate; overwhelmed and yet constantly tempted by the mass of cultural contents, even if they know that they are incapable of appropriating them.

This *divorce* defines the *tragedy of culture*. The task of mediation is to reduce the gap, thus introducing two distinct perspectives, defining either a political pedagogy of culture, which implies an instrumentalization of institutions to educational ends, or a political praxeology in which mediators promote a kind of freedom, or better, carry out a political action in the strong sense of the word, instituting a way of living together and creating close, intense links between individuals.

1.2. The Political Aspect of the "Divorce"

Mediation can thus be seen as a practical imperative or a norm of public action. Because, since at least 1959, the democratization of culture has, from a political point of view, provided the foundations of public intervention in the field of culture in France, it has served as a point of reference for all cultural policies deployed since then. Against the background of the institutionalization of a cultural administration, the professionalization of the artistic field, and the elaboration of successive definitions of public action (cultural action, cultural animation, cultural development, cultural mediation), a technocratic conception of cultural policy has been replaced by a more symbolic approach. An interdependent relationship between *culture* and *politics* has given way to an articulation between the *sociology of culture* and *public policy*. For forty years, the concern of sociologists with analyzing the cultural practices of people in France has been accompanied by the political question of whether access to culture has been democratized and by a practical intuition about the need to improve mediation approaches in order to reduce the gap between individuals and works of art.

What does it mean for art to be, if not "democratized," then at least institutionalized? How can a form of culture, proposed by the institution, be consonant with the demands of free individuals? Otherwise expressed, the question is whether the cultural institution plays a role in the creation of a "positivity," or, in other words, an approach which, due to its dogmatic, institutional character, risks transforming art into a form alien to the community, an ideology foreign to a population made up of free individuals; or, conversely, whether it contributes to the elaboration of a culture shared within a critical public space. The very fact that such a question can be asked suggests that the institution of a public space goes hand-in-hand with procedures and processes of mediation.

The genealogy of the imperative of cultural mediation is thus rooted in a historical awareness of the divorce between art and the individual that has characterized cultural policy since Condorcet's inaugural *Report on the General Organization of Public Instruction* (1792), the objective of which was to "make reason popular," a position emblematic of a popular education project which already presupposed a gap between culture and the people (Fleury, 2004a). Another acknowledgment of this phenomenon is to be found in the emphasis placed on popular educational movements in France's Third Republic (1870–1940) by Jean Zay and Léo Lagrange, who applied the heritage of the Enlightenment in the Popular Front's ephemeral work in the field of culture, or again, after the Second

World War, in the work of Jean Guéhenno and Jeanne Laurent who also pursued, in their different ways, the ideal of bridging the gap between art and ordinary people. "Encouraging access on the part of the people to the capital works of humanity," the project announced in the Decree of July 24, 1959, written by André Malraux to mark the founding of the Ministry of Culture, also presupposed the existence of a gap between culture and the people.

1.3. The Sociological Thematization of "The Gap"

In France, the origins of the sociology of culture can be traced to the elaboration by Pierre Bourdieu of a theoretical framework combining elements of a sociology of education, developed with Jean-Claude Passeron in *The Inheritors*, originally published in 1964, and *Reproduction*, originally published in 1970, and an emerging sociology of cultural legitimacy, outlined in *The Love of Art* (1966 and 1969) and further developed in *Distinction*, first published in 1979. Numerous surveys pointed to a recurrent phenomenon, namely differentials in the rate of visits to cultural facilities that highlighted the existence of a hierarchical social distribution of cultural practices. In 1966, Bourdieu, writing about the social distribution of cultural practices, advanced the idea that the problem did not lie in the absence of a relationship with art, but in "the absence of a feeling of absence."

The second, revised, and augmented edition of *The Love of Art* (1969) popularized this observation among professionals of culture. The publication of *Distinction* in 1979 completed the conceptual edifice. Indeed, such is the influence of Bourdieu's work that his ideas, which have not been seriously challenged since the 1960s, are more or less accepted today as a fact. One of the major contributions of the sociology of culture is, in offering an explanation for differentials in numbers of visitors to cultural institutions, to have posited that obstacles to culture are more symbolic (socialization, cultivated *habitus*) than material (spatial distance, price barriers). This is, at least, what the fourth and fifth editions of the longitudinal survey, *Les pratiques culturelles des Français*, have tended to confirm (Donnat, 1998; 2008).

Thus, from a variety of perspectives, the sociological tradition has, since the outset, particularly since Simmel, as well as in recent works in the sociology of culture tradition, focused on the question of how to bridge the gap between individuals and culture. This question has haunted politicians, sociologists, and professionals of culture, who have attempted to address it by applying various mediation techniques. This, at least, is what we have been able to observe in an analysis of policies concerning the public successively developed by institutions such as Vilar's National Popular Theater (Fleury, 2006c) and the Pompidou Center (Fleury, 2007). One of the original approaches taken by Vilar, both at the

National Popular Theater and the Avignon Festival, was to work with "relays" or mentors. The success of this idea is apparent even today in that the Festival's public is thought of in terms of a *mediator* public (Ethis, 2003). Another example of mediation is provided by the Beaubourg Center's "correspondents," who will be the object of the remarks that follow.

2. THE BEAUBOURG "CORRESPONDENTS": CULTURAL MEDIATION IN ACTION

The Pompidou Center's attitude to members of the public was entirely original (Stiegler, 2007). Indeed, any temptation to attribute the success of the Center to its architecture alone should be avoided; instead, the origins of its enigmatic triumph should be sought in the kind of relations it attempted to develop with potential visitors. How did the Center's policy of institutional innovations further its relationship with the public? Dispensing with the notion that cultural practices are free of all external influences, the Center sought to encourage those practices by introducing a membership system instituting a link between "members" and "Beaubourg correspondents," two distinct statuses which rendered *correspondents* central to the institution's membership policy for almost twenty years—between 1977, the year in which it opened, and 1996, when the membership system was reappraised.

2.1 The Invention of the Status of Correspondent

Condemned to success by the alarmist predictions of the Cour des comptes in terms of the number of people it was likely to attract, the Pompidou Center developed a series of innovations designed to define target markets, attract visitors, provide them with information, and ensure that they stayed loyal. The policy distinguishing the simple member from the correspondent, responsible for at least ten members, was originally defined in Georges Guette's report, *Embarquons pour le vingtième siècle*[1] ("Let's embark for the twentieth century"). The maritime or aviation metaphor[2] contained in the idea of embarkation is redolent of the idea of departure, of a journey to Utopia. The twentieth century, presented as an unknown realm waiting to be discovered, is offered to the citizen who is, paradoxically, presumed to be ignorant of her own era. The report, once established, contained the membership formula and the right to access all the cultural content the Center had to offer. Designed to generate cultural practices, these innovative techniques, developed by Guette, were implemented and given meaning by Claude Fourteau, who developed their pedagogical aspect.

The originality of the Center's approach to its relationship with the public quickly became apparent. The task of conquering a particular section of the public presupposed the idea of providing it with information, thereby encouraging its loyalty and ensuring that it contributed to the development of the Center itself. This notion prompted the elaboration of an original policy based on the figure of the *correspondent*, which was to become central to the Center's membership strategy. On average, the Center's 2,000 correspondents introduced 36,000 of the 50,000 new members the institution attracted every year. The success of the approach, which led to the development of similar *apparatuses, instruments, techniques, mechanisms*, and *machineries* in other museums, made membership a model to be followed.

The success of the Pompidou Center's membership scheme as a public service management tool can be measured in terms of how often it has been copied. The Pompidou Center was, for example, a precursor in the field of public policy in the plastic arts. The fact that the Center's membership system served as a model was underlined by the ease with which it could be reproduced. Among the most prestigious examples are to be found the Bordeaux Center for Contemporary Art, the Museums of Marseille, the Musée d'Orsay, the Institute of the Arab World, the City of Science and Industry, and, in a renewed form, the Louvre. The Beaubourg's "correspondents" provided an example of a successful approach to mediation that was later applied in a wide range of cultural institutions, museums and media libraries set up in the 1980s and 1990s.

2.2 Using "Relays" to Conquer Different Target Markets

The idea of "relays"—or mentors—presupposes an interpersonal relationship or a relationship based on mutual knowledge. Working with friends and relations in neighborhoods and apartment blocks and with people they knew around the city, correspondents were, in their role as representatives, able to provide the Center with a presence where it would otherwise have been absent. The correspondents no longer constituted a public that had been *conquered* by the Pompidou Center; now, they were a *conquering* public developing an original form of reticular communication. Most correspondents were recruited from works committees in leisure associations, local neighborhoods, youth movements, and schools and *lycées*. They were able to contribute to the development of a network of people loyal to the institution by providing members with cultural guidance.

By representing a link between the cultural institution and its real or potential public, who were distanced from the Pompidou Center for geographical or social reasons or due to a lack of interest in cultural matters, the correspondents assumed a central role in the membership system. They carried out a number of functions designed to bolster their relationship with members, including recruitment, distributing passes, organizing the enrollment of new members in an initiation cycle, enlarging the circle of members, and organizing group visits. But their role also involved distributing information, acting as "relays" on behalf of those who visited the museum—or who did not yet visit the museum—and providing added value. Furthermore, their role of assessing the criticisms and desires of members meant that correspondents were effectively *representatives* of the institution in the eyes of members and members in the eyes of the Pompidou Center.

2.3 The Development of Social Bonds and Sociability

Given a pivotal role by the Pompidou Center, correspondents were central to networks of sociability, a factor long neglected in the analysis of cultural practices. Sociability, the importance of which as a key to understanding the life of social forms was highlighted by Simmel (1997), is central to grasping a number of exceptions to the classical rule of cultural socialization. Effects of social contiguity applied to explaining singular trajectories serve as a useful guide to understanding the practices of many users of the Center and are crucial for grasping the specificity of the relationship between correspondents and their members (Fleury, 1991). The influence of *sociability* in the formation of aesthetic judgments explains the dynamic of the role and the range of relationships they were able to develop.

In comparing the many and various cultural practices of different individuals, Bernard Lahire (2001) insists on the multiplicity of contexts at play. Studies on practices of sociability in museums (Caillet, 1995; Davallon, 1999) and movie theaters (Allard, 1999) reveal how they structure cultural practices (DiMaggio, 1996). Similarly, literary mediation demonstrates that readers are not the solitary, introspective characters that they are too often imagined to be (Burgos, 1995), but, on the contrary, that they develop a real or imaginary sociability—with other readers or authors (Burgos, Evans, Buch, 1996)—and that the creation of a new profession— that of the library mediator—is entirely justified (Leturcq, 1999).

Relations between correspondents and members were framed against the backdrop of various networks. Correspondents thus found themselves at the root of a social arborescence that enabled them to develop a kind of reticular communication. Responsible for recruiting and managing at least ten members each, their role was to promote the Pompidou Center to potential new publics and provide a source of information facilitating access to its enormous cultural offer.

3. THE VIRTUE OF MEDIATION PROCESSES: RESISTANCE TO CONSUMERIST REDUCTION

The "Beaubourg Case" provides an emblematic example of the tension characterizing modernity and suggests a need for mediation for those who want to encourage the process of subjectivization. For mediation is becoming increasingly necessary at a time in which consumerism, with its destructive immediacy, is invading the sphere of culture. Long since described by Adorno, the transformation of culture into a commodity now affects the very definition of the cultural act by reducing it to an act of consumerism, thereby diluting the very idea of culture. Today, Bernard Stiegler observes the multiplicity of tasks, flows, and channels of information, and industries that "vie for our attention like sharks. . . . And it is because this *hyper-stimulation* generates *infra-attention* that mediation is so necessary and useful" (Stiegler, 2008a: 148). The main objective of this chapter is to reveal the effects of mediation approaches, which represent a kind of resistance to processes which tend to reduce cultural practices to acts of consumerism.

3.1 From Confusion to Trust Through Mediation

According to a number of commentators, the Pompidou Center condemns anyone who enters it to a distinctly confusing experience. Jean Baudrillard talks of "implosion" (Baudrillard, 1977); Jacques Rigaud of "ignorance" (Rigaud, 1990: 432); Jean Chesneaux of *a loss of the self* (Chesneau, 1989: 86–102); and Michel de Certeau of the power of a new *Panopticon* (de Certeau, 1987: 70). All of them describe an anomic, alienating world in which an absence of rules is a potential source of de-socialization and confusion. But here again, the fact that correspondents listened to and observed the public makes it possible to nuance or even invalidate such descriptions, as convergent as they are complacent in terms of the denunciation of the democratization of culture. The work of correspondents produced regulatory effects and encouraged loyalty. In both cases, trust constituted a springboard for these positive effects, enabling correspondents to become the agents of a transformation of the relationship between the Pompidou Center and its public and to move from confusion to concrete forms of mutual confidence.

How to decide without knowing? When one is uncertain about exactly what particular names represent, choosing from a vast array is a difficult task. Interpersonal relations help to overcome this problem. Without being actively sought, useful information is imparted either by friends and family or by correspondents, a personalized, word-of-mouth process that facilitates new discoveries. In this context, the correspondent introduced a triangular relationship between the individual and the Pompidou Center, a relationship in which she played the role of a third party.

Through their capacity to orient and inform with discernment, correspondents developed their qualities as both a *receptacle of trust* and a *source of judgment*,[3] in a context in which their value as a *source of judgment* was directly proportional to the lack of knowledge about contemporary forms of artistic expression of the member or potential member.

Due to the information of which they disposed and which members expected to receive from them, correspondents were able to act as guides for members. The exhibitions, conferences and debates, concerts, theater and dance productions, and introductory courses on architecture, the plastic arts, contemporary music and film offered by the Center were a kind of maze that was extremely difficult to negotiate. It was nigh on impossible to take everything in. In this regard, the Center's *Magazine* did not always provide all the necessary pointers. However, correspondents made it possible to overcome the opacity of the Pompidou Center's offer, which, for the uninitiated, implied a degree of uncertainty, if not in terms of quantity then at least about the value to be accorded to any relationship with contemporary works of art. The mutual trust built up between correspondents and members was all the more important in that visitors who are not experts on contemporary art find it impossible to recognize the originality of works or to discern their aesthetic value.

Members were able to delegate responsibility to correspondents for judging the quality of a work of art or an exhibition. The judgment of individuals was based on personal trust in that members recognized that their correspondents had an aesthetic competence and a body of knowledge which enabled them to judge with discernment. The logical result of a generally high level of education and of the level of culture procured by the initiation to contemporary art dispensed by the Liaison-Membership Department, the correspondent's faculty of judgment was seen as worthy of respect. At the head of a network, correspondents used the *surest* approach, according to members, of reducing uncertainty about aesthetic values. That approach was word-of-mouth. The correspondent both saved time and reduced uncertainty. "Experience shows us that we can *trust* our correspondent and therefore, it's true, we can trust word-of-mouth." "And it really saves time," something for which members were grateful.

3.2. Apparatuses of Trust, Apparatuses of Promise

Correspondents thus served as coordinators and sources of information. In terms of the Center's voluminous offer, where communication strategies and hierarchy seemed to be accorded little place, expert advice delivered by a person one knew was of great value. For members, correspondents became informants, delivering expert advice directly, thus boosting the Center's communication strategy, which was distinctly non-hierarchical. People with whom members had a personal relationship, correspondents were seen and understood as crucial sources of information in whom trust could be placed. This trust was tantamount to a recognition of authority, a surrendering of the self characteristic of a paradoxical relationship that was at once egalitarian and asymmetrical.[4]

Trust indicates a relationship based on sharing governed by a norm of reciprocity. Indeed, there were two concrete forms of trust. The first, corresponding to the personal forms of trust implicit in an apparatus of promise, was formed between the individual and her correspondent; the second, meanwhile, was established between the individual and the Pompidou Center and characterized the impersonal forms of the same apparatus. Located at the opposite end of the spectrum to consumerist discourse, the practice of putting people in contact with one another allowed for a reappropriation of meaning. According to the correspondents, the Liaison-Membership Department enabled them to provide a conceptual framework. By avoiding reducing the status of culture to that of a *culture-consuming* public, by offering a space for a *culture-debating* public (Habermas, 1989: 159–175), a space that certain correspondents termed a *space of resistance*, the Pompidou Center was able, between 1975 and 1995, to turn a consumerist ethos into a sphere in which a rapport with meaning was guaranteed.

Consequently, the approach applied by correspondents to members took the form of an incitement which the former did not hesitate to term *decisive*. "Encouraging people to go out" and "trying to make them discover contemporary art" were phrases often employed by correspondents, who regarded members as being passive and lazy, frequently displaying a form of ignorance and even a lack of curiosity. Correspondents ensured that the apparatus of promise functioned effectively. According to Lucien Karpik, the role of apparatuses of promise is to guarantee the commitments of partners, thereby ensuring the execution of a contract (Karpik, 1996: 540). Because correspondents could guarantee the permanence and equilibrium of the contract between the institution and its public, they were able to command trust in two ways: first, thanks to a dynamic of interactions; and, second, through their personal qualities.

The actions of correspondents thus constituted an apparatus of judgment and an apparatus of promise as a personal form of trust all the more valuable in that the visitor, unfamiliar with contemporary art, was often at a loss to recognize the singularity of the works on display and discern their aesthetic value. However, making decisions without the benefit of prior knowledge is a challenging prospect. When one is uncertain about quality, rational choice seems out of reach. But the interpersonal relationship seems to solve this problem. Useful information is actively sought among friends and it is through the personalized advice of word-to-mouth that discoveries are made. In this context, correspondents introduce a triangular relationship between themselves, the member, and the

Pompidou Center, a relationship in which they play the role of a third party trusted by the other parties in the triangle.

3.3 The Normative Impacts of Mediation

As modest as it may seem, by capitalizing on the experience of other people, this approach to mediation is foundational in that it makes it possible to at least partially overcome uncertainties rooted in an ignorance of the qualities of contemporary art and in difficulties in assessing its value. Members delegate responsibility to correspondents for judging the quality of a work of art or an exhibition. Providing a source of judgment, correspondents commanded the trust of members, who considered them to be better informed and more highly qualified than themselves. Correspondents therefore played the role of an interface capable of reducing, or even overcoming the kind of *dissuasion* effect predicted, as we have seen, by certain commentators since 1977.

By mediating between two spheres which might otherwise have remained separate, correspondents provided an interface between the individual and the institution, thus fulfilling their role as "relays" or mentors. Alongside its cultural aspect, the human dimension of the mediation process was important, or even decisive—decisive because it was not dissuasive—in terms of encouraging people to visit the institution. The difficulty of appreciating, or even approaching contemporary art—which can often be put down to a lack of knowledge of appropriate cultural codes—as well as resistance to the complexity of a place such as the Pompidou Center, highlighted the usefulness of correspondents to neophyte members. In effect, this function was particularly apparent among young correspondents, who considered the members for whom they were responsible, and who were no older than themselves, to be racked with anxiety due to the sheer size of the Center. Indeed, this "carcass of flows and signs," this "black hole devouring cultural energy," instilled in them a sense of dread manifesting itself as a form of "cultural dissuasion" (Baudrillard, 1977). The machine, or "refinery" as it was called in 1977, retained such characteristics for a number of years. A correspondent, who was a high school student when interviewed, stated that his friends-members felt "safer" due to the fact that they had a pass: "it's rather reassuring to be able to go into this enormous, hyper-concentrated cube armed with a map," he said. In the same way, after a correspondents' meeting, a female student expressed how happy she was to see that "this enormous building and the thousands of people in it still had a human dimension." Mediation thus has the power to structure cultural practices by transforming ways of experiencing relationships with art and artistic practices.

These effects can be seen as having two impacts. The first, of a normative type, underpins evolutions in the frequency with which cultural venues are visited. The second, of a more cognitive kind, influences representations of the relationship between the individual and art, and structures registers of identification with the institution. While policies concerning the public influence visitor rates, they also produce normative and cognitive impacts on the way in which members of the public think about the institution. The normative impact prompts a transformation in cultural practices. Although definitively marginal in regard to the working class, the increased number of middle class visitors makes it possible to nuance the discourse on the failure of democratization. But even more than an impact on numbers, the qualitative effect of policies concerning the public transforms the individual's relationship with art. More frequent, this effect can encourage people from all kinds of social backgrounds to develop a relationship with the arts that they would never have experienced had it not been for the Center's policies. Thanks to the routines that they define and implement, those policies provide a practical precondition for the elaboration of new norms of behavior.

The cognitive impact of policies concerning the public manifested itself in a qualitative effect: the Beaubourg's mediation policy transformed the public's self-image by enabling the individuals of which it was composed to divorce themselves from the framework of socialization in which they were previously enmeshed by providing them with a new principle of association. The second effect was inversely reciprocal. Partially but substantially transformed by the institution, individuals were able, in turn, to transform the institution's identity. Whereas, before, the institution presented a barrier to visitors, a separation from society, an obstacle sometimes incarnated materially by the price of entry, individuals making up the public were now able to establish a *bridge*, since, as we have seen, apparatuses of judgment and promise constituted by the correspondents of the Beaubourg Center guaranteed a transition from confusion to trust.

3.4 The Invisible Powers of Cultural Mediation

The effects of mediation suggest that cultural institutions possess a certain degree of power. Similarly, highlighting the *cognitive* and *normative* impacts of these effects on individuals demonstrates that the logic of cultural practices cannot be reduced to a logic of distinction. Other logics are at work, revealed in the transformation of approaches to the reception of works of art and of forms of sociability favored by mediation mechanisms.

These two impacts highlight the role of intermediaries in actively helping members of the public to access artistic and cultural works and their contribution to developing original approaches to promoting a deep and unbroken relationship with art and culture. Last, their no less active role in the introduction of a shared, public space demonstrates the effectiveness of mediation processes.

For far from being impotent in the face of the traditional determinants of cultural practices, cultural mediation possesses a capacity to fashion the relationship between individuals and art and to produce social effects including the acceptance or rejection of the influence of the cultivated *habitus*. Cultural mediation thus exercises a specific power, defined by Michel Foucault as "an action on other actions" (Foucault, 1992). By their actions, the "mediators" of the Beaubourg Center, in their role as correspondents, exercised genuine power in terms of the ability to structure cultural practices. Cultural mediation as a process defines the invisible element of cultural policies, an invisible element which can be explained in reference to the unknown power of its own action. Mediation exercised within the public itself defines a space in which collective identification, ways of experiencing relations to art, and social practices are expressed and crystallized.

It seems that the power of cultural mediation is ignored. As such, its social and political effectiveness remains invisible. Similarly invisible is the capacity of institutions to influence activities, govern practices, and introduce "regimes of familiarity" between individuals and culture. Cultural institutions such as the Beaubourg have produced a series of norms and rules, as well as a number of apparently insignificant routines. That is why it is possible to conclude with the idea that the unrecognized power of cultural institutions represents the invisible content of cultural policy. In this sense, such institutions not only contribute to the implementation of cultural policies but, even more importantly, to their very definition.

CONCLUSION: THE MEANINGS OF MEDIATION

In conclusion, cultural mediation is characterized by a number of intertwined aspects and meanings. A *political project* when used to favor the access of members of the public to cultural works; a *technical procedure* when it defines a way of putting people in contact with one another; and a *socio-political project* when it condenses the consequences of this approach and reveals that the tools used are not neutral. Indeed, those tools produce political effects, social norms, and cultural expectations. Project, procedure, process: the common point between these three aspects of mediation resides in the fact that they each encourage the development of a relationship with meaning. The meaning of cultural action is thus, in the end, retained as a condition of possibility of the development of a shared world (Tassin, 1999). Mediation creates a sphere of potential by rooting itself in past experiences and historical thought, while encompassing events occurring in the present.

Part of an old problematic associated with the ancient political question of the reception of symbols, mediation is a contemporary theme for both the sociology of culture and political sociology. As Hannah Arendt pointed out, *action* gives birth to the *actor*, facilitating the development of social bonds *via* the pleasure of sociability derived from action, thereby encouraging a process of subjectivization. Mediation thus reveals the constitution of a public space of appearance in which mediators are produced, exhibited, and born from their own actions and "dis-identified" vis-à-vis their cultural substrate in a process that Arendt termed a *second birth*, this one political. Mediation can thus define a political phenomenon, which makes it possible to more accurately judge the ways in which political actors appear and are subjectivized on the cultural scene, since acts of mediation favor the creation of the identity of the cultural actor.

Cultural mediation thus defines what makes it possible to *depart, deviate,* and *differentiate* oneself from the continuity of life itself. This gap— this *"deviance"*—institutes an opening of meaning, enabling cultural practices to retain their meaning as acts of culture irreducible to acts of consumerism. For, as we have seen, cultural mediation as a process makes it possible to work on what Simmel called the *tragedy of culture* by encouraging a subjectivization of objective culture and an objectivization of subjective culture. Mediation could thus be applied to ease the tension between the hypertrophy of objective culture and the relative atrophy of subjective culture. From this perspective, cultural mediation could facilitate the institution of *regimes of familiarity* capable of diminishing the authority of certain forms of culture and contributing to what Jean-Claude Passeron calls the *democratization of a social rapport* by introducing "a practice of familiarity and personalization of contact for the impersonal recourse to a statutory power of authority" (Passeron, 2003: 378).[5] On a methodological level, the analysis of processes of mediation could thus prove to be equally crucial.

On a more programmatic level, such a conclusion makes it possible to disassociate the sometimes overly linear continuity that analytically distinguishes production, mediation, and reception, since what is revealed is a *reciprocal action*, a *Wechselwirkung* (Simmel) between these intertwining moments in which modes of reception are entangled with modalities of mediation. This invites one to think of the indissociable character of a sociology of culture, a sociology of reception, and a sociology of mediation for those anxious to grasp the dynamic of the elaboration of judgments of taste and the evolution of such judgments. Because individuals develop by differentiating themselves from others and personalizing themselves in reciprocal actions that they entertain among themselves, with others, and with the objects that surround them, their very personalities are marked by such relationships. In this sense, analyses of processes of individuation and subjectivization are indissociable from a sociological understanding of mediation considered as a process of reciprocal action.

NOTES

This chapter was originally published as: « L'influence des dispositifs de médiation dans la structuration des pratiques culturelles. Le cas des correspondants du Centre Pompidou, » in « La médiation culturelle : enjeux, dispositifs et pratiques », *Lien social et politiques* 60 (2008): 13–24.

1. After having been secretary general of the TNP, Georges Guette directed the Théâtre de la Ville, alongside Jean Mercure, until 1970, before acting as secretary general of the Comédie-Française, this time alongside Pierre Dux. Better yet, as manager of the Inter-Théâtres, he was "the man who filled the Paris theaters." It was thanks to his image and reputation that the Pompidou Center called upon his expertise with a view to developing an appropriate relationship with the public.

2. The Beaubourg Center was compared to the supersonic airliner, Concord.

3. The terms are borrowed from Karpik, Lucien. « Dispositifs de confiance et engagements crédibles. » *Sociologie du travail* 4 (1996): 527–550.

4. Émile Benvéniste recalls that the etymological origin of "trust," or, rather, of its French equivalent, "confiance," namely *fides*, has two main meanings, the first based on the equivalent of credit, the second rooted in an inequality of conditions linked to a recognition of authority. See Benveniste, Émile. 1969. « La fidélité personnelle.» In *Le vocabulaire des institutions indo-européennes*. t. I, *Économie, parenté, société*. Paris: Éditions de Minuit. 102–121.

5. This is the fourth definition applied by Jean-Claude Passeron to the democratization of culture.

EIGHT

The Discourse of the "Failure" of the Democratization of Culture

Sociological Observation or Ideological Assertion?

That sociologists of art and culture are regularly consulted by various political and administrative bodies suggests that the relationship between sociology and public policy is a close one. This entanglement between academe and politics is a characteristic of the sociology of culture, the foundations of which, in France, are as much intellectual as they are institutional. The *institutional* basis of the sociology of culture is associated with the establishment by André Malraux in 1959 of the French Ministry of Cultural Affairs. In 1961, the first commission made specifically responsible for the cultural and artistic sector within the framework of France's Fourth Plan bore the name "Cultural Facilities and Artistic Heritages"; its secretary, Augustin Girard, was charged by Jacques Delors with the task of creating a research department within the newly created Ministry of Cultural Affairs. In 1963, just after having been set up, the Department of Studies and Research requested from Pierre Bourdieu a survey of the number of visitors to museums in Europe. The initial results of the survey were published in 1966 (Bourdieu and Darbel, 1966). The first INSEE survey on leisure activities was published in 1967.

    The *intellectual* foundations of the sociology of culture are to be found in the concomitant elaboration of a theoretical framework by Pierre Bourdieu, at the crossroads between the sociology of education developed by Jean-Claude Passeron and an emerging sociology of cultural legitimacy outlined in *The Love of Art* and later fully developed in *Distinction*, published in France in 1979. A conclusion drawn again and again from the results of Bourdieu's surveys is that social practices are hierarchical. Differing rates in the number of visits to cultural venues bring to light a top-down social distribution of cultural practices. Indeed, this conclusion, which has rarely been challenged since the mid-1960s, is now considered to be self-evident. One of the main contributions of the sociology of culture has been to point out that the reasons for not visiting cultural facilities are more often symbolic (socialization, cultivated *habitus*) than material (distance, prices).

Thus, the *sociological* question: "what are the cultural practices of the French?" is often followed by the *political* question, "has access to culture been democratized?," or by a more prophetic question: "will we one day realize the ideal of the democratization of culture?" Posed in such broad terms, these questions can be discouraging, especially in that today it is fashionable to take the view that "the failure of democratization" is a given.

1. UPS AND DOWNS IN THE FORTUNES OF AN IDEAL

In France, the democratization of culture has known its hours of glory as well as its darker moments. Supported by troupes encouraged by the French government's theatrical decentralization program introduced after the Second World War, and by Vilar's National Popular Theater at the Palais Chaillot in Paris and at the Festival of Avignon, and given a stamp of approval by André Malraux in the Decree of July 24, 1959, officially setting up the Ministry of Cultural Affairs, the democratization of culture was criticized in 1968, then constantly depreciated as, at the same time, the sociology of culture, which considered the ideal to be unattainable, gained ground. In spite of it all, however, cultural policies were introduced which attempted to give it the status of doctrine.

1.1 The Historical Formation of a Contested Idea

Because, at least since 1959, the ideal of democratization has provided the political basis of public intervention in the field of culture, cultural policies have regularly been judged in the light of this ideal. Against the background of the institutionalization of a cultural administration, of the professionalization of the artistic field and of the elaboration of successive definitions of public action (cultural action in the 1960s, cultural development in the 1970s, cultural mediation in the 1990s), a technocratic conception of cultural policies replaced a more symbolic conception of policy: solving "problems" became more important than elaborating a political order focusing on the issue of how people can best live together and an emphasis on the power of public action to establish new configurations. In fact, an interdependence between culture and politics gave way to an articulation between the sociology of culture and public policy.

Almost as soon as it was announced, the ideal of the democratization of culture was negatively impacted by a sociological observation concerning the social distribution of cultural practices made by Pierre Bourdieu in his initial work on museum visitor rates in Europe published in 1966. A little later, the surveys of the Ministry of Cultural Affairs tended to confirm empirically the explanations advanced at the time by articulating three concepts: socialization, *habitus*, and distinction. Differences in visitor numbers can, firstly, be explained by the process of *cultural socialization*. By insisting on instances of primary socialization, Bourdieu demonstrated that the relationship with culture is experienced as self-evident by *inheritors* who forge a *free culture* for themselves within their families (precocious, continuous, and diffuse learning), a process which the author distinguishes from *scholarly culture* (accelerated, late, methodical learning). These differences can also be explained by the cultivated *habitus* characteristic of a particular lifestyle. Thus, at an equivalent *standard of living* practices can vary in reference to a past *way of life*.

Bourdieu correlates cultural practices with the "cultural capital" of the individual. The problem of those without cultural capital is not so much to be found in the absence of a relationship with culture, but in "the absence of a sentiment of absence." Last, inequalities in access to culture are explained by the concept of *distinction*, according to which a relationship with culture encourages the practical manifestations of social differences by asserting at once a differentiation with the group from which one wants to distinguish oneself, and an imitation of the group with which one wants to identify. Cultural practices are linked to a *status group*, characterized by a way of life. Even today, the social distribution of cultural practices confirms the continued existence of such inequalities. In spite of several decades of public action in the field of culture, these inequalities have never diminished: successive waves of studies on *Les Pratiques culturelles des Français*[1] ("The cultural practices of the French") have hammered home the idea of a "failure of democratization," just as the explanations advanced lead to a conclusion that could be described as determinist: that it is impossible to realize such an ideal.

1.2. The Effects of the Diffusion of Knowledge from the Social Sciences

This repeated discourse, which is more closely associated with the ideological effects of the diffusion of knowledge from the social sciences than with simple indifference and resignation, invites not only an analysis of the reasons for which the democratization process is regarded by some as unattainable but also, and perhaps more importantly, an examination of the forms and functions of the distrust evoked by the ideal itself. The simultaneous emergence in France of a cultural administration and of the sociology of culture explains how the two discourses reinforced one another and why the democratization of culture was not able to accede to the status of an object of research.

The development of the notion of *social reproduction* seemed to render the idea of democratization almost worthless, to the point of relegating it to the status of inanity and depriving it of all positive aspects. But worse was to follow: democratization was to acquire a sulphurous tinge as claims were made that it was "normative," a negative quality in the eyes of the advocates of a certain sociological tradition. The democratization of culture was also the object of a second accusation, that of abandoning politics in favor of supporting artistic creation. The priority accorded to the arts was seen as detrimental to the democratic ideal. The notion of the failure of democratization was thus replaced by a more ideological discourse focusing on the alleged lack of validity of the democratization project itself as well as of the many institutional innovations which accompanied it. The close relationship between knowledge and power thus revealed makes it necessary to challenge the "self-evident" nature of such a discourse which, in certain cultural spheres, has acquired the force of law. Indeed, in some cultural milieus an argument based on the notion of sociological determinism is advanced to explain the absence of political reflection on the most effective ways of attenuating (if not effacing) the effects of symbolic obstacles revealed in the late 1960s, symbolic obstacles that limit most people's access to culture.

Jean-Claude Passeron distinguishes four different approaches to the democratization of culture (Passeron, 2003). The first focuses on analyzing the growing number of different cultural practices. The surveys of the Ministry of Culture on the cultural practices of the French reveal a substantial growth in the number of such practices and in cultural consumerism in general. However, this development is above all the result of a transformation in the socio-professional structure of the active population. The consumption of cultural goods and cultural practices is correlated to academic qualifications. In fact, the phenomenon can be explained by the growth in the numbers of people with tertiary qualifications (upper middle managers, intermediate occupations), which in turn is due to transformations in the system of production and the expansion of the university system. A statutory mechanism of assignation encourages individuals moving up through the social hierarchy to adopt the cultural norms of their milieu of destination. The democratization of culture is therefore the indirect result of educational democratization. In spite of this growth in the volume of cultural practices, no real reduction in the gap between social classes has been observed. This is the second approach to measuring democratization identified by Jean-Claude Passeron. Insofar as cultural outings are concerned (theater, concerts, museums, opera), increases in the number of visits to cultural facilities have not led to a substantial diversification of publics. The third measurement approach is based on the probability of accessing culture according to social category. This approach, first applied in studies on the equality of chances in the education system, makes it possible to analyze not only the social composition of a particular public, which partially depends on the demographic weight of various categories, but also the opportunities for each of the members of an initial category to indulge in a particular cultural practice and to what degree of intensity. The last meaning adduced by Passeron is that of a social rapport. Any decrease in the authority of one individual or group over another is thus considered democratic. This poses the question of the maintenance or decline of the power of legitimization of cultural practices possessed by certain social groups.

2. THE DISCOURSE ON *FAILURE*: THE FORMAL COHERENCE OF AN IDEOLOGICAL DISCOURSE

Due to the multifaceted nature of the idea, the democratization of culture, a doctrine underlying cultural policy in France since André Malraux, is difficult to define.

2.1 Three Definitions of the Democratization of Culture

In effect, cultural democratization can be understood either as a *political project*, an *historical process*, or a *technical procedure*: these three potential definitions are worthy of further examination. Jean-Claude Passeron (1991: 293–299) identified the first meaning, according to which the democratization of culture is a *political project*. A project designed to *convert* the public to aesthetic values adjudged to be legitimate can coincide with a political project characterized to some degree by a form of proselytism encouraging the masses to appropriate learned culture and inspiring them to visit cultural establishments. More broadly, it can be seen as a *project to rehabilitate* popular forms of culture. And, finally, within the *political perspective*, democratization corresponds to a *project of revolutionary renewal* of the creative process, of the legitimization of proletarian culture, as developed in the 1920s and 1930s with the name *Agitprop*.

Democratization can be understood as a *historical process*, or, in more Tocquevillian terms, as a long, slow progression toward equal conditions, in this case, in the field of access to culture. The popular theater advocated by Victor Hugo (1848), the setting up of the Théâtre du Peuple by Maurice Pottecher (1895), the direction of the National Popular Theater by Firmin Gémier, from 1920, and Jean Vilar, from 1951, are milestones in the history of the popular theater, a history characterized in this context by an implicit evolutionism in which the battles and dramas constituting its continuities and discontinuities are obscured.

A third and last reading casts democratization as a *technical procedure*. This procedural conception of democratization focuses on the approaches implemented to render it possible. Examples of such a conception of democratization include the decentralization of the French theater network, a project equipped with the means to "cover the territory," conquering and ensuring the loyalty of a new theater public across the country. The innovations introduced by Vilar's National Popular Theater again demonstrate the possibility of developing artistic activity capable of arousing public interest and boosting attendance figures. Indeed, Vilar's goal was to assert the principle of "theater as a public service," thought of in terms of a theater that excludes no one (Fleury, 2005a), from the conquest of the popular public and efforts to ensure that it stayed loyal, to the introduction of a series of approaches breaking with the intimidating rituals of the bourgeois theater, including earlier performance times, reservations, a ban on tipping, free cloakrooms, and cheap subscriptions for rehearsals, all of which succeeded in adding warmth to the somewhat impersonal Palais de Chaillot and moving away from the rituals of distinction that had previously held sway. Last, the innovations introduced by the Pompidou Center in the 1970s should be mentioned (free entry to certain areas such as the contemporary art galleries and the CCI's design and architecture exhibitions). In the 1990s, innovations such as a free Sunday every month at the Louvre were introduced. However, the approach taken often consisted of applying the discourse of "positive discrimination" to certain target populations, often, but not necessarily from the culturally and economically less favored classes, the members of which did not generally visit cultural institutions. Targeting certain populations rather than others is the same thing as favoring certain potential publics over others. This new aspect of the policy aimed at democratizing culture reveals a certain detachment from the Republican ideal according to which everyone should receive equal treatment. Taking note that, in terms of access to the arts, certain individuals are advantaged, while others are disadvantaged, this last meaning of democratization is linked to an ensemble of procedures characterized by an attempt to reduce the gap between individuals in terms of their relationship with art. If we are to agree that these different aspects of the democratization of culture are not mutually exclusive, but that, on the contrary, cultural institutions help to articulate them, then sociological observation becomes possible.

2.2 Three Topics on the Discourse on the Failure of Democratization

In a more analytical fashion, it is possible to distinguish three discursive figures applied to undermining the ideal of cultural democratization: the first claims that it had no legitimacy; the second attempts to demonstrate its lack of equity; and the third concludes that it is impossible due to the supposed ineffectiveness of public action in the field of culture. Each of these figures deserves to be analyzed.

The democratization of culture has been accused of illegitimacy. This accusation is aimed at cultural policies which supposedly produce the opposite of what they are designed to achieve: they are said to destroy rather than protect the creative process. This approach, defended by authors including Marc Fumaroli (*L'Etat culturel*, 1991), focuses on demonstrating the shortcomings of public cultural policy, what Raymond Boudon would have termed its "perverse effects," and concludes that culture has declined due to the "anthropologization" of the way in which it is defined, itself a consequence of the advances of cultural relativism. But not far beneath the surface of this critique lurks a dispute over values, which, for Weber, was impossible to resolve.

Democratization has also been accused of a lack of equity, largely on the grounds of its "anti-redistributive effects." This argument is based on the idea that using public money to fund the arts is questionable due to the fact that only a small percentage of the population visits cultural institutions. But it is a specious argument since withdrawing public funding would only accentuate already existing inequalities.

Last, efforts to democratize culture have often been criticized on the grounds of their supposed inefficiency; this is especially true of the approaches developed by cultural institutions to conquer new publics and encourage them to remain loyal. This kind of criticism of public cultural policy is based on the disappointingly slow evolution of cultural practices in the field of the performing arts—for which ministerial surveys reveal large differences in visitor rates defined by socio-demographic variables. The advocates of this approach often refer to Pierre Bourdieu's theory, based on the concepts of socialization, *habitus,* and distinction, in an attempt to prove once and for all that approaches to cultural democratization are inefficient and that the ideal itself is unattainable. This denunciation of inefficiency is often used to justify the disappearance of institutional innovations which, leading to a loss of spectators, provides an example of Robert Merton's "self-fulfilling prophecy" (Merton, 1948). An alternative approach would be to think about how symbolic obstacles could be overcome instead of resigning oneself to the fact of their eternal existence. Pierre Bourdieu alluded to one such alternative when he wrote that it has been "established that an intensification of the action of the school is the most efficient means of increasing cultural practice [. . .] at the same time as being the necessary condition for the effectiveness of all other approaches" (Bourdieu and Darbel, 1997).

Political project, historical process, technical procedure, the democratization of culture can be understood in a number of different ways. But it should be noted that the three accusations correspond to the three stated definitions: the political project is illegitimate; the historical process lacking in equity, which accentuates rather than diminishes inequalities; and, last, the procedural approach is dismissed as being inefficient.

In his description of "reactionary rhetoric," Albert O. Hirschman distinguished three discursive figures: jeopardy, perversity, and futility (Hirschman, 1991). The fact that the three criticisms leveled at the ideal of cultural democratization can be said to correspond to Hirschman's categories, indicates their ideological nature. There is a fairly large step between the objective *sociological* observation of varying visitor rates, and the more *ideological* discourse on the invalidation of the very project of democratization, as evidenced in the positions taken by researchers intent on developing an unequivocal discourse which concludes that "the democratization of culture is a failure" (Donnat, 1991; 1994). As Karl Mannheim pointed out, the denunciation of an ideology is often itself ideological (Mannheim, 1985).

The charge of the failure of democratization is thus replaced by a more ideological discourse invalidating the project itself, and, along with it, a whole series of institutional innovations by which it is accompanied. Yet empirical surveys of the publics of cultural institutions such as Vilar's National Popular Theater and the Beaubourg Center have made it possible to render the question more complex by showing that, contrary to received ideas, the democratization of culture has enjoyed a number of successes.

3. AN EMPIRICAL CASE OF THE REALIZATION OF THE IDEAL OF DEMOCRATIZATION

Vilar's National Popular Theater is a brilliant riposte to the discourse on the "failure of democratization," which is based on the idea of the inability of cultural institutions to combat the determinants of the social distribution of cultural practices. However, since, in an entirely contrary sense, those institutions make a powerful contribution to crafting cultural experiences, social practices and ways of experiencing relationships to art, and because Vilar's National Popular Theater defined a way forward in the public theater, and, more broadly, in other cultural institutions, it is important to understand how these identities were formed, how sociabilities discovered within groups constituting the public were deployed, and how a desire for culture was born and reborn in the hearts and minds of the spectators of the Vilar's productions.

3.1 The Democratization of Culture in the Light of Vilar's TNP

Vilar's National Popular Theater prefigured the development of public policies on culture. The popular success of Jean Vilar rendered *legitimate* what had previously been considered *illegitimate*. Associating high-quality artistic productions with an approach guaranteeing a democratization of culture, Vilar's work made the idea of public intervention in the artistic field legitimate, thus providing the Ministry of Culture, set up under the stewardship of André Malraux a few years later, with an operational template. Vilar's National Popular Theater represents a historical moment since his approach became a yardstick for the reconciliation between the arts and the State which occurred in the second half of the twentieth century.

Thus, for thousands of people, the *incredible* became *imaginable*. If going to the theater was unthinkable for a worker or a secretary in 1945, it became thinkable in 1951. Vilar's National Popular Theater threw a new light on the social and cultural practices of individuals, many of whom admitted, not without emotion, that it had "changed their lives." The transformation of their lives and relationship with the arts recalls the idea of the potential emancipatory effect of culture dear to the Enlightenment tradition, but sometimes forgotten due to the influence of perspectives insisting on the effects of domination or reproduction. Vilar's approach was characterized by its undying commitment to the democratization of culture, and it was in dedicating his life to the cause that he was able to associate his name with the ideal. This explains the enigmatic nature of his success and the emotion he still provokes in anybody who knew him, either directly or indirectly. Vilar's National Popular Theater provided spectators with the possibility of changing their lives by creating, albeit temporarily, conditions of equality with others and by offering the chance to access the power within themselves.

These three approaches contributed to the "event" that Vilar represents in the history of the democratization of culture. If it is possible today to conceptualize the emancipatory aspects of culture, it is because Jean Vilar created the very possibility of accessing a new figure of truth, both in the political field and the theatrical sphere.

3.2 A Programmatic Invitation to Sociological Research

A number of research perspectives thus emerge. The *possibility* of instituting an approach to the democratization of culture auguring a *possible* "new beginning" initially serves to arouse interest in a subject sometimes ignored in sociological research: that of the "possible." Eschewing all deterministic conceptions of history, this approach not only makes of the future a realm of endless potentialities but also opens up the past and the ways in which it can be interpreted. The concept of *possibility* to which Max Weber attracted our attention with his work on causal imputation or on *Möglichkeit* (possibility) is an invitation to carry out further research on the idea that things could have been different than they are. The sociological imagination thus makes it possible to elaborate more sophisticated causal explanations, to avoid, thanks to past experiences, the traps of crystallized forms, and to pose questions about what Michel Foucault might have called the unthought elements of an *episteme* or, to quote

Thomas Kuhn, a "paradigm." The influence of hypotheses and results that are regarded as stable can lead to the emergence of a number of blind spots or unthought elements, which in turn become obstacles to research.

The second avenue of research takes the form of a confirmation. That of the value of the Weberian method of sociological analysis deliberately adopted over the course of these surveys, with a view to developing a sociology of decision-making, which accords a certain importance both to political motivations and historical configurations, and to understanding the revolutionary approaches applied by Jean Vilar and the kind of reception they received from theater-goers (Fleury, 2006c). More broadly, this avenue of research reveals the value of a sociological perspective to those attempting to produce a deeper, more open-ended analysis of cultural socialization, or, in other words, an analysis not definitively determined by the influential instances of socialization represented by school and family. Socialization is once more seen as a continuous process that lasts throughout the individual's lifetime.

In other words, there is no simple, unequivocal link between childhood attitudes and adult behaviors in the field of culture. The cultural institution forms and informs practices, both in terms of behaviors and representations. In this sense, it presents itself as a sphere in which norms and values are learned, or, in other words, as an instance of socialization capable of confirming, or, inversely, rebutting the effects of primary socialization, able to institute public spaces and a shared world, to fashion social bonds, forms of identity, and sociability.

The last avenue of research implies carrying out yet more sophisticated surveys of cultural institutions and their publics (Fleury, 2007). The democratization of culture reveals itself as the product of a series of reciprocal actions involving the institution and its public which makes it possible to take a relational approach to the development and deployment of policies concerning the public. An object of study in itself, the cultural institution thus becomes a gateway to the understanding of both cultural policies and cultural practices.

In light of Vilar's National Popular Theater, cultural institutions appear not only as the result but also as the condition of possibility of public policies on culture. *Instituted* by the policy, the National Popular Theater acted as an agent *instituting* not only new cultural practices but also new cultural policies thanks to the norms of public action that it introduced. The National Popular Theater played a central role in defining public policies on culture, and still serves, first as an event and later a model, as a potential vector of the realization of the ideal of the democratization of culture (Fleury, 2009).

CONCLUSION: AN INVITATION TO REFLECT

In conclusion, the mere possibility of calling the status of the discourse on the failure of the democratization of culture into question suggests the importance of reexamining the issue in its entirety. For, to sum up, the social distribution of cultural practices highlighted in the work of Pierre Bourdieu on visitor rates to European museums, later confirmed by the surveys of the French Ministry of Culture, is now widely known, both by sociologists and professionals in the artistic field and the cultural sector, to the point that it now enjoys the status of a self-evident truth and serves as the basis for a belief in the "failure of the democratization of culture." But, in regard to empirical cases suggesting other results and in view of the formal coherence of the discourse which frames it, such a conclusion is both univocal and normative.

Why should we therefore choose to translate social *determinants* as "*determinisms*"? Isn't the discourse on the "failure of democratization" typical of "reactionary rhetoric," in which Albert O. Hirschman identified three topics (jeopardy, perversity, and futility)? Rather than accepting the apparent coherence between the unquestionable *sociological* explanation for differing numbers of visitors to cultural institutions and the more *ideological* discourse calling into question the very validity of the ideal of the democratization of culture, a discourse used by certain researchers who like to talk of "failure," this chapter suggests, on the basis of empirical surveys, that any approach to the subject should be nuanced. The chapter will have proven worthwhile if it has encouraged its readers to take such a possibility into account.

Instead of concluding on that point, it should be recalled that sociologists find themselves not so much *confronted* by political, economic, and media discourses, as *inserted* into them, or even *traversed* by those *orders of discourse*, to borrow a phrase from Michel Foucault. This chapter has attempted to illustrate that observation by showing how interpretations of the "failure of the democratization of culture" proposed by sociologists of culture should be seen in their socio-historical context and in terms of an intellectual horizon against which those interpretations take on a more circumscribed meaning. One final remark: modesty in research in the field of the sociology of culture is always a good thing. Using empirical surveys to invalidate globalizing explanations is one of the tasks incumbent on social scientists, a task that implies, as Max Weber observed, a *refusal of causal monism*. This involves not only rejecting all forms of simplification in the description of cultural practices but also, and above all in this context, undertaking the necessary mission of elucidating one's own *relationship to values*. Indeed, the author of *Science as a Vocation* strongly suggested that sociologists develop an axiological neutrality in order to overcome the confusion between the *learned* and *political* orders, a confusion which is all the more problematic in that sociological observation and ideological assertion have more than a little in common.

NOTES

This chapter was originally published as « Le discours d'"échec" de la démocratisation de la culture : constat sociologique ou assertion idéologique?» In Sylvia Girel and Serge Proust (eds.), Les usages de la sociologie de l'art: constructions théoriques, cas pratiques.L'Harmattan, « Logiques sociales—Sociologie de l'art », 2007, pp. 75-100.

1. For the latest edition, see Olivier Donnat. 2008. Les pratiques culturelles des Français à l'ère numérique. Paris: La Découverte / Ministère de la Culture et de la Communication.

Bibliography

Adorno, Theodor W. 1989. *Prismes, Critique de la culture et société*. Paris: Payot.
———. [1970]. 1997. *Aesthetic Theory*. Translated, edited and with an introduction by Robert Hullot Kentor. Minneapolis: University of Minnesota Press.
Alexander, Jeffrey C. 2000. La subjectivation des forces objectives : l'habitus. In *La Réduction. Critique de Bourdieu*, translated by Nathalie Zaccai-Reyners with Julie Lejeune. Paris: Éditions du Cerf. 39–70.
Alexander, Victoria. 2003. *Sociology of the Arts: Exploring Fine and Popular Forms*. London: Wiley-Blackwell.
Allard, Laurence. 1999. Espace public et sociabilité esthétique. *Communications* 68: 207–237.
Amrani, Younes, and Stéphane Beaud. 2005. *Pays de malheur! Un jeune de cité écrit à un sociologue*. Paris: La Découverte.
Amselle, Jean-Loup. 2001. *Branchements. Anthropologie de l'universalité des cultures*. Paris: Flammarion.
Ancel, Pascale, and Alain Pessin. (eds.) 2004. *Les non-publics*. Tome 1, *Les arts en réceptions & Les non-publics*; Tome 2, *Les arts en réceptions*. Paris: L'Harmattan.
Arendt, Hannah. 1993. *The Crisis in Culture: Its Social and Its Political Significance*. Harmondsworth: Penguin Books.
Austin, John L. 1962. *How to Do Things with Words*. Oxford: Clarendon Press.
Barrault, Jean-Louis. *Arts* (February 1957), 1.
Baudrillard, Jean. 1977. *L'effet Beaubourg. Implosion et dissuasion*. Paris: Galilée.
Baxandall, Michael. 1991. *Patterns of Intention: On the Historical Explanation of Pictures*. New Haven: Yale University Press.
———. 1972. *Painting and Experience in 15th Century Italy*. Oxford: Oxford University Press.
Beaud, Stéphane. 2002. *80% au bac . . . et après? Les enfants de la démocratisation scolaire*. Paris: La Découverte.
Beaud, Stéphane, and Michel Pialoux. 2005. *Retour sur la condition ouvrière : enquête aux usines Peugeot de Sochaux-Montbéliard*. Paris: Fayard.
Baudelot, Christian, Marie Cartier, and Christine Detrez. 1999. *Et pourtant ils lisent . . .* Paris: Seuil.
Beaudry, Lucille, and Lawrence Olivier. (eds.) 2001. *La politique par le détour de l'art, de l'éthique et de la philosophie*. Quebec: Presses de l'Université du Québec.
Becker, Howard. 1982. *Art Worlds*. Berkeley: University of California Press.
———. 1999. *Propos sur l'art*. Paris: L'Harmattan.
Bellavance, Guy. 2004. Non-public et publics cultivés. Le répertoire culturel des élites. In Pascale Ancel and Alain Pession (eds.), *Les non-publics. Les arts en réception*, Tome II. Paris: L'Harmattan, « Logiques sociales ». 277–315.
———. 2008. "Where's high? Who's low? What's new?" Classification and stratification inside cultural 'repertoire.' In A. Warde, M. Ollivier, K. Van Eijck, (eds). Models of Omnivorous Cultural Consumption: New Directions in Research *Poetics* 36(2–3): 189–216.
Bellavance, Guy and Fournier, Marcel. 1996. Les publics des arts à Montréal : le cas des chevauchements de publics. In Viviana Fridman and Michèle Ollivier (eds.), *Les Publics du secteur culturel : nouvelles approches*. Québec: Presses de l'Université Laval. 29–57.
Benedict, Ruth. 1934. *Patterns of Culture*. Boston: Houghton Mifflin Co.

Benjamin, Walter. 2008. *The Work of Art in the Age of Mechanical Reproduction*. Harmondsworth: Penguin Books.
Benveniste, Émile. 1969. La fidélité personnelle. In *Le vocabulaire des institutions indo-européennes*. t. I. *Économie, parenté, société*. Paris: Éditions de Minuit. 103–121.
Bernstein, Basil. 1971. *Class, Codes and Control: Theoretical Studies Towards a Sociology of Language*. London: Routledge & Keegan Paul.
Bertrand, Anne-Marie. 2003. Le peuple, le non-public et le bon public. In Olivier Donnat and Paul Tolila (eds.), *Le(s) Public(s) de la culture*. Paris: Presses de Sciences Po. 139–154.
Boudon, Raymond. 1999. « De l'objectivité des valeurs artistiques ou les valeurs artistiques entre le platonisme et le conventionnalisme. » In *Le Sens des valeurs*. Paris: Presses Universitaires de France PUF, « Quadrige ». 251–294.
Bourdieu, Pierre. 1987. *Chose dites*. Paris: Éditions de Minuit.
———. 1984. *Distinction: A Social Critique of the Judgment of Taste*, translated by Richard Nice. London: Routledge & Keegan Paul.
———. 1990. The Logic of Practice. Cambridge: Polity Press.
Bourdieu, Pierre, and Alain Darbel (with Dominique Schnapper). 1997. *The Love of Art: European Art Museums and their Public*. Cambridge: Polity Press.
———. 1977. *Reproduction in Education, Society and Culture*. Translated by Richard Nice; foreword by Tom Bottomore. London: Sage.
———. 1979. *The Inheritors: French Students and their Reaction to Culture*. Translated by Richard Nice. Chicago, London: University of Chicago Press, 1979.
Burgos, Martine. 1995. La sociologie de la littérature : médiation, contextualisation et modes de lecture. In B. Veck and J. Verrier (eds.), *La littérature des autres*. Paris: I.N.R.P. 172–177.
Burgos, Martine, Christophe Evans, and Esteban Buch. 1996. *Sociabilités du livre et communautés de lecteurs : trois études sur la sociabilité du livre*. Paris: Centre Georges-Pompidou, Bibliothèque publique d'information.
Caillet, Elizabeth (with Lehalle, Evelyne). 1995. *À l'approche du musée, la médiation culturelle*. Lyon: Presses Universitaires de Lyon.
Callon, Michel, and Bruno Latour. 1981. Unscrewing the Big Leviathan: how actors macrostructure reality and how actors help them do so. In K. D. Knorr-Cetina and A. Cicourel (eds.), *Advances in Social Theory and Methodology*. London: Routledge and Keegan Paul. 277–303.
Caune, Jean. 1992. *La Culture en action. De Vilar à Lang : le sens perdu*. Grenoble: Presses universitaires de Grenoble.
Certeau, Michel de. 1977. *La Culture au pluriel*. Paris: Christian Bourgeois.
———. 1987. « Le sabbat encyclopédique du voir ». L'utopie Beaubourg dix ans après. *Esprit* 123: 66–82.
———. 1990. Lire : un braconnage. In Michel de Certeau, Luce Giard and Pierre Mayol (eds.), *L'invention du quotidien*, t. I, *Les arts de faire*. Paris: Gallimard, «Folio-Essais». 239–255.
Chaney, David. 1994. *The Cultural Turn. Scene-Setting Essays on Contemporary Cultural History*. London: Routledge.
Chartier, Roger. 1996. *Culture écrite et société : l'ordre des livres (XIVème–XVIIIème siècles)*. Paris: Albin Michel.
Chesneaux, Jean. 1989. La modernité comme culture et idéologie. In Jean Chesneaux, *Modernité-monde*. Paris: La Découverte, 1989. 86–102.
Clark, Terry Nichols, and Felipe Carreira da Silva. Culture matters. How and why arts participation fosters democratic politics, forthcoming.
Clark, Terry Nichols. 2007. Making culture into magic: how can it bring tourists and residents together? *International Review of Public Administration* 12 (1): 13–25.
Clark, Terry Nichols. 2011. *The City as an Entertainment Machine*. Lanham, Maryland: Lexington Books.

Clark, Terry Nichols and Stephen Sawyer. 2009–2010. Villes créatives ou voisinages dynamiques ? Développement métropolitain et ambiances urbaines. *L'Observatoire, La revue des politiques culturelles* 36 (Winter): 44–49.
Clark, Terry Nichols and Vincent Hoffmann-Martinot. 1998. *The New Political Culture*. Boulder, CO: Westview Press.
Colas, Dominique. 2006. *Sociologie politique*. Paris: Presses universitaires de France.
Coulangeon, Philippe. 2011. Les métamorphoses de la distinction. Inégalités culturelle dans la France d'aujourd'hui. Paris: Grasset, « Mondes vécus ».
———. Philippe. 2005. *Sociologie des pratiques culturelles*. Paris: La Découverte, « Repères ».
Crane, Diana. 1994. *The Sociology of Culture. Emerging Theoretical Perspectives*. Oxford, UK and Cambridge, Mass.: USA: Basil Blackwell Ltd.
Cuche, Denys. 1997. *La notion de culture dans les sciences sociales*. Paris: La Découverte, « Repères ».
Danesi, Marcel. 2008. *Popular Culture: Introductory Perspectives*. Lanham: Rowman & Littlefield.
Davallon, Jean. 1999. *L'exposition à l'œuvre. Stratégies de communication et médiation symbolique*. Paris: L'Harmattan.
Denizot, Marion. 2005. *Jeanne Laurent. Une fondatrice du service public pour la culture (1946–1952)*. Paris: La Documentation française, Comité d'histoire du ministère de la Culture.
Deroche-Gurcel, Lilyane. 1993. La sociabilité : variations sur un thème de Simmel. *L'Année sociologique* 43: 159–188.
———. 1997. *Simmel et la modernité*. Paris: Presses Universitaires de France.
DiMaggio, Paul. 1996. Are art-museum visitors different from other people? The relationship between attendance and social and political attitudes in the United States. *Poetics* 24: 161–180.
———. 1997. Culture and cognition. *Annual Review of Sociology* 23: 263–287.
DiMaggio, Paul and Michael Useem. 1983. Cultural democracy in a period of cultural expansion: the Social composition of arts audiences in the United States. In Jack B. Kamerman and Rosanne Martorella (eds.), *Performers and Performances: the Social Organization of Artistic Work*. New York: Praeger, 199–225.
———. 1985. Why do some theaters innovate more than others? An empirical analysis. *Poetics* 14, 107–122.
———. 1982. The arts in class reproduction. In Michael W. Apple (ed.), *Cultural and Economic Reproduction in Education: Essays on Class, Ideology and the State*. London: Routledge & Keegan Paul, 181–201.
———. 1978. Cultural property and public policy: emerging tensions in government support for the arts. In "The Production of Culture." Special Issue, *Social Research* 45 (2): 356–389.
DiMaggio, Paul and Toqir Mukhtar. 2004. Arts participation as cultural capital in the United States (1982–2002). Signs of decline? *Poetics* 32: 168–194.
Donnat, Olivier. 1991. Démocratisation culturelle : la fin d'un mythe. *Esprit* 3–4: 65–79.
———. 1994. L'épuisement des utopies. In *Les Français face à la culture. De l'exclusion à l'éclectisme*, Éditions La Découverte. 366–369.
———. 1994. *Les Français face à la culture. De l'exclusion à l'éclectisme*. Paris: La Découverte.
———. 2009. *Les pratiques culturelles des Français à l'ère numérique. Enquête 2008*. Paris: La Découverte/Ministère de la Culture et de la Communication.
———. 1998. *Les pratiques culturelles des Français. Enquête 1997*. Paris : La Documentation française.
———. 2003. *Regards croisés sur les pratiques culturelles*. La Documentation française.
Donnat, Olivier, and Sylvie Octobre. 2001. *Les publics des établissements culturels. Méthodes et résultats d'enquête*. Paris: La Documentation française.
Donnat, Olivier, and Paul Tolila (eds.). 2003. *Le(s) Public(s) de la culture*. Paris: Presses de Sciences Po.

Dubet, François. 2003. Paradoxes et enjeux de l'école de masse. In Olivier Donnat and Paul Tolila (eds.), *Le(s) Public(s) de la culture*. Paris : Presses de Sciences Po. 25–42.
———. 2002. *Le Déclin de l'institution*. Paris: Seuil.
Dubois, Vincent. 1993. Les prémices de la "démocratisation culturelle. Les intellectuels, l'art et le peuple au tournant du siècle. *Politix. Travaux de science politique* 24 (4): 36–56.
Ducret, André. 2005. *Teddie goes to Hollywood*. Du jazz au cinéma : la genèse du concept d' « industrie culturelle ». In Laurent Creton, Michael Palmer and Jean Pierre Sarrazec (eds.), *Arts du spectacle, métiers et industries culturelles*. Paris: Presses de la Sorbonne Nouvelle. 23–40.
Ducret, André, and Olivier Moeschler, eds. 2001. *Nouveaux regards sur les pratiques culturelles. Nouveaux regards sur les pratiques culturelles. Contraintes collectives, logiques individuelles et transformation des modes de vie*. Paris: L'Harmattan.
Dumazedier, Joffre. 1996. *Le Loisir et la ville*. Paris: Seuil.
———. 1996. *Société éducative et pouvoir culturel*. Paris: Seuil.
———. 1974. *Sociologie empirique du loisir*. Paris: Seuil.
Dumont, Louis. [1966] 1990. *Homo hierarchicus. Le système des castes et ses implications*. Paris: Gallimard.
Dumontier, Françoise, Françoise de Singly and Clark Thélok. 1990. La lecture moins attractive qu'il ya vingle ans. Economie et Statistique, 233, 63–80.
Durkheim, Émile. 1975. *Textes III. Fonctions sociales et institutions*. Paris: Éditions de Minuit.
———. 2001. *The Elementary Forms of the Religious Life*. Translated by Carol Gossman. Oxford: Oxford University Press.
Eidelman, Jacqueline, and Benoît Céroux. 2009. *Culture et études. Pratiques et publiques*. Paris: Ministère de la Culture et de la Communication.
Elias, Norbert. [1969] 2006. *The Court Society*, edited by Stephen Mennel. Dublin: UCD Press.
———. [1965] 1994. *The Established and the Outsiders. A Sociological Enquiry into Community Problems*. London: Sage.
———. [1969] 2000. The development of the antithesis between *Kultur* and *Zivilisation*. In *The Civilizing Process* Oxford: Blackwell Publishing, 9–10.
Esquenazi, Jean-Pierre. 2007. *Sociologie des œuvres. De la production à l'interprétation*. Paris: Armand Colin, « U ».
———. 2003. *Sociologie des publics*. Paris: La Découverte.
Ethis Emmanuel. 2002. *Avignon, le public réinventé. Le Festival sous le regard des sciences sociales*. Paris: La Documentation française.
———. 2001. *Aux marches du palais. Le festival de Cannes sous le regard des sciences sociales*. Paris: La Documentation française.
———. 2003. « La forme Festival à l'œuvre : Avignon, ou l'invention d'un "public médiateur" », in Olivier Donnat & Paul Tolila, ed., *Le(s) public(s) de la culture*, Presses de Sciences Po. 181–196
———. 2005. *Sociologie du cinéma et de ses publics*. Paris: Armand Colin.
Fabiani, Jean-Louis. 2004. Publics constatés, publics inventés, publics déniés. *Enseigner la musique* 6–7, Lyon.
———. 2007. De l'analyse des objets culturels. In Jean-Louis Fabiani (ed.), *Après la culture légitime. Objets, publics, autorités*. Paris: L'Harmattan.
———. 2003. Éléments de synthèse. In Olivier Donnat and Paul Tolila (eds.), *Le(s) Public(s) de la culture*. Paris: Presses de Science Po. 309.
———. 2003b. Peut-on encore parler de légitimité culturelle ? In Olivier Donnat and Paul Tolila (eds.), *Le(s) Public(s) de la culture*. Paris: Presses de Sciences Po. 305–319.
———. 1993. Sur quelques progrès récents de la sociologie des œuvres. *Genèses* 11: 148–167.
Fleury, Laurent. 2004. Abolition des classes sociales ou production d'une fiction d'égalité ? La réalisation d'un espace utopique au TNP de Vilar. In Jean-Noël Cho-

part and Claude Martin (eds.), *Que reste-t-il des classes sociales* ? Paris: Éditions de l'École nationale de la santé publique. 121–136.

———. 2014. Forthcoming. *Max Weber et les ambivalences de la modernité*. Paris: Armand Colin.

———. 2002. De quelques désirs insoupçonnés de spectateurs du TNP de Jean Vilar. *Théâtres en Bretagne*, 13–14. Rennes: Presses Universitaires de Rennes. 34–48.

———. 2005. Efficacité des pratiques rituelles et temporalité des pratiques culturelles. In *Rites et rythmes de l'œuvre*. Paris: L'Harmattan, 2005. 117–139.

———. 2004a. Généalogie d'un théâtre "sans qualités". Le théâtre amateur, l'Éducation populaire et l'État culturel. In Marie-Madeleine Mervant-Roux (ed.), *Du théâtre amateur. Approches historiques et anthropologiques*. Paris: CNRS-Éditions. 51–57.

———. 2006. L'analyse des politiques et des pratiques culturelles à l'intersection de la science politique et de la sociologie. In Sylvie Girel (ed.), *Sociologie des arts et de la culture. Un état de la recherche. Premier Congrès de l'Association Française de Sociologie*. Paris: L'Harmattan. 37–58.

———. 2006a. L'art, l'émotion et les valeurs. In *Vingt ans de Sociologie de l'art. Bilan et perspectives*. Paris, L'Harmattan. 149–162.

———. 2007. *Le cas Beaubourg. Mécénat d'Etat et démocratisation de la culture*, preface by Bernard Stiegler. Paris: Armand Colin.

———. 2002a. Le pouvoir des institutions culturelles. In Claude Fourteau (ed.), *Les institutions culturelles au plus près du public*. Paris: La Documentation française. 31–49.

———. 2003. Le public du T.N.P. comme critique autorisé : l'inversion du protocole de la critique par Jean Vilar. *Sociologie de l'art* 3: 49–77.

———. 2006b. Le public populaire : une catégorie réalisée au TNP de Jean Vilar. In *Les Peuples de l'art*. Paris: L'Harmattan. 291–311.

———. 1991. Les correspondants du Centre Pompidou. Photocopy.

———. 1999. *Le T.N.P. et le Centre Pompidou : deux institutions culturelles entre l'État et le public. Contribution à une sociologie des politiques publiques de la culture en France après 1945*. Paris: Université de Paris IX.

———. 2006c. *Le T.N.P. de Vilar. Une expérience de démocratisation de la culture* . Presses Universitaires de Rennes, « Res Publica ».

———. 2004b. L'invention de la notion de non-public. In Pascale Ancel and Alain Pessin (eds.), *Les non-publics. Les arts en réceptions*. Paris: L'Harmattan. 53–82.

———. 2009. Le travail d'institution : la démocratisation de la culture à la lumière des héritages du TNP, » In Olivier Moeschler and Olivier Thévenin (eds.), *Les territoires de la démocratisation culturelle. Équipements, événements, patrimoines*. Paris: L'Harmattan, « Logiques sociales ». 21–34.

———. 2006d. Maurice Halbwachs Précurseur d'une sociologie des émotions. In Bruno Péquignot (ed.). *Maurice Halbwachs : le temps, la mémoire et l'émotion*. Paris: L'Harmattan. 61–98.

———. 2009a. *Max Weber*. Paris: Presses universitaires de France, « Que Sais-je ? ».

———. 2005a. *Omnes et singulatim* : l'adresse à tous et à chacun. Le "théâtre, service public" de Jean Vilar. *Théâtre public* « Espace Privé / Espace Public » (December): 29–34.

———. 2003a. Retour sur les origines : le modèle du TNP de Jean Vilar. In Olivier Donnat and Paul Tolila (eds.), *Le(s) Public(s) de la culture*. Paris: Presses de Sciences Po. 123–138.

———. 2005b. Weber sur les traces de Nietzsche ? In *Revue française de sociologie* 46 (4). 117–149.

Fleury, Laurent, and Isabelle Vazereau. 2005. L'attente du spectateur. Pour une compréhension des formes de la réception esthétique. *Carnets de bord* 8, Special Issue, « Des goûts et des couleurs. La réception des biens culturels ». 5–15.

Florida, Richard. 2004. *The Rise of the Creative Class: And How It's Transforming Work, Leisure, Community and Everyday Life*, New York: Perseus Book Group.

Foucault, Michel. 1992. Deux essais sur le sujet et le pouvoir. In Hubert Dreyfus and Paul Rabinow (eds.), *Michel Foucault. Un parcours philosophique*. Paris: Gallimard, « Folio-Essais ». 296–321.

Fournier, Marcel, and Michèle Lamont. 1992. *Cultivating Differences: Symbolic Boundaries and the Making of Inequality*. Chicago: University of Chicago Press.

Fourteau, Claude. 2007. La gratuité, point aveugle des politiques culturelles. *La Lettre de l'OCIM* (Summer): 15–22.

———. (eds.) 2002. *Les Institutions culturelles au plus près du public*. Paris: La Documentation française, Louvre, « Conférences et colloques ».

Fourteau, Claude, and Maurice Godelier, Maurice. 2002. Signe et symbole : l'exemple de la gratuité. In *Les institutions culturelles au plus près du public*. Louvre, « Conférences et colloques. » Paris: La Documentation Française. 61–143.

Freud, Sigmund. 1990. *Totem and Taboo*. New York: W. W. Norton.

Fridman, Viviana, and Michèle Ollivier. 2004. *Goûts, pratiques culturelles et inégalités sociales : branchés et exclus*. Montreal: Les Presses de l'Université de Montréal.

Frith, Simon. 1998. Literary studies as cultural studies. Whose literature? Whose culture? *Critical Quarterly* 43 (Spring): 3–26.

Fumaroli, Marc. 1991. *L'État culturel. Essai sur une religion moderne*. Paris: Éditions de Fallois.

Gans, Herbert. 1974. *Popular Culture and High Culture. An Analysis and Evaluation of Taste*. New York: Basic Books.

———. 1985. American Popular Culture and High Culture in a Changing Class Structure. In *Art, Ideology and Politics*. Judith H. Balfe and Margaret Jane Wyszomirski, editors. New York: Praeger. 40–57.

Gartman, David. 1991. Culture as class symbolization or mass reification? A critique of Bourdieu's distinction. *American Journal of Sociology* 97 (2): 421–447.

Geertz, Clifford. 1973. *The Interpretation of Culture*. New York: Basic Books.

Gellner, Ernest. *Nations and Nationalism*. Ithaca, NY: Cornell University Press, 1983.

Girel, Sylvia. 2006. *Sociologie des arts et de la culture. Un état de la recherche*, Premier Congrès de l'Association Française de Sociologie. Paris: L'Harmattan.

Goblot, Edmond. [1925] 1967. *La Barrière et le niveau. Étude sociologique sur la bourgeoisie française moderne*. Paris: Presses universitaires de France.

Grignon, Claude, and Jean-Claude Passeron. 1989. *Le savant et le populaire. Misérabilisme et populisme en sociologie et en littérature*. Paris: Gallimard-Le Seuil, « Hautes-Études ».

Grossein, Jean-Pierre. 2003. Présentation. In Weber. Max. L'Éthique protestante et l'esprit du capitalisme suivi d'autres essais , edited, translated and with an introduction by Jean-Pierre Grossein. Paris: Gallimard. V–LXV.

Gruel, Louis. 2005. *Pierre Bourdieu illusionniste*. Rennes: Presses Universitaires de Rennes.

Guy, Jean-Michel. 1991. *Les Publics de la Comédie-Française*. Paris: La Documentation française.

Habermas, Jürgen. 1989. From a culture-debating public (kulturrasonierend) to a culture-consuming public. In *The Structural Transformation of the Public Sphere: An Inquiry into a Category of Bourgeois Society*, translated from the German by Thomas Burger with the assistance of Frederick Lawrence, 159–175. Cambridge: Polity Press, 159–175.

———. 1970. Technology and science as ideology. In *Toward a Rational Society*. Translated by J. Shapiro. Boston: Beacon Press.

Halbwachs, Maurice. 1950. *La mémoire collective*. Paris: Presses universitaires de France.

———. 1925. *Les cadres sociaux de la mémoire*, Paris: Alcan.

Hall, Stuart. 1992. Cultural studies and its theoretical legacies. In Lawrence Grossberg, Cary Nelson, and Paula Treichler (eds.), *Cultural Studies*. New York: Routledge. 277–286.

———. 1980. Cultural studies and the centre: some problematics and problems. In Stuart Hall, Dorothy Hobson, Andrew Lowe and Paul Willis (eds.), *Culture, Media, Language*. London: Hutchinson. 15–47.

———. 1990. The emergence of cultural studies and the crisis of the humanities. *October* 53, 11–90.

Halley, Jeffrey A. 2004. Culture, politique et vie quotidienne. In Pascale Ancel and Alain Pessin (eds.), *Les non-publics. Les arts en réception*. Tome II. Paris: L'Harmattan, « Logiques sociales ». 85–105.

Hamel, Jacques. 1998. Défense et illustration de la méthode des études de cas en sociologie et en anthropologie. Quelques notes et rappels. *Cahiers internationaux de Sociologie* 45 (CIV). 121–138.

Hebdige, Dick. 1988. *Hiding in the Light*. London: Routledge.

———. 1979. *Subcultures. The Meaning of Style*. London: Methuen.

Heinich, Nathalie. Gérer l'inconciliable : les médiateurs culturels, entre consensus politique et dissensions artistiques. In *Res publica et culture. Actes du colloque, 1993*. Ville de Montreuil: 1994.

———. *La gloire de Van Gogh. Essai d'anthropologie de l'admiration*. Paris: Éditions de Minuit, 1991.

Hennion, Antoine. 1993. *La passion musicale. Une sociologie de la médiation*. Paris: Métailié.

———. 2003. Ce que ne disent pas les chiffres . . . Vers une pragmatique du goût. In *Le(s) Public(s) de la culture*. Olivier Donnat and Paul Tolila, editors. Paris: Presses de Science Po, 287–304.

Hirschman, Albert O. 1991. *The Rhetoric of Reaction: Perversity, Futility, Jeopardy*. Cambridge: Harvard University Press.

Hoggart, Richard. 1957. *The Uses of Literacy: Aspects of Working Class Life with Special References to Publications and Entertainments*. London: Chatto and Windus.

Horkheimer, Max, and Theodor W. Adorno. 2000. The Culture industry: Enlightenment as mass deception. In *Dialectic of Enlightenment: Philosophical Fragments*. Translated by Edmond Jephcott. Stanford: Stanford University Press, 94–136.

Infield, Henrik F. 1955. *Utopia and Experiment*. New York: Praeger.

Iser, Wolfgang. 1978. *The Act of Reading: A Theory of Aesthetic Response*. Baltimore and London: The Johns Hopkins Press.

Jauss, Hans-Robert. 1978. *Toward an Aesthetic of Reception*. Minneapolis: University of Minnesota Press.

———. 1988. *Aesthetic Experience and Literary Hermeneutics*. Translated by Michael Shaw. Minneapolis: University of Minneapolis Press.

Jeanson, Francis. 1972. Déclaration de Villeurbanne. In *L'action culturelle dans la cité*. Paris: Éditions du Seuil. 119–120.

Kane, Danielle. 2003. Distinction worldwide? Bourdieu's theory of taste in an international context. *Poetics* 31: 403–421.

Kardiner, Abraham. 1939. *The Individual and His Society: the Psychodynamics of Primitive Social Organization*. New York, Columbia University Press.

Karpik, Lucien. 1996. Dispositifs de confiance et engagements crédibles. *Sociologie du travail* 4: 527–550.

———. 2007. *L'économie des singularités*. Paris: Gallimard, « Bibliothèque des sciences humaines ».

Katz, Elihu, and Paul F. Klarsfeld. 1955. *Personal Influence: The Part Played by People in Mass Communication*. Glencoe, Ill.: Free Press.

Kingston, Paul W. 2001. The unfulfilled promise of cultural capital theory. *Sociology of Education* 74 Extra Issue: 88–99.

Koselleck, Reinhart. 1988. *Critique and Crises. Enlightenment and the Pathogenesis of Modern Society*. Oxford: Berg Publishers Ltd.

Labourie, Raymond. 1978. *Les institutions socioculturelles. Les mots-clés*. Paris: Presses Universitaires de France.

Lacouture, Jean. 1995. Jean Vilar et les pouvoirs. In Jacques Téphany (ed.), *Jean Vilar*. Paris: Éditions de l'Herne. 65–69.

Lahire, Bernard. 1999. Esquisse du programme scientifique d'une sociologie psychologique. *Cahiers Internationaux de Sociologie* CVI: 25–55.

———. 2004. *La culture des individus. Dissonances culturelles et distinction de soi*. Paris: La Découverte, « Textes à l'appui ».

———. 1996. La variation des contextes en sciences sociales. Remarques épistémologiques. *Annales. Histoire, sciences sociales* 2 (April-March): 381–407.

———. 2001. *Le travail sociologique de Pierre Bourdieu. Dettes et critiques*, Paris: La Découverte.

———. 2005. *L'homme pluriel. Les ressorts de l'action*. Paris: Armand Colin.

Lamont, Michèle. 2009. Critères d'évaluation et structures culturelles. In Marc Breviglieri, Claudette Lafaye, and Danny Trom (eds.), *Compétences critiques et sens de la justice*. Paris: Economica. 437–446.

———. 1994. *Money, Morals, and Manners: The Culture of the French and the American Upper-Middle Class*. Chicago: University of Chicago Press.

Lamont, Michèle, and Annette Lareau. 1988. Cultural capital: allusions, gaps, and glissandos in recent theoretical developments. *Sociological Theory* 6: 153–168.

Latour, Bruno. 1986. *Laboratory Life. The Construction of Scientific Facts*. Princeton: Princeton University Press.

Le Bart, Christian. 2000. *Les Fans des Beatles. Sociologie d'une passion*. Rennes: Presses Universitaires de Rennes.

Le Queau, Pierre, ed. 2007. *Vingt ans de sociologie de l'art : bilan et perspectives*, 2 tomes Paris: L'Harmattan, « Logiques sociales », série « Sociologie des arts », 2007.

Le Wita, Beatrix. 1988. *Ni vue, ni connue. Approche ethnographique de la culture bourgeoise*. Paris: Éditions de la Maison des Sciences de l'Homme, 1988.

Leenhardt, Jacques. 1978. La réception de l'œuvre d'art. In Michaël Dufrenne *et al.* « L'esthétique et les sciences de l'art », *Tendances principales de la recherche dans les sciences sociales*, t. II, *Sciences anthropologiques et historiques. Esthétique et sciences de l'art*. UNESCO. 784–797.

Leenhardt, Jacques, and Pierre Jozsa. 1999. *Lire la lecture. Essai de sociologie de la lecture* Paris: L'Harmattan.

Leontsini, Mary, and Jean-Marc Leveratto. 2006. Online reading practices and reading pleasure in a transnational context: The reception of Coetzee's disgraceon Amazon sites. In Anna Guttmann, Michael Hockx, George Paizis (eds.), *The Global Literary Field*. Cambridge: Cambridge Scholars Press. 163–178.

Levine, Lawrence W. 1988. *Highbrow/Lowbrow: The Emergence of Cultural Hierarchy in America*. Cambridge: Cambridge University Press.

Leturcq, Sandrine. 1999. *Les médiateurs en bibliothèques*. Preface by Anne Kupiec. Villeurbanne: ENSSIB.

Lewis, David-K. 1974. *Convention: A Philosophical Study*. Cambridge: Harvard University Press, Cambridge.

Lichtblau, Klaus. 1996. *Kulturkrise und Soziologie um die Jahrhundertwende. Zur Genealogie der Kultursoziologie in Deutschland*, Frankfurt am Main: Suhrkamp.

Linton, Ralph. 1947. *The Cultural Background of Personality*. London: Keegan Paul.

Long, Elizabeth. 1992. *From Sociology to Cultural Studies*. Oxford: Blackwell.

Macé, Éric. 2000. Qu'est-ce qu'une sociologie de la télévision? 1. Esquisse d'une théorie des rapports sociaux médiatisés. *Réseaux* 18, (104): 245–288.

———. 2001. Qu'est-ce qu'une sociologie de la télévision ? 2. Les trois moments de la configuration médiatique de la réalité : production, usages, représentations. *Réseaux* 19 (105): 199–242.

Mannheim, Karl. 1956. *Essays in the Sociology of Culture*, London: Routledge and Keegan Paul Ltd, 1956.

———. [1929] 1985. *Ideology and Utopia: An Introduction to the Sociology of Knowledge*, translated and with a preface by Louis Wirth. New York, NY: Harcourt Brace Jovanovich.

Marcuse, Herbert. 1964. *One Dimensional Man. Studies in the Ideology of Advanced Industrial Society.* Boston: Beacon.
———. 1970. *Culture et société.* Paris: Éditions de Minuit.
Marx, Karl. 1998. *The Civil War in France and Other Writings on the Paris Commune.* Chicago: Charles H. Kerr.
———. 2007. *The Class Struggles in France, 1848–1850.* Whitefish, Montana: Kessinger Publishing.
———. 1985. *The Eighteenth Brumaire of Louis Bonaparte.* London: Lawrence and Wishart.
Marx, Karl, and Friedrich Engels. *The German Ideology.* [1932] 1998. New York: Prometheus Books.
Mattelart, Armand. 2005. *Diversité culturelle et mondialisation.* Paris: La Découverte, 2005.
Mauss, Marcel. 1991. Essai sur le don. Forme et raison de l'échange dans les sociétés archaïques. [1923–1924]. In *Sociologie et anthropologie.* Preface by Claude Lévi-Strauss. Paris: Presses Universitaires de France. 142–284.
Mauger, Gérard, Claude Poliak and Bernard Pudal. 1999. *Histoires de lecteurs.* Paris: Nathan.
Mead, Margaret. 1935. *Sex and Temperament in Three Primitive Societies.* New York: W. Morrow & Co.
Menger, Pierre-Michel. 1997. Durkheim et la question de l'art. In Jean-Louis Fabiani (ed.), *Le goût de l'enquête. Pour Jean-Claude Passeron.* Paris: L'Harmattan. 313–347.
———. 1986. L'oreille spéculative. Consommation et perception de la musique contemporaine. *Revue française de sociologie*, XXVII, (3): 445–479.
———. 2009. *Le travail créateur. S'accomplir dans l'incertain.* Paris: Gallimard-Seuil, « Hautes études ».
———. 2003. *Portrait de l'artiste en travailleur. Métamorphoses du capitalisme.* Paris: Seuil.
Merton, Robert K. The self-fulfilling prophecy. *Antioch Review* 8 (1948):193–210.
Mervant-Roux, Marie-Madeleine. 1998. *L'assise du théâtre. Pour une étude du spectateur.* Paris: CNRS Éditions.
Miller, Toby, and George Yudice. 2002. *Cultural Policy.* London: Sage.
Milner, Jean-Claude. 1997. *Le salaire de l'idéal. La théorie des classes et de la culture.* Paris: Le Seuil.
Moeschler, Olivier, and Olivier Thevenin, (eds). 2009. *Les territoires de la démocratisation culturelle. Équipements, événements, patrimoines : perspectives franco-suisse.* L'Harmattan, « Logiques sociales ».
Moulin, Raymonde. 1992. *L'Artiste, l'institution et le marché.* Paris: Flammarion.
Moulin, Raymonde, and Paul Veyne. 1996. Entretien avec Jean Claude Passeron. *Revue européenne des sciences sociales* XXXIV(103): 275–354.
Muller, Lara. 2005. *Participation culturelle et sportive : tableaux issus de l'enquête permanente sur les conditions de vie de mai 2003.* Paris: Insee.
Nègre, Fabien. « L'esthétique de l'existence dans le dernier Foucault, » *Raison présente* 120 (1996): 47–72.
Neveu, Erik and Armand Mattelart. 2003. *Introduction aux Cultural Studies.* Paris: La Découverte, « Repères ».
Octobre, Sylvie. 2004. *Les Loisirs culturels des 6 – 14 ans.* Paris: La Documentation française.
Ostrower, Francie. 1998. The arts as cultural capital among elites: Bourdieu's Theory Reconsidered. *Poetics* 26: 43–53.
Papilloud, Christian. 2002. *Le don de relation. Georg Simmel-Marcel Mauss.* Preface by Otthein Rammstedt. Paris: L'Harmattan, 2002.
Pasquier, Dominique. 2005. *Cultures lycéennes. La tyrannie de la majorité.* Paris: Autrement, « Mutations ».
Passeron, Jean-Claude. 2004. À propos de l'écriture et des lectures de La reproduction . Interview with Natalia Chmatko. Afterword to the Russian translation of *La*

Reproduction by Pierre Bourdieu and Jean-Claude Passeron. Moscow Academy of Sciences.

———. 2003. Consommation et réception de la culture : la démocratisation des publics. In Olivier Donnat and Paul Tolila (eds.), *Le(s) Public(s) de la culture*. Paris: Presses de Sciences Po. 361–390.

———. 2006. Figures et contestations de la culture. Légitimité et relativisme culturel. In Jean-Claude Passeron, *Le raisonnement sociologique. L'espace non-poppérien du raisonnement naturel. Nouvelle édition revue et augmentée*. Paris: Albin Michel. 445–508.

———. 2006a. Les yeux et les oreilles : à propos de l'audio-visuel. In Jean-Claude Passeron, *Le raisonnement sociologique. L'espace non-poppérien du raisonnement naturel. Nouvelle édition revue et augmentée*. Paris: Albin Michel. 289–299.

———. 2006b. L'usage faible des images. Enquête sur la réception de la peinture. In Jean-Claude Passeron, *Le Raisonnement sociologique. L'espace non-poppérien du raisonnement naturel. Nouvelle édition revue et augmentée*. Paris: Albin Michel. 399–422.

Passeron, Jean-Claude, and Emmanuel Pedler. 1999. Le temps donné au regard : enquête sur la réception de la peinture. La réception. *Protée*, UQAM, Québec, Chicoutimi, Quebec, 27 (2): 93–116.

———. 1991. *Le Temps donné aux tableaux*. Marseille: IMEREC, 1991.

Passeron, Jean-Claude, and Jacques Revel. 2005. Penser par cas. Raisonner à partir des singularités. In Jean-Claude Passeron and Jacques Revel (eds.), *Penser par cas*. Paris: EHESS. 9–44.

Passeron, Jean-Claude, Michel Grumbach, François de Singly et al. 1984. L'Œil à la page. Enquête sur les images et les bibliothèques. Paris: Centre Georges-Pompidou, Bibliothèque publique d'information, Service des études et de la recherche. 5–24.

Passeron, Jean-Claude, Pierre Mayol, and Éric Macé. 2003a. *Culture(s) : entre fragmentation et recompositions*. Paris: CNDP.

Paul-Boncour, Joseph. 1912. *Art et démocratie*. Paris: Librairie Paul Ollendorff.

Pedler, Emmanuel. 2003. *Entendre l'opéra. Une sociologie du théâtre lyrique*. Paris: L'Harmattan.

Péquignot, Bruno. 2007. *La question des œuvres en sociologie des arts et de la culture*. Paris: L'Harmattan, « Logiques sociales », série « Sociologie des arts ».

———. 1991. *La Relation amoureuse. Analyse sociologique du roman sentimental*. Paris: L'Harmattan, « Logiques sociales ».

———. La sociologie de l'art et de la culture. In Jean-Michel Berthelot (ed.), *La sociologie française contemporaine*. Paris: Presses Universitaires de France, 2000. 251–264.

———. 1993. *Pour une sociologie esthétique*. Paris: L'Harmattan, « Logiques sociales ».

———. 2008. *Recherches sociologiques sur l'image*. Paris: L'Harmattan, « Logiques sociales », série « Sociologie des arts ».

———. 2009. *Sociologie des arts*. Paris: Armand Colin, « 128 ».

Peterson, Richard A., and Roger M. Kern. 1996. Changing highbrow taste: From snob to omnivore. *American Sociological Review*, 61: 900–907.

Peterson, Richard A. 1999. *Creating Country Music: Fabricating Authenticity*. Chicago: University of Chicago Press.

———. 1992. Understanding audience segmentation: From elite and mass omnivore and univore. *Poetics* 21: 243–258.

Peterson, Richard A., and Albert Simkus. 1992. How musical tastes mark occupational status groups. In Marcel Fournier and Michèle Lamont (eds.), *Cultivating Differences: Symbolic Boundaries and the Making of Inequality*. Chicago: University of Chicago Press. 152–168

Petit, Michèle et al. 1997. *De la bibliothèque au droit de cité. Parcours de jeunes*. Paris: Éditions du Centre Georges-Pompidou, Service des Études et Recherche de la Bibliothèque publique d'information.

Petit, Michèle. 2002. *Éloge de la lecture. La construction de soi*. Paris: Belin.

Pfister, Joel.1996. The Americanization of Cultural Studies. In John Storey (ed.), *What is Cultural Studies?* London: Arnold. 287–299.

Pinçon, Michel, and Monique Pinçon-Chariot. 2000. *Sociologie de la bourgeoisie*. Paris: La Découverte.
Poulain, Martine. 1990. *Constances et variances : les publics de la Bibliothèque publique d'information (1982–1989)*. Paris: Éditions du Centre Georges-Pompidou, Bibliothèque publique d'information.
Poulot, Dominique. 1986. Les mutations de la sociabilité dans les musées français et les stratégies des conservateurs : 1960–1980. In Raymonde Moulin (ed.), *Sociologie de l'art*. Paris: La Documentation française. 95–109.
Proust, Françoise. 1991. *Kant. Le ton de l'histoire*. Paris: Payot, « Critique de la politique ».
Putnam, Robert D. 2000. *Bowling Alone: The Collapse and Revival of American Community*. New York: Simon & Schuster.
———. 2004. *Democracies in Flux: The Evolution of Social Capital in Contemporary Society*. Oxford: Oxford University Press.
Queiroz de, Jean-Manuel. 2005. *L'École et ses sociologues*. Paris: Nathan, « 128 ». 19.
Revel, Jacques (ed.). 1996. *Jeux d'échelles. La micro-analyse à l'expérience*. Paris: Hautes-Études-Gallimard-Le Seuil: 1996.
Rigaud, Jacques. 1990. *Libre culture*. Paris: Gallimard, Le Débat.
Saez, Guy. 1985. Les politiques de la culture. In Madeleine Grawitz and Jean Leca (eds.), *Traité de science politique*, IV. Paris: Presses Universitaires de France. 387–422.
Sawyer, Stephen, and Terry N. Clark. 2012. Politique culturelle et la démocratie métropolitaine à l'âge de la défiance. In Guy Saez and Jean-Pierre Saez (eds.) *Politiques culturelles* 21 : Débats et enjeux en Europe. Paris: Editions de la découverte. 81–95.
Sawyer, Stephen. 2010. Is there a place for more Molière? Cultural planning and metropolitan politics in the Grand Paris. *Territorio*. Paris.
Scaff, Lawrence A. 1994. Max Webers Begriff der Kultur. In Gerhard Wagnerand Heinz Zipprian (ed.), *Max Webers Wissenschaftslehre. Interpretation und Kritik*. Frankfurt-am-Main: Suhrkamp: 1994. 678–699.
Sartre. Jean-Paul. [1960]. 1985. *Critique de la raison dialectique*. Paris: Gallimard, « Bibliothèque de philosophie ».
———. 1955. Jean-Paul Sartre nous parle du théâtre. Interview with Jean-Paul Sartre conducted by Bernard Dort. *Théâtre populaire* 15 (1955): 3–9.
Schiller, Friedrich. [1793] 1962. *Lettres sur l'éducation esthétique de l'homme*. In *œ uvres choisies*, t. VIII. Paris: Hachette.
Scott, James. 1990. *Domination and the Arts of Resistance*. New Haven: Yale University Press.
Shroederer, Ralph. 1992. *Max Weber and the Sociology of Culture*. London: Sage.
Silver, Daniel, Terry Nichols Clark, and Clemente J. Navarro. 2010. Scenes: Social Context in an Age of Contingency. *Social Forces* 88 (5): 2293–2324.
Silverstone, Roger. 1994. The power of the ordinary: on cultural studies and the sociology of culture. *Sociology* 28: 991–1001.
Simmel, Georg. 1950. [Excursus on] fidelity and gratitude. *The Sociology of Georg Simmel*. New York: The Free Press.
———. 2004. *The Philosophy of Money, Third Enlarged Version*, edited by David Frisby, translated Tom Bottomore and David Frisby from a first draft by Kaethe Mengelberg. London: Routledge.
———. 1997. Sociability (an example of pure sociology). In *Simmel on Culture: Selected Writings*, edited and translated by David Frisby and Mike Featherstone. London: Sage.
———. 2009. *Sociology: Inquiries into the Construction of Social Forms Volumes 1 and 2*, translated and edited by Anthony J. Blasi, Anton K. Jacobs & Mathew Kanjirathinkal; introduced by Horst J. Helle. Leiden and Boston: Brill.
———. 1997a. The concept and the tragedy of culture. In *Simmel on Culture: Selected Writings*, edited and translated by David Frisby and Mike Featherstone. London: Sage.

———. 1997b. The philosophy of fashion. In *Simmel on Culture: Selected Writings*, edited and translated by David Frisby and Mike Featherstone. London: Sage, 187–205.
———. 1984. *On Women, Sexuality and Love*, translated and edited by Guy Oaks. New Haven: Yale University Press.
Singly, François de. 1996. Le travail de l'héritage. *Revue européenne des Sciences sociales* XXXIV (103) : 61–80.
———. 2003. *Les Uns avec les autres. Quand l'individualisme crée du lien.* Paris: Armand Colin.
———. 1989. *Lire à 12 ans.* Paris: Nathan.
———. 2007. *Sociologie de la famille contemporaine.* Paris: Armand Colin. 16–33.
———. 2003a. La famille individualiste face aux pratiques culturelles. In Olivier Donnat and Paul Tolila (eds.), *Le(s) Public(s) de la culture.* Paris : Presses de Sciences Po. 43–60.
Singly, François de, and Émilia Vaillant. 1997. « L'espace public. In *Le Musée et la bibliothèque, vrais parents ou faux amis.* Paris: Centre Georges-Pompidou, Bibliothèque publique d'information, « Études et recherche ». 100–130.
Stauth, Georg. 1992. Nietzsche, Weber, and the Affirmative Sociology of Culture. *Archives européennes de Sociologie* XXXIII (2): 219–247.
Stiegler, Bernard. 2005. *De la misère symbolique. 2. La catastrophè du sensible.* Paris: Éditions Galilée.
Stiegler, Bernard. 2007. La modernité enchantée. Preface to Laurent Fleury. *Le cas Beaubourg. Mécénat d'Etat et démocratisation de la culture.* Paris: Armand Colin. 13–21.
———. 2008a. L'hyper-sollicitation de l'attention et le déficit attentionnel. In *Prendre soin. 1. De la jeunesse et des générations.* Paris: Flammarion. 144–149.
———. 2004. *Mécréance et discrédit. 1. La décadence des démocraties industrielles.* Paris: Éditions Galilée.
———. 2008. *Prendre soin de la jeunesse et des générations.* Paris: Flammarion.
Swingewood, Alan. 1977. *The Myth of Mass Culture.* London: Macmillan.
Tassin, Étienne. 1999. *Le trésor perdu. Hannah Arendt l'intelligence de l'action politique.* Paris: Payot, « Critique de la politique ».
———. 2003. *Un monde commun. Pour une cosmo-politique des conflits.* Paris: Éditions du Seuil, « La couleur des idées ».
Tocqueville, Alexis de. [1856]. 1986. *L'Ancien régime et la révolution.* Paris: Robert Laffont.
Thompson, E. P. 1963. *The Making of the English Working Class.* London: Victor Gollancz.
Urfalino, Philippe. 1996. *L'invention de la politique culturelle,* edited by the Comité d'histoire du Ministère de la Culture. Paris: La Documentation française.
———. 1996. Mai 68 ou la fausse désillusion. », *L'invention de la politique culturelle,* Comité d'histoire du Ministère de la Culture et La Documentation française, «Travaux et documents». 215–242.
Uzel, Jean-Philippe. 2001. Le conflit art et politique. In Lucille Beaudry and Lawrence Olivier (eds.), *La politique par le détour de l'art, de l'éthique et de la philosophie.* Québec, Presses de l'Université du Québec. 44–45.
Veblen, Thorstein. 1970. *La théorie de la classe de loisir.* Paris: Gallimard.
Verret, Michel. 1996. *L'Ouvrier français. La culture ouvrière.* Paris: L'Harmattan.
Veyne, Paul. 1988. Conduites sans croyance et œuvre d'art sans spectateurs. *Diogène* 143: 3–22.
———. 1990. *Bread and Circuses. Historical sociology and political pluralism,* translated by Brian Pearce. 1990. London: Penguin.
Viala, Alain. 1985. *Naissance de l'écrivain.* Paris: Minuit, 124.
Vilar, Jean. 1971. « Deux lettres et un ballet. » *Chronique romanesque.* Paris: Grasset.
----. 1986. Le petit manifeste de Suresnes. In *Le Théâtre , service public (et autres textes).* Introduction and notes by Armand Delcampe. Paris: Gallimard.
———. 1965. Le public des associations populaires françaises est le plus aristocratique qui soit. Il arrive à l'heure. *Le Figaro*, February 23.

———. 1986a. *Le Théâtre, service public (et autres textes)*. Introduction and notes by Armand Delcampe. Paris: Gallimard.

———. 1981. *Mémento, du 29 novembre 1952 au 1er septembre 1955*. Introduction and notes by Armand Delcampe. Paris: Gallimard, « Pratique du théâtre ».

Weber, Max. [1908] 1951. « Die Grenznutzlehre und das 'psychophysische Grundgesetz' », *Archiv für Sozialwissenschaft und Sozialpolitik*. Reprinted in Weber, Max. *Gesammelte Aufsätze zur Wissenschaftslehre*, Tübingen, Verlag J.C.B. Mohr (Paul Siebeck). 384–399.

———. 1977. Religious rejections of the world and their directions. *From Max Weber: Essays in Sociology*, translated, edited and with an introduction by H. H. Gerth and C. Wright Mills. New York: Oxford University Press. 323–359.

———. 2012. The "objectivity" of knowledge in social science and social policy. *Max Weber: Collected Methodological Writings*, edited by Hans Henrik Bruun and Sam Whimster. Translated by Hans Henrik Bruun. Abingdon: Routledge. 100–138.

———. 2011. *The Protestant Ethic and the Spirit of Capitalism*. Translated and introduced by Stephen Kalberg. Oxford: Oxford University Press.

———. 2005. Science as a vocation. *Max Weber: The Vocation Lectures*. "*Science as a Vocation*"; "*Politics as a Vocation*", edited and with an introduction by David Owen and Tracy B. Strong; translated by Rodney Livingstone. Indianapolis/Cambridge: Hackett Publishing Company.

———. 1920. Zwischenbetrachtung. Gesammelte Aufsätze zur Religionssoziologie, Tübingen, C. B. Mohr, 1920.

Weiß, Johannes. 1981. "Max Weber : die Entzauberung der Welt." In J. Speck (ed.), *Grundprobleme der großen Philosophen. Die Philosophie der Gegenwart—II*. Gottingen. 9–47.

Williams, Raymond. 1958. *Culture and Society*. Harmondsworth: Pelican Books.

———. 1961. *The Long Revolution*. London: Chatto & Windus.

———. 1985. *The Sociology of Culture*. Chicago: University of Chicago Press.

Wolff, Janet. 1999. Cultural Studies and the Sociology of Culture." In *Visible Culture. An Electronic Journal for Visual Studies*. (http://www.rochester.edu/in_visible_culture/issue1/wolff/).

Zolberg, Vera L. 1990. *Constructing a Sociology of the Arts*. Cambridge: Cambridge University Press.

Zuzanek, Jiri. 1988. Démocratisation de la culture ou démocratie culturelle : un débat enterré ? In Augustin Girard (ed.), *Économie et culture*. t. II : *Culture en devenir et volonté publique* Paris: La Documentation française. 49–56.

FURTHER READING

Valuable studies on the themes and problematics of the sociology of culture and cultural practices have appeared in a number of journals. For example, *Protée* (*Théories et pratiques sémiologiques*) devoted an issue to « La réception » (Quebec, Chicoutimi, 27 (2), Fall 1999), *Mots* produced a special edition on emotion in the media (75, July 2004), while *Réseaux* focused on reception theory (Paris, CNET, 68, 1994) and cultural studies (Paris, CNET, no. 80, 1996), and the special editions of the journal *Hermès*, « Espaces publics, traditions et communautés » (no. 10, 1992); « À la recherche du public : réception, télévision, médias » (nos. 11–12, 1993); and « Toutes les pratiques culturelles se valent-elles ? Création artistique, développement culturel et politique publique » (no. 20, 1997), as well as the special edition of the journal of sociology and anthropology, *Utinam*, on « Arts et culture » (no. 24, 1998). Furthermore, a number of issues of the journal *Sociologie de l'art* are dedicated to questions concerning the sociology of culture, including « Les arts et le public » (No. 12, 1999) and two issues dedicated to « La question de la critique » (OPuS 3, and OPuS 4, 2003). For a critique of Pierre Bourdieu's model of cultural consumption, see the special issue of *Theory, Culture and Society* (no. 10, 1993). Lastly, the journal, *Poetics (Journal of Empirical Research on Literature, the Media and the Arts)*, founded in 2007, publishes sociology studies on cultural policy and serves as a platform for debate concerning the contemporary themes, concepts and methods of the sociology of culture.

Index

Adorno, Theodor W., x, 9, 10, 74, 107
Allard, Laurence, 106
Althusser, Louis, x
Amrani, Younes, 39
Amselle, Jean-Loup, 69
Aragon, Louis, 90
Arendt, Hannah, xxiii, 11, 113
Ariès, Philippe, 37
Aristotle, xxiii
Aubert, Yvette, 96n6
Austin, John L., 21

Bakhtin, Mikhail, xi
Barrault, Jean-Louis, 90
Baudelaire, Charles, xxxi
Baudelot, Christian, 71
Baudrillard, Jean, 107, 110
Beaud, Stéphane, 39, 42
Beaumarchais, 44
Bellavance, Guy, 66, 69
Benjamin, Walter, 9, 72, 95
Benvéniste, Émile, 114n4
Bertrand, Anne-Marie, 22
Beauvoir, Simone de, 87
Benedict, Ruth, 3
Berg, Alban, 9
Bernstein, Basil, 37
Bloch, Ernst, 8
Bouchindhomme, Christian, xxxi
Boudon, Raymond, 121
Bourdieu, Pierre, x, xivn1, xv, xvi, xxiv, 13, 14, 15, 16n1, 28, 35, 37, 40, 41, 42, 43, 45, 48n1, 57, 58, 65, 67, 68, 69, 71, 72, 74, 103, 115, 117, 121, 125
Brecht, Bertolt, ix, x, xxv
Broch, Hermann, xv, xxxi
Brown, Alan, xii
Buch, Esteban, 71, 106
Burgos, Martine, 71, 106

Caillet, Elizabeth, Jean, 106
Callon, Michel, 72
Cartier, Marie, 71
Catu, Robert, 96n5
Céroux, Benoît, 57
Certeau, Michel de, 26, 107
Chéreau, Patrice, 90
Chesneaux, Jean, 107
Chmatko, Natalia, 48n1
Chaney, David, 12
Chartier, Roger, 75
Chomsky, Noam, 41
Christie, Agatha, 47
Clark, Terry Nichols, ix–xivn1, xiii, xix, xvi, xvii, xviii, xxx, xxxi, 69, 70, 81n3
Colas, Dominique, 44
Coleman, James S., xiii
Condorcet, Nicolas de, 52, 102
Corneille, Pierre, 96n6

Da Silva, Felipe, xiii, xvii, 70
Darbel, Alain, 57, 58, 115, 121
Davallon, Jean, 106
De Gaulle, Charles, xxv, xxvi
Delors, Jacques, 13
Denizot, Marion, 95
Deroche-Gurcel, Lilyane, 8, 94
Detrez, Christine, 71
DiMaggio, Paul, xii, xv, 62, 66, 72, 73, 106
Donnat, Olivier, 14, 15, 24, 25, 27, 28, 29, 30, 31, 32, 33n2, 59, 103, 122, 126n1
Dorival, Bernard, 90
Drieu La Rochelle, Pierre, 47
Dubet, François, 39, 69
Ducret, André, 10
Duhamel, Jacques, 90, 99
Dumazedier, Joffre, 13
Dumont, Louis, 45

Dumontier, Françoise, 26
Durkheim, Émile, xv, 4, 14, 37, 38, 92, 96n4, 97n14
Dux, Pierre, 114n2

Eidelman, Jacqueline, 57
Elias, Norbert, xv, 41, 43, 44, 45, 47, 48, 68
Esquenazi, Jean-Pierre, 27
Ethis, Emmanuel, xv, 27, 72, 103
Evans, Christophe, 71, 106

Fabiani, Jean-Louis, xv, 15, 22, 23, 27
Ferry, Jules, 51
Fine, Gary Allen, xi
Fleury, Laurent, ix, xii, xiii, xivn1, xvi, 7, 19, 50, 56, 59, 60, 61, 62, 73, 74, 75, 78, 79, 88, 90, 93, 94, 102, 103, 119, 124
Foucault, Michel, x, 77, 81n8, 112, 124, 125
Fournier, Marcel, 69
Fourteau, Claude, xxx, 15, 74, 104
Freud, Sigmund, 41, 97n14
Fumaroli, Marc, 121

Gans, Herbert, 68
Gartman, David, 66
Gates, Bill, xiii
Geertz, Clifford, 12
Gellner, Ernest, 51
Gémier, Firmin, 56, 96n2, 96n3, 119
George, Stefan, 8
Gerth, Hedwig Ida, 5
Giddens, Anthony, 39
Gilbert, Roger, 90
Girard, Augustin, 13, 115
Girel, Sylvia, 126
Goblot, Edmond, xvi, 45, 96n1
Godelier, Maurice, 74
Gordon, Colin, 81n8
Gramsci, Antonio, x
Grignon, Claude, 67
Gruel, Louis, 67
Grumbach, Michel, 76
Guéhenno, Jean, 52
Guette, Georges, xxix, 104, 114n1
Guitry, Sacha, 47
Guy, Jean-Michel, 27, 28

Guyau, Jean-Marie, 4
Grossein, Jean-Pierre, 6

Habermas, Jürgen, x, xi, xxiii, 10, 18, 93, 109
Hennion, Antoine, 72
Halbwachs, Maurice, 42, 73, 92
Hall, Stuart, 11
Halley, Jeffrey A., 72
Hebdige, Dick, 12
Heinich, Nathalie, xxii, 15, 49, 72
Herder, Johann Gottfried, 51
Hirschman, Albert O., 59, 122
Hoffmann-Martinot, Vincent, 70
Hoggart, Richard, 11, 42
Horkheimer, Max, x, 9, 10
Hugo, Victor, 56, 119

Iser, Wolfgang, 74, 77

Jauss, Hans-Robert, 74, 75
Jeanson, Francis, 19
Jacno, Marcel, 91
Jacobs, P., xiii
Jeffrey, Alexander, 41
Joas, Hans, xi
Jobs, Steve, xiii
Jozsa, Pierre, 75

Kant, Immanuel, 72, 74
Kardiner, Abraham, 3
Karpik, Lucien, 71, 109, 114n3
Katz, Elihu, xi, 71
Kern, Roger, 28, 66
Kingston, Paul, 66
Kosseleck, Reinhart, 93
Kracauer, Siegfried, 27
Kuhn, Thomas, 124

Lacouture, Jean, xxiii
Lagrange, Léo, 102
Lahire, Bernard, xvi, 38, 40, 41, 60, 68, 71, 73, 92, 106
Lamont, Michèle, 66
Lang, Jack, xix
Lareau, Annette, 66
Lash, Scott, 81n8
Latour, Bruno, 72
Laurent, Jeanne, 52, 87, 102

Index

Lazarsfeld, Paul, xi, 71

Le Wita, Beatrix, 42

Leenhardt, Jacques, 75
Leontsini, Mary, 81n1
Leturq, Sandrine, 106
Lévi-Strauss, Claude, 4
Linton, Ralph, 3
Long, Elizabeth, 12
Lukács, Georg, 8
Luther, Martin, 51

Macé, Éric, 12
Mahler, Gustav, 9
Malinas, Damien, 27
Malraux, André, xix, xxv, 10, 13, 51, 103, 115, 119, 123
Mannheim, Karl, 59, 122
Marcuse, Herbert, x, 10
Marx, Karl, 10, 42, 52
Mattelart, Armand, 10
Mauger, Gérard, 28
Mauss, Marcel, xvi, 4, 41
Mayol, Pierre, 12
Mead, Margaret, 3
Menger, Pierre-Michel, 4, 15, 28
Mercure, Jean, 114n1
Merton, Robert K., 21, 121
Mervant-Roux, Marie-Madeleine, 73, 94, 97n15
Michelangelo, Lodovico Buonarotti Simonidi, 8
Miller, Toby, 62
Mills, C. Wright, 5
Milner, Jean-Claude, 45, 46, 47
Mitterrand, François, xix
Moeschler, Olivier, 96
Molière, ix, xxv
Montaigne, 95
Morin, Edgar, 27
Moulin, Raymonde, 69, 77, 81n7
Muller, Lara, 24, 32n1
Mukhtar, Toqir, 66

Navarro, Clemente Jesus, 70
Nègre, Fabien, 77
Newcomb, T.W., xiii

Nietzsche, Friedrich, 5, 50, 72, 81n8, 100
Novak-Leonard, Jennifer, xii

Octobre, Sylvie, 15, 71
Orwell, George, 11
Ostrower, Francie, 65

Parsons, Talcott, 37
Pasquier, Dominique, 39, 71
Passeron, Jean-Claude, xivn1, xvi, xvii, 12, 13, 23, 37, 38, 48n1, 54, 55, 67, 73, 76, 77, 81n7, 103, 113, 114n5, 115, 118, 119
Paul-Boncour, Joseph, 96n3
Pavis, Patrice, 91
Pedler, Emmanuel, 27, 76
Petit, Michèle, 40
Péquignot, Bruno, xvi, 15
Peterson, Richard, xvi, 28, 32, 66, 69
Pialoux, Michel, 42
Pinçon, Michel, 42
Pinçon-Chariot, Monique, 42
Pfister, Joël, 13
Philipe, Gérard, 89, 96n6
Planchon, Roger, 19, 90
Poliak, Claude, 28
Pompidou, Georges, xix, xxvi
Pottecher, Maurice, 56, 90, 96n2, 119
Poulot, Dominique, 71
Pudal, Bernard, 28
Putnam, Robert, xi, 70
Proust, Françoise, xxvi
Proust, Serge, 126

Queiroz, Jean-Manuel de, 39

Raudenbush, Stephen, xiii
Revel, Jacques, 23, 60
Rickert, Heinrich, 8
Rigaud, Jacques, 107
Rilke, Rainer Maria, 8
Rodin, Auguste, 8
Rolland, Romain, 96n2
Rouet, François, 73
Rusch, Pierre, xxxi

Sartre, Jean-Paul, 44, 45, 48, 90
Saussure, Ferdinand de, 4

Sawyer, Stephen, xvii, 70
Scaff, Lawrence, 6
Schönberg, Arnold, 9
Scott, James., 12
Shakespeare, William, ix, xxv
Silver, Daniel, 70
Silverstone, Roger, 12
Singly, François de, 26, 37, 38, 71, 76
Simkus, Albert, 32
Simmel, Georg, xvi, xvii, 4, 7, 8, 9, 20, 45, 49, 50, 65, 75, 94, 97n10, 97n11, 100, 101, 103, 106, 113
Sorlin, Pierre, 27
Spira, Françoise, 96n6
Stauth, Georg, 6
Stiegler, Bernard, 11, 107
Stravinsky, Igor, 9

Tarragoni, Federico, 81n4
Tassin, Etienne, 112
Thélot, Claude, 26
Thévenot, Laurent, 88
Thévenin, Olivier, 96
Thompson, E.P., 11
Throsby, David, xiii
Tolila, Paul, 15
Tocqueville, Alexis de, 43, 48, 50, 119
Triolet, Elsa, 90
Turner, Victor, xi, 97n16

Urfalino, Philippe, 57
Useem, Michael, 62
Uzel, Jean-Philippe, 72

Vazereau, Isabelle, 75
Veblen, Thorstein, xvi, 45, 46
Verret, Michel, 42
Veyne, Paul, 50, 72, 77, 81n7, 99
Viala, Alain, 75
Vilar, Jean, ix, xv, xvi, xvii, xx, xxiii, xxiv, xxv, xxvi, xxvii, xxviii, 18, 56, 61, 85, 86, 87, 89, 90, 91, 92, 93, 95, 96n1, 96n2, 97n12, 103, 116, 119, 122, 123, 124

Weber, Marianne, 8
Weber, Max, xvi, xvii, xxx, 4, 5, 6, 7, 8, 23, 41, 50, 51, 67, 80, 81n5, 81n8, 94, 95, 97n18, 123, 124, 125
Weiß, Johannes, 6
Whimster, Sam, 81n8
Williams, Raymond, 11
Wilson, Georges, xx, xxviii, 90

Yudice, George, 62

Zay, Jean, 102

The author

Laurent Fleury is professor of sociology at the Université Paris Diderot/Sorbonne Paris Cité where he is director of the master's course in Cultural Policies and the master's course in Sociology and Anthropology: Politics, Culture, Migrations. He is also an *agrégé* in Social Sciences and holds a doctorate in Political Science.

Laurent Fleury is the author of a number of books, including two on French institutions that have had a revolutionary impact on the way in which cultural practices are structured: *Le T.N.P. de Vilar. Une expérience de démocratisation de la culture* (Presses Universitaires de Rennes, 2006), and *Le cas Beaubourg. Mécénat d'Etat et démocratisation de la culture* (with a preface by Bernard Stiegler, Armand Colin, 2007). He is also the author of *Max Weber* (Presses Universitaires de France, 2009). *Sociology of Culture and Cultural Practices* was published as *Sociologie de la culture et des pratiques culturelles* (Armand Colin, 2011).

Member of the editorial board of the journal, *Sociologie de l'art* and of the editorial board of the *Revue de l'Institut de Sociologie* (Brussels), Laurent Fleury is president of the Research Committee (CR18) on the Sociology of Art and Culture at the Association Internationale des Sociologues de Langue Française (A.I.S.L.F.). He is also member of the editorial board of the *Arts and Social Sciences Journal*.